America's Allies and War

America's Allies and War

Kosovo, Afghanistan, and Iraq

Jason W. Davidson

AMERICA'S ALLIES AND WAR
Copyright © Jason W. Davidson, 2011.
All rights reserved.

First published in 2011 by
PALGRAVE MACMILLAN®
in the United States – a division of St. Martin's Press LLC,
175 Fifth Avenue, New York, NY 10010.

Where this book is distributed in the UK, Europe and the rest of the world, this is by Palgrave Macmillan, a division of Macmillan Publishers Limited, registered in England, company number 785998, of Houndmills, Basingstoke, Hampshire RG21 6XS.

Palgrave Macmillan is the global academic imprint of the above companies and has companies and representatives throughout the world.

Palgrave® and Macmillan® are registered trademarks in the United States, the United Kingdom, Europe and other countries.

ISBN: 978-0-230-61482-6

Library of Congress Cataloging-in-Publication Data

Davidson, Jason.
  America's allies and war : Kosovo, Afghanistan, and Iraq / Jason W. Davidson.
    p. cm.
  ISBN 978-0-230-61482-6 (hardback)
  1. United States—Military relations—Europe. 2. Europe—Military relations—United States. 3. United States—Military relations—Europe—Case studies. 4. Europe—Military relations—United States—Case studies. 5. Alliances—Case studies. 6. World politics—1989– I. Title.
  UA646.3.D35 2010
  355'.0310973094—dc22   2010035423

A catalogue record of the book is available from the British Library.

Design by MPS Limited, A Macmillan Company

First edition: April 2011

10 9 8 7 6 5 4 3 2 1

Printed and bound in Great Britain by
CPI Antony Rowe, Chippenham, Wiltshire

Contents

List of Tables and Figure	vii
Acknowledgments	ix
1 Transatlantic Alliance Burden-Sharing: Defining and Justifying the Question	1
2 A Neoclassical Realist Explanation of Transatlantic Alliance Burden-Sharing	11
3 Vietnam, Lebanon, Persian Gulf, and Somalia	31
4 Kosovo	75
5 Afghanistan	105
6 Iraq	133
7 Improving Transatlantic Alliance Burden-Sharing	169
Notes	181
Index	239

List of Tables and Figure

Table 1.1	The Transatlantic burden-sharing record	3
Table 7.1	Evaluating the propositions	170
Table 7.2	Evaluating the causal factors	174
Figure 2.1	The neoclassical realist argument.	21

Acknowledgments

One might think that researching and writing a book in Rome, Paris, and London would be all *bucatini all'amatriciana* and *croissants aux amandes*. In fact, it entailed bearing some rather imposing burdens on both sides of the Atlantic. I am very fortunate to have friends, family, and colleagues who shared those burdens—and the occasional plate of bucatini—with me.

I owe a great many of the interviews I conducted to personal connections, so I offer sincere thanks to the friends and colleagues who helped in that regard. I am especially grateful to Charlie Kupchan, who was at the center of the web of personal connections that made the book possible. Roberto Menotti put me in touch with an extraordinary number of people in Rome, Paris, and London. Raffaello Matarazzo was of tremendous help in Rome, as were Marta Dassù and Ettore Greco. For contacts and connections in Paris, I drew on Jean-Pierre Darnis, Nicolas Jabko, Daniel Keohane, François Lafond, and Edouard de Tinguy. In London, Dana Allin and Robin Niblett were of great use.

I owe the greatest debt to those who took the time to speak with me about their government's decisions regarding Kosovo, Afghanistan, and Iraq. I am grateful to those I cite by name later in the book, those I cite anonymously, and those who agreed to be interviewed only on background.

The University of Mary Washington also provided essential support. A sabbatical made the interviews possible. Carla Bailey of Simpson Library did an excellent job getting me obscure books and articles. My *Alliance Politics* students in spring 2008 and spring 2010 offered good questions and comments. My departmental colleagues provided feedback and advice: I am especially grateful to Robert Barr, Rosalyn Cooperman, Emile Lester, and Ranjit Singh.

While in Rome, I served as Visiting Scholar at Aspen Institute Italia and very much appreciate the support Gyneth Sick and others provided during my time there. I am also grateful to Alessandra Bertino, librarian of the Istituto Affari Internazionali, for her assistance with my research.

x • Acknowledgments

Toby Wahl, Farideh Koohi-Kamali, and Robyn Curtis at Palgrave all contributed in important ways to the final product. An anonymous external reviewer for Palgrave offered excellent comments as well.

I am grateful to the friends and colleagues who commented on the draft book proposal, paper presentations, or draft chapters: David Auerswald, Joshua Busby, Oliver Daddow, Brian Dempsey, Rebecca Johnson, Karl Mueller, Itai Sneh, Craig Nation, Ken Kennard, Christopher Preble, Brian Rathbun, and Patricia Weitsman. Fabrizio Coticchia and Luca Ratti provided excellent comments and made it possible for me to present my research at the Università degli Studi, Roma Tre, IMT Lucca, and the Università di Bologna, where the audiences provided useful comments and questions.

I owe a special debt to the few who read and provided comments on the entire manuscript: Roni Bart, Jack Kramer, Roberto Menotti, and Justin Simeone. Their feedback made the final product much better than it otherwise would have been.

The book's findings should not be attributed to any of those who helped with it. I alone am responsible for any flaws herein.

I also offer my heartfelt gratitude to family and friends on both sides of the Atlantic for their support, which was essential: Tom and Debby Davidson, Jeffrey McClurken, and Evelyn Schnee in the United States, Elisabeth Dardenne and Fabrizio Stefanini in Italy, and Philippe and Mireille Dardenne and Monique Lallier in France.

Alessia Stefanini Davidson deserves special thanks: she offered advice on myriad issues, tracked down articles, corrected my Italian and French grammar, completed citation details, and managed the permission request form endeavor. While this book is clearly not *Pride and Prejudice*, I still hope she will take pride in it.

I dedicate this book to Elisa and Livia. The time apart from the two of you was the hardest part of writing it.

CHAPTER 1

Transatlantic Alliance Burden-Sharing: Defining and Justifying the Question

George W. Bush responded to those who criticized his administration of waging a unilateral war against Iraq in 2003 by pointing to an over forty-nation "coalition of the willing" supporting the United States. When U.S. troops crossed into Iraqi territory on the morning of March 20, 2003, however, they had only three allied countries' troops at their sides: Britain (46,000 troops), Australia (2,000), and Poland (180).[1] British Prime Minister Tony Blair had been Bush's closest diplomatic ally in the period preceding the war, so his country's contribution came as no surprise. French President Jacques Chirac and Foreign Minister Dominique de Villepin refused their country's military support, instead becoming Washington's loudest international critics. Italian troops were conspicuously absent as American and British forces raced toward Baghdad—while Silvio Berlusconi's government in Rome had politically supported Washington in the lead-up to the war, Italy did not commit its military to the fight.[2] Why was Britain the only one of these transatlantic allies to provide military support for the 2003 Iraq War?

The casual observer might believe the 2003 Iraq case reflects a broader imbalance in transatlantic burden-sharing between the United States and its allies: that is, that America's allies rarely contribute to U.S.-led military deployments. Some analysts and politicians favor such a view. The historical record paints a very different picture, however. Over the past half century, the United States has led military operations abroad and asked Britain, France, and Italy for military support (or they believed the United States wanted support) on seven occasions. The United States received allied support on six of seven occasions from Vietnam through the 2003 Iraq War

2 • America's Allies and War

(see Table 1.1). Why do America's allies—Britain, France, and Italy—sometimes provide military support to U.S.-led uses of force and sometimes refuse? This book provides the first ever multiple-case study analysis of allied decisions to provide or refuse military support for U.S.-led military operations since 1945.

This chapter provides specification of the book's core question and argues that the question is worth studying. The chapter begins with a summary of scholarship on alliance burden-sharing, which suggests that if America's allies are rational, they will contribute little or nothing to U.S.-led uses of force, and analyst and policymaker statements asserting that America's allies contribute little of value to U.S.-led operations. The next section documents the pattern of America's allies' military contributions since Vietnam. That accomplished, the chapter argues that the United States benefits from having allies at its side when it uses force. A final substantive section elaborates on the scope of the book: it justifies the focus on Britain, France, and Italy and provides a defense of the seven cases. The chapter concludes with a brief summary of the book's explanation of transatlantic alliance burden-sharing and an outline of the coming chapters.

Allies and Burden-Sharing in Academia and Washington

Scholarship on public goods and defense burden-sharing shows that it would be fully rational for America's allies to refuse to contribute military support when the United States leads a military operation. A generation ago Mancur Olson and Richard Zeckhauser showed that the logic of public goods and free riding applied to defense spending in an alliance of asymmetric powers, such as North Atlantic Treaty Organization (NATO).[3] Olson and Zeckhauser pointed out that it was rational for America's NATO allies to underspend on defense, knowing that the United States would spend enough to provide security—a public good—for its allies. More recent scholarship confirms that the free-riding logic explains gaps in defense spending between the United States and its allies, at least for the early Cold War.[4] The public goods logic points to graver free-riding problems when applied to contributions to military operations.[5] Consider a scenario like the 1991 Persian Gulf War wherein allies view a military response to an external threat as a public good. If allies see successful action as a public good and know the United States will act successfully to eliminate the threat, their smartest move would be to refrain from providing *any* military support.

After World War II, the United States extended an alliance commitment to Western Europe to share the burden of defense against the Soviet Union.[6]

Table 1.1 The Transatlantic burden-sharing record

	VIETNAM	*LEBANON*	*P. GULF*	*SOMALIA*	*KOSOVO*	*AFGHANISTAN*	*IRAQ '03*
BRITAIN							
Contribution	*None*	80	45,000	*None*	39 planes	Air, naval, and Special Forces	46,000
FRANCE							
Contribution	*None*	1,000	10,000	1,500	84 planes	Air and Special Forces	*None*
ITALY							
Contribution	*None*	1,100	4 ships, 8 Tornadoes	2,500	58 planes	Air and naval	*None*

4 • America's Allies and War

Many today believe, however, that America's European allies get much out of but contribute little to their relationship with the United States. Donald Rumsfeld's September 2001 statement that " . . . we ought not to think that a coalition should define the mission" was rooted in the view—based on lessons learned from the 1999 Kosovo War—that America's allies provide little of value but require too much consultation.[7] At the height of the transatlantic split over Iraq, neoconservative Robert Kagan posed the question of whether the United States could provide global stability without its European allies and then responded: "The simple answer is that it already does."[8] This view is restricted neither to the Bush administration nor to the period leading up to the 2003 Iraq War. Rajan Menon makes the case that the United States should cut its alliance ties to NATO, Japan, and South Korea because the allies contribute too little to American interests relative to what they cost the United States.[9] The Cato Institute's Christopher Preble argues that only if the United States significantly cuts its defense spending and uses force less frequently will its allies start to spend and act at a level commensurate with their interests and ability.[10] Stephen Cimbala and Peter Forster suggest that a more comprehensive definition of burden-sharing is necessary: they argue that in deploying troops abroad the United States often bears more international and domestic political risk than its allies.[11]

Recently, American policymakers have been highly critical of NATO burden-sharing in Afghanistan. House Armed Services Committee Chairman Ike Skelton began a December 2007 hearing on Afghanistan contending: " . . . our NATO allies must do much more in fulfilling their commitments and freeing their forces from so-called national caveats that limit their ability to fight. . . . "[12] In that hearing Secretary of Defense Robert Gates, Chairman of the Joint Chiefs of Staff Admiral Mike Mullen, and a bipartisan host of committee members expressed similar sentiments.[13] In March 2008, Joe Biden, then Chairman of the Senate Foreign Relations Committee, noted: "This was not a war of choice. It was a war of necessity. Our allies have as much at stake as we do. . . . You're either in the fight or you are not. It is time for NATO to be fully in the fight."[14] A December 2009 Congressional Research Service report documents continued concern that NATO members need to contribute more troops and that they often attach overly restrictive caveats on the troops they do deploy.[15]

The Record: America's Allies Contribute

The scholarly literature on alliance burden-sharing and contemporary policymaker and analyst assessments suggests that America's allies contribute rarely or never to U.S.-led uses of force. The historical record, however, shows that allies have regularly contributed troops, planes, and ships to U.S.-led uses of force over the past half century. True, when the Johnson administration pressed allies to contribute to U.S.-led efforts in Vietnam—from April 1964 onwards—Britain, France, and Italy refused to provide troops.[16] In each of the other cases, however, America's allies contributed (see Table 1.1).

In August 1982, Ronald Reagan's administration led the creation of the Multinational Force (MNF) in Lebanon (which it later reconstituted as MNF II) and asked allies for troops. France initially pledged 1,000 troops to MNF II, whereas Italy offered to provide 1,100 troops, and Britain said it would deploy 80 troops.[17] After Saddam Hussein's August 1990 invasion of Kuwait, the United States led a coalition of countries to defend Saudi Arabia and expel Iraqi forces from Kuwait. George H. W. Bush's administration requested allied military support and received 45,000 British troops, 10,000 French troops, and four ships and eight Tornado fighter-bombers from Italy.[18] In December 1992, the United States led an international effort termed the Unified Task Force (UNITAF) to provide a secure environment to enable famine relief efforts in Somalia. France responded to American requests by promising at least 1,500 troops whereas Italy pledged 2,500 troops.[19] John Major's government in London refused to contribute.[20]

In March 1999, the United States joined allies in launching an air war against Serbia over the treatment of Albanians in Kosovo. The United States was by far the largest contributor to the air war and it sought to get allies to share the burden of fighting the war. In the end Britain contributed thirty-nine planes, France offered eighty-four, and Italy provided fifty-eight.[21] In the aftermath of the September 11, 2001, terrorist attacks, the United States led a military effort to kill and capture Taliban and Al Qaeda forces in Afghanistan. While not seeking large commitments from allies, it did receive British and French contributions of special forces, air and naval assets, and an Italian contribution of air and naval forces.[22] Britain provided a 46,000-troop contribution to the U.S.-led 2003 Iraq War.

The record of regular allied contribution across these six cases is striking because it is not what we would expect from the aforementioned scholarly literature and policymaker and analyst statements. Why would America's allies make rather costly contributions when they could have taken a free ride off American military might (especially given that many in the United States expect them to do so)? As such, the question of why Britain, France, and Italy contribute to U.S.-led military actions is a true theoretical and policy puzzle.

Why Allies' Contributions Matter: Legitimacy and Blood

Why should the reader care whether America's allies provide or refuse military support for U.S.-led military operations? First, analysts suggest that the larger the coalition of supporters, the greater the military action's legitimacy.[23] The use of force is almost always controversial but the more support it has, the more likely it is for undecided governments to see it as legitimate. It is also important that allies make a *military* contribution because it is costly (as the chapter discusses later) and, thus, others often see it as a truer indicator of the country's assessment of the action than political or financial support. A contrast between the Persian Gulf War and the 2003 Iraq War is illustrative. Thirty-four nations contributed troops to the Persian Gulf War. While the Bush administration claimed a forty-five-nation "coalition of the willing" supported the 2003 Iraq War, only four countries contributed troops.[24] In turn, few would dispute that the 2003 Iraq War commanded far less international legitimacy than the Persian Gulf War. Globally, there was much more widespread and vociferous opposition to the Iraq War than to the Persian Gulf War.[25]

Even those who defended the 2003 Iraq War recognized the link between coalition size and legitimacy. Robert Kagan wrote: "Nor can there be any question that the Bush administration has suffered from its failure to gain the full approval of Europe, and thus a broader international legitimacy for the invasion of Iraq—and suffered at home as well as abroad."[26] Jeremy Greenstock, the British Ambassador to the UN at the time, recently admitted that the war was of "questionable legitimacy" because it did not have the clear backing of a majority of UN member states.[27] Legitimacy matters because it can play an important role in the success or failure of the use of force in the short, medium, or long term. As Walter Wells of the *International Herald Tribune* put it, ". . . the wider the coalition the more effective the effort."[28]

Second, allies bear costs in blood and treasure, which means that all things held equal, American taxpayers pay less and fewer American soldiers' lives are imperiled. Allied troops do things that otherwise would not get done or would get done by American troops (which would have less time for other tasks or the United States would have to deploy more troops). This is not to say that every allied soldier is necessarily the equivalent of an additional American soldier. Patricia Weitsman argues, for example, that wartime alliances suffer from overly rigid decision-making structures, thus making them relatively inefficient wagers of war.[29] One should not overemphasize the negatives of fighting with allies, however. For example, while American military officials complain that allies limited their ability to effectively wage the Kosovo War, a retired Italian General pointed out that allied restraint can help prevent damaging errors like the United States' 1999 bombing of the Chinese Embassy in Belgrade.[30] Leaving aside the coordination question, the point is that if the United States were to have engaged in the aforementioned uses of force without allies, it would have had to deploy more force and/or have been less effective at the tasks it undertook. As of April 2010, the United States had 62,415 troops in Afghanistan, whereas allies provided 40,139.[31] While American officials would prefer more allied troops and fewer caveats on their use, if those allies exited Afghanistan the United States would have to deploy more troops, existing forces would have to do more, or some mission-critical tasks would not be accomplished. One final point: while the United States sometimes has to use its resources (e.g., transport planes) to get allies to the theater of operations and maintain them there, allies also sometimes have valuable skills or equipment that enhance mission effectiveness.[32]

Third, U.S. domestic political support—by the mass public and the Congress—is greater when allies contribute. In a 2006 survey by the Program on International Policy Attitudes, 72 percent agreed that the United States "should do its share in efforts to solve international problems together with other countries."[33] Allied contributions increase domestic political support because the public wants to know the burden of using force is being shared and because it is sensitive to the fact that legitimacy comes with a coalition. Secretary of State James Baker recalled that the United States could not go it alone in the Persian Gulf War because " . . . we would need the support of the American people and the Congress," and allied contributions would make that political support significantly more likely.[34] When allies contribute, American presidents gain domestic political support, which is a good in itself and is also a critical component of a successful military operation.

Defining the Question

This book analyzes all cases since World War II where the United States led a military operation in which American troops were in harm's way and it requested military support from Britain, France, and Italy or the governments of those countries could have reasonably perceived that the U.S. government desired a contribution.[35] How do we know whether a deployment of troops was in harm's way? First, they may be deployed with the intent to wage war or the knowledge that war is likely (Vietnam, Persian Gulf, Kosovo, Afghanistan, and Iraq).[36] Second, they may be deployed to

8 • America's Allies and War

conduct another type of mission (e.g., peace operations) with the knowledge that the mission puts the troops' lives at risk (Lebanon and Somalia).

This book seeks to explain whether allies make a military contribution or not. It does not claim to explain all cases of political or financial support, although a good theoretical explanation should clarify why an ally would provide only political but not military support (such as Italy in the 2003 Iraq War). As the previous discussion of the record of allied contribution makes clear, there is great diversity in the military contributions under review, from Italy's ships and planes in the 1991 Persian Gulf War to Britain's 46,000 troops in the 2003 Iraq War. What they all share in common is that they require allies to put members of their military at risk of losing their lives and, thus, are ceteris paribus a more costly contribution than money or public statements of support. Even small military contributions (like Britain's 120 troops to Lebanon) are costly because they could lead to the loss of life. In the post–World War II era, democratic societies have become casualty averse—that is, reluctant to risk the lives of their citizens on the battlefield. As a recent survey of the subject concludes: " . . . there are sufficient grounds to conclude that [casualty aversion] is more prominent now than ever before in Western democracies. . . ."[37]

The notion of request also requires elaboration. In most of the seven cases there is a record that the U.S. government formally requested that allies make a military contribution. There is frequently also a record that the allied government or analysts in the allied countries were responding to the request. There is not always a record of a request, however. When the United States leads a military operation its allies sometimes (though not always) have the impression that officials in Washington would like them to contribute and will reward them for doing so. Each of the case studies in the coming chapters includes evidence that at least one of these criteria was present. Some might take issue with the inclusion of cases where an ally was seen to push the United States to use force (e.g., Britain and the Kosovo War). Such cases should be included, however, because pushing for action is not the same as contributing to it, and as the leader of the military operation the United States has an interest in getting allies to make and maintain significant contributions. The book excludes cases where neither the United States requested that these allies contribute nor did the allies have the impression that the United States wanted them to contribute, such as Operation Uphold Democracy in Haiti in 1994.

Why these three transatlantic allies? Britain and France are obvious choices because of their importance in the policy debate and because the conventional wisdom sees Britain as most likely to support the United

States and France as most likely to oppose it. Why Italy rather than Germany?

Germany's post–World War II relations with the United States have been more thoroughly studied than Italy-U.S. relations covering the same period.[38] Italy's post–World War II foreign policy has also been less well covered than Germany's in rigorous comparative studies with other Western democracies.[39] Moreover, as noted, Italy is an increasingly consistent and significant contributor to U.S.-led uses of force alongside Britain and France, so its decisions are increasingly relevant in policy terms.[40]

The Neoclassical Realist Explanation in Brief: Alliance, Threat, and Electoral Politics

The neoclassical realist explanation of allies' support decisions stresses the value of alliance relationships, threat, prestige, and—rarely—public opinion. First, a state is more likely to provide military support if it values its relationship with the powerful ally. If a state values its relationship with a powerful ally, it makes sense to provide military support as in so doing the state will strengthen and even reinforce its existing relationship. Second, the state is more likely to provide military support to address a threat. A state is more likely to bear the burden associated with providing military support if the target of the use of force threatens the state's national interest (territorial integrity and citizen safety, economy or natural resources, or the potential to spread to impact national interest). The state is also more likely to provide military support when its prestige—its reputation for power—is implicated in the particular case. The state provides military support to demonstrate what it is willing and able to do relative to its peers. Finally, because governments desire reelection they are sensitive to public opinion—when it is likely to have electoral ramifications. Specifically, if a politically viable opposition party/coalition stands with the public against a government considering military support (a rare occurrence), the government is highly unlikely to provide support.

Conclusion: A Roadmap

The rest of this book seeks to explain British, French, and Italian decisions to provide or refuse military support for U.S.-led uses of force. The book is novel in that it attempts to explain all cases where the United States put its troops in harm's way and asked transatlantic allies to provide military support. Chapter 2 outlines a theoretical explanation rooted in the international relations theory of neoclassical realism and an alternative explanation generated from constructivist theory. Chapter 3 applies the neoclassical realist and constructivist explanations to the first four cases: Vietnam, Lebanon, the Persian Gulf War, and Somalia. Chapter 4 offers the first of three more detailed case studies, applying the theoretical explanations to British, French, and Italian decisions to contribute to the 1999 Kosovo War. Chapter 5 explores the allies' decisions to join U.S.-led efforts to overthrow the Taliban in Afghanistan. Chapter 6 provides a detailed analysis of the British decision to provide and the French and Italian decisions to refuse contributions to the 2003 Iraq War. Chapter 7 assesses the overall empirical accuracy of the neoclassical realist and constructivist explanations, concluding that the former is substantially more accurate than the latter. Chapter 7 also offers advice for American policymakers seeking to garner allied military contributions in the future.

CHAPTER 2

A Neoclassical Realist Explanation of Transatlantic Alliance Burden-Sharing

This chapter provides a theoretical explanation for why leading transatlantic allies—Britain, France, and Italy—sometimes provide and sometimes refuse military support when the United States leads military operations abroad. I posit a neoclassical realist (i.e., based in international power and security but also sensitive to domestic factors) explanation of variance in allied support. I argue that each ally was more likely to support the United States if it valued its alliance relationship with the United States and if the state perceived the target of intervention as a threat to its national interest. I also argue that each ally was more likely to support the United States if its domestic public opinion favored support and if public opinion on the issue was likely to impact the government's future electoral prospects.

The chapter first reviews the contemporary policy debate and the scholarly literature on this topic. The chapter then outlines the book's neoclassical realist argument. It provides an abstract sketch of alliance value, threat, prestige, and electoral politics. Having discussed each of the factors individually, the chapter then discusses their interaction effects and provides seven propositions linking the factors to the likelihood that a state will provide or refuse support. Development of a constructivist alternative explanation follows, including three alternative propositions. The chapter then addresses methodological issues and concludes by discussing the value of the project for contemporary scholarship.

The Policy Debate and the 2003 Iraq War

The current policy debate on this issue has been almost entirely focused on the 2003 Iraq War. Many have sought to explain France's refusal to support

12 • America's Allies and War

the United States. Perhaps the most popular argument is that Europeans—especially those on the continent—are more reluctant to use force than Americans. Robert Kagan is responsible for the most popular formulation of this argument, arguing that the European preference for peaceful means is rooted in their weakness in capabilities relative to the United States.[1] Some articulate a similar argument that countries oppose the United States when it uses force because of resentment or jealousy of American power in the post–Cold War world.[2] Others argue that the French are instinctively, almost genetically, predisposed to say "no" to the United States.[3] Finally, some stress that French opposition to the 2003 Iraq War can best be explained by the profits French companies and politicians gained (and stood to gain) from Iraq's oil.[4] Aside from their merit in explaining allied behavior in the 2003 Iraq War, these arguments cannot account for France's military contribution in five of this study's seven cases.

In explaining Britain's support for the United States in the 2003 Iraq War, analysts point to shared values and the history of the "special relationship."[5] One problem with this explanation is that it cannot make sense of all the cases. While Britain also provided support for the United States in Lebanon, the Persian Gulf, Kosovo, and Afghanistan, it chose not to contribute to U.S. efforts in Vietnam or Somalia. Britain's special relationship with the United States may explain some of the cases where it provided military contributions but it cannot explain Britain's failure to contribute in other cases.

Many have argued that the Bush administration's arrogance and impatience best explain the lack of support for the 2003 Iraq War.[6] They argue that if only the Bush administration had been more sensitive to the concerns of its major allies and had been willing to wait longer for UN weapons inspectors, allied support would have been forthcoming.[7] This argument cannot explain Italy's political support or Britain's political and military support.

In their book on the alliance dynamics preceding the 2003 Iraq War, analysts Philip Gordon and Jeremy Shapiro argued that governments that chose not to support the United States were less concerned with the threat from Iraq's weapons of mass destruction than the United States was and more concerned with the war's anticipated negative strategic ramifications.[8] Gordon and Shapiro's explanation is more generalizable than the aforementioned alternatives but it cannot make sense of the Italian government's political support for and sympathy with the American position. Gordon and Shapiro's book also did not consider alternative explanations of transatlantic burden-sharing during the 2003 Iraq War and it only focuses on that case.

The blind spots in the current policy debate demonstrate why a comprehensive study is necessary. Most of the explanations of alliance burden-sharing in the 2003 Iraq War case are only plausible explanations of that case and many cannot explain all three states' choices for that case. Some of the arguments have the potential to explain other cases but have not been evaluated across a range of cases over time.

The Scholarly Literature

The existing scholarly literature on alliance burden-sharing provides important moorings for this book but also demonstrates that the field lacks a comprehensive, comparative study. Andrew Bennett, Joseph Lepgold, and Danny Unger's 1994 article examined the ability of five hypotheses (drawn from the scholarly literature on alliances) to explain the decisions of six countries to contribute to the 1991 Persian Gulf War.[9] Bennett, Lepgold, and Unger found that international factors, like the dependence of a state on its alliance with the United States and the view that Iraqi control of Kuwait was threatening to them, explained the state's desire to contribute. The authors also found that domestic political factors often constrained states' ability to contribute. In a later book-length study, Bennett, Lepgold, and Unger enlisted an array of country specialists to engage in detailed case studies of countries that contributed (or might have) to the U.S.-led coalition.[10] The book found that alliance dependence—or anticipation of alliance dependence—was a particularly important factor in explaining state decisions to provide support, whereas domestic politics was most helpful in explaining the nature of a state's contribution (e.g., financial or military).[11] While the article and book provided good explanations of many countries' decisions, they only looked at the 1991 Gulf War.

David Auerswald developed a theoretical model to explain the level of support France, Germany, Italy, Britain, and the United States provided during the 1999 Kosovo War.[12] He argued that government institutional structure, public opinion, and collective action theory—whether a state stood to benefit from the war and whether its contribution would have made a difference to the effort—best explain the varying levels of support allies provided during the war.[13] Auerswald's study posits that a state's likelihood of benefiting from the war is a causal factor but it does not provide a theoretical basis for why benefit varies and what variance in benefit means. Moreover, Auerswald's study sets out to explain varying contribution during a war whereas this book seeks to explain the initial decision to provide or refuse military support.

Jürgen Schuster and Herbert Maier analyzed twenty European governments' stances on the 2003 Iraq War.[14] They found that power relationships explained

14 • America's Allies and War

the East European governments' decisions whereas the ideological orientations of the governing party explained the West European governments' decisions. Schuster and Maier's study is based on an extremely broad notion of support. They categorize countries that provided political—but no military—support as having "supported" the Iraq War (e.g., Italy). This book is focused on the costly decision to deploy a state's military. Moreover, the Schuster and Maier study examines only correlative relationships between posited independent and dependent variables—they do not engage in detailed, process-tracing analysis to expose the links between cause and effect.

Finally, Daniel Baltrusaitis's recent book attempts to explain state decisions to support the 2003 Iraq War and its aftermath. Baltrusaitis developed a complex decision model to explain the decisions of South Korea, Germany, and Turkey. His model stresses historical learning, balance of threat, collective action, alliance dependence, public opinion, and domestic structure.[15] Baltrusaitis's book confirms that burden-sharing explanations must include international and domestic factors. The book does not exhaust the need for further study of alliance burden-sharing, however. First, none of the three countries provided a military contribution during the formal hostilities phase of the war (South Korea provided troops only for the stabilization phase). Second, it is not clear that explaining burden-sharing decisions requires six independent variables. Third, as it only covers the 2003 Iraq case, it cannot fully assess any of that case's idiosyncrasies.

These scholarly studies suggest that analytical approaches that combine international-level power and security elements with domestic politics can provide accurate explanations of transatlantic alliance burden-sharing. Unfortunately, each of these existing studies only examines one case where the United States used force. A study that compares cases has the advantage of allowing many factors of potential interest (e.g., threat from target of intervention) to vary, permitting a more thorough study of their importance.[16]

The Neoclassical Realist Argument: Alliance, Threat, Prestige, and Electoral Politics

This book's argument is rooted in neoclassical realist theory. Neoclassical realism departs from Kenneth Waltz's structural realism in that it seeks to explain state behavior (v. the pattern of major international political outcomes).[17] The theory is realist as it stresses the impact of the anarchic international system on states: it expects states to seek to maximize their security in a world where relative power is paramount. Neoclassical realism also suggests, however, that domestic-level variables can significantly influence how security and power affect state behavior. This book begins with the view that decision makers face pressures from both the international and domestic levels. While the anarchic international system motivates states to be concerned with their security and relative power, democratic governments must also consider their domestic political survival.

Alliance Value

Much existing scholarship uses characteristics of the alliance relationship to explain variance in alliance burden-sharing.[18] I begin by observing that state value for an alliance relationship varies across countries and across time (discussion of why alliance value varies follows). Varying value for the alliance impacts a government's decision to provide or refuse support. The anticipation of future benefit from the alliance leads states to provide military support when a valued ally requests it.[19] When the state values its relationship with its ally, it has more incentive to contribute to maintaining and strengthening the alliance. The state provides requested military support with the expectation that the ally will see support as a reason to continue the alliance relationship. Conversely, if a government has low value for an alliance, it has little incentive to make sacrifices for its ally. If the state has low value for its alliance with the larger state, it will care little if the larger ally reacts to a lack of support by ending or weakening the alliance relationship.[20]

Some caveats are necessary. First, while this study covers cases where the United States requested military support from its allies, not all such cases would necessarily impact the alliance relationship. The United States may request support but not value support so much that it is willing to put its relationship with the state on the line. Second, while previous scholarship has examined alliance "dependence," or the relative power of the choosing states, I prefer alliance value.[21] I use the term value because I take into account that a government may value an ally for myriad reasons and value does not necessarily entail dependence. I determine alliance value in the cases by examining elite statements and actions prior to and during the period between the request for support and the government's decision, looking to general claims about alliance value and specific references to it as a causal factor.

What explains variance in alliance value? Alliance value varies depending on influence, external threat, and the ally's relative power.[22] Influence is critical: a state's value for an ally varies depending on the ally's sensitivity to its concerns and perspectives.[23] States value allies that listen to their views and incorporate those views into policy more than those who ignore the states' perspectives. A state may seek to be heard and to impact an ally's policy on issues related to the alliance, decisions on whether and how to use force, or on other matters of importance to them. As a support decision

16 • America's Allies and War

looms, the state will consider its influence with the ally in the recent past as the basis for its expectations about future influence. The more influence a state expects to have, the more it will value the alliance and the more likely it will be to provide support as a way of preserving it.

External threat and the ally's relative power also impact alliance value. States are more likely to value allies like the United States when they perceive a large, menacing existential threat like the Soviet Union (note: this notion of threat differs from target threat outlined in the next section). This claim is rooted in the view that alliances are a way to aggregate capabilities.[24] Variance in external threat is relevant because it tells the smaller ally whether the greater ally's capabilities are likely to be necessary to deter aggression or defend against an attack.[25] States also value an ally more when the ally is powerful relative to other states. The more power the ally has, the more power there is to aggregate with the state's own.[26] Influence is the critical factor in alliance value because of how it interacts with threat and power. When threat is high, a state's influence over an ally reduces the likelihood that the state will be abandoned or entrapped by the ally. When threat is low, influence is important because it can make the ally more predictable and can help the state achieve its goals. States care about influence over powerful allies because if they have it, they may be able to leverage their ally's power into outcomes in their favor and they have less reason to fear the ally's power will be used against them.[27]

Threat: Target Threat to National Interest and Prestige

The extent to which the target of the use of force is a threat to the state's national interest plays an important role in the decision to offer or refuse support. Analysts have used extant national interest to explain a country's costly decision to elect to use force whereas policymakers have used it as an important criterion in deciding to use force.[28] I argue that states will be more willing to incur the costs—the potential of life lost and money spent—of providing military support when the target threatens their national interest. Conversely, low threat from the target makes it harder to justify incurring costs. I define threat to national interest as a direct or potential—due to geographic proximity—threat to the state's territorial integrity or its citizens, the state's economy (including significant economic interests abroad), or a natural resource of major economic or security significance.[29] Government statements and actions are critical in determining whether a country perceived the target to be a threat to its national interest. High target threat to national interest makes intervention likely whereas low target threat makes intervention unlikely. Note: this book's notion of threat to national interest excludes existential threats to a country's fundamental survival (e.g., Nazi Germany relative to France in May 1940).[30]

A number of clarifications are in order. First, the ally has to believe the U.S.-led operation is likely to succeed. If the use of force is unlikely to succeed, the state will not benefit from a reduction in threat to its national interest. Second, a state's ability to contribute should be seen in terms of threat. Allies the United States asks for military support almost always have the capability to provide a minimum acceptable contribution if threat to national interest warrants (e.g., Britain's 120 troops in Lebanon or Italy's ships and planes in the Persian Gulf War). A government's claim that it is unable to contribute is often an indicator that insufficient national interest is at stake. Third, one should expect the costs the state is willing to bear—that is, the size of the contribution and the danger to troops it is willing to accept—to be positively correlated with threat.[31] Finally, a state's contribution must be critical for the success of the military operation. If the state thinks the United States will act successfully against the threat alone, the state can take a free ride (as discussed previously): it need not provide military support to defend against threat.

A critic might argue that the link between threat to national interest and military support borders on tautology because when states incur the costs of deploying troops it must be in their national interest, and elites often use national interest terms to justify military action. This criticism is unfounded. First, there have been cases where a government has engaged its military abroad and did not even attempt to argue that doing so was in response to a threat to its national interest. George H. W. Bush did not make a national interest case for the 1992 military deployment to Somalia, instead he made a moral case: "[t]he people of Somalia, especially the children of Somalia, need our help."[32] Second, the previously specified definition of national interest is relatively strict: it emphasizes a real or potential threat to the state's territory, citizens, or economy. The definition intentionally excludes things like threats to a country's values or international law. Thus, only statements consistent with the book's definition of threat to national interest will be seen as support for the relevant propositions.

Whether a state's prestige—the social recognition of its relative power—is implicated in the case of intervention can also have a critical bearing on the outcome.[33] States seek prestige as it makes it easier for them to achieve their goals. Providing military support for the United States can contribute to a state's prestige whereas a refusal to provide support could lead others to believe the state is neither willing nor able to engage in military action. Across case variance in the implication of prestige occurs for two reasons. First, a state's international peers (i.e., the judges of a state's prestige) may

18 • America's Allies and War

be more or less divided on the operation. If the international community is united in favoring an operation, participating will contribute to a state's prestige whereas stark divisions in the international community mean that prestige gains from contribution are not guaranteed. Second, a state's prestige may also be implicated in a case if it has historical ties or is geographically close to the target. Such ties lead the state's peers to expect it to provide support and they are likely to see a failure to do so as a lack of will or ability, justifying a devaluation of the state's prestige. Prestige concerns also vary over time: states are likely to be particularly sensitive about their prestige when they believe their peers underestimate their power. In short, a government is likely to provide military support when it perceives its prestige at stake in a particular case whereas support is less likely if the government does not perceive its prestige to be at stake in the case.

From a realist perspective it makes sense for states to emphasize alliance value, eliminate threats, and maximize prestige. These three activities are related but distinct. Consistent with realist logic, retaining valuable allies and maximizing prestige serve the national interest. They are simply indirect means of defending or enhancing the national interest that should be distinguished from direct defense of the national interest by eliminating or reducing threats to the country's territorial integrity, citizens, or economy. Note also the threat/prestige logic differs from, but does not contradict, the previous discussion of alliance value. While a state might provide support because a valued ally asks them, it might also provide support because of characteristics of the case of intervention itself: the target may be a threat to the state's national interest or the case may implicate the state's prestige.

Public Opinion and Electoral Relevance

To know whether a particular country will provide or refuse support for a large ally one must also look inside the state's government, especially given that this is a study of transatlantic democracies. While democratic leaders must consider their country's alliance relationships, threats to national interest, and prestige, they must also take their (and their party's) electoral future seriously. Governments seek to survive because election is a prerequisite to pursuing all other goals.[34] Given that the public plays a significant role in government survival, it makes sense for governments to be sensitive to public opinion when considering whether to provide support.

A country's public may have an assessment of the costs and benefits of providing support at variance with the assessment of the government—even after the latter has done its best to "educate" the former. First, the public may emphasize factors that the governing elite does not, such as the suffering of the people in the target state. The media may play a role in this process, emphasizing certain conflicts over others and framing conflicts in a way that encourages public outrage.[35] Second, the public may assess the aforementioned international-level factors discussed previously—alliance value and threat—differently than the government. If the government and public disagree on whether their country should provide or refuse support, a government concerned with its survival should defer to the public, if it expects public opinion to be relevant to its future electoral prospects. Governments that defy an electorally relevant public will be replaced by those more sensitive to the public's preferences.

While the public and governing elite may disagree on the best foreign policy for their country, governments do not always expect the disagreement to have electoral ramifications. The opposition's stance on the issue is the single most important factor in whether the public is electorally relevant. Governments fear the electoral ramifications that occur when they (the governing party or coalition) lose voters to the opposition.[36] The opposition does not always provide the public with a clear alternative to the government, however. For this to occur, the opposition must take a policy line consistent with a majority of the public and opposed to the likely governmental policy.[37] Consider a scenario wherein the government perceives high alliance value and strong national interest at stake in the target of intervention and is leaning toward providing support but the public is opposed. If the opposition joins the public in opposing a military contribution, it puts a lethal weapon in the hands of the public as the public can simultaneously punish the government and reward the opposition by voting for it. If the opposition favors support, however, the government will be less afraid of losing votes to its rivals, as it makes no sense for voters to cast their ballot for the opposition. Of course, in such a case angry voters may abstain from voting: in so doing they hurt the government but the opposition does not gain votes, so the damage to the government is less significant.

The decision to provide or refuse support must also have the potential to influence the next national election, which requires several prerequisites. The decision to provide or refuse support must be sufficiently salient to determine the vote choice of a significant portion of the public.[38] Moreover, the majority margin on providing or refusing support must be great relative to the government's general margin of support against the opposition.[39] That is, governments with a commanding lead over the opposition would be unlikely to fear a slight margin of public opposition to providing support. The next election must also loom in the government's near-to-medium-term future.[40]

If—for the reasons previously outlined—public opinion is unlikely to be relevant, it is unlikely to play a role in the decision to provide or refuse

20 • America's Allies and War

support.[41] If public opinion is relevant for the government's electoral future, the government will likely provide support when the public supports it and likely withhold if the public opposes it.

It is rare for governments to face an electorally relevant public opposed to their policy. Why? First, the public and/or opposition often agree with the government's assessment of alliance value, threat, and prestige.[42] Second, competitive opposition parties rarely side with the public against a government considering providing military support. At first glance, the opposition's unity with the government is puzzling as it appears to be electorally suboptimal: the opposition would seem to be more likely to maximize electoral gains by siding with the public. The opposition defers to the government because the latter has privileged access to secret intelligence and more resources devoted to threat analysis than the former. Thus, the opposition defers because it believes the government is better equipped to make good military support decisions. The opposition also realizes that the prospective electoral gains from opposing military support are not as clear as polls might suggest. If it later emerges that the government simply had better information than the public and opposition about threat, expected electoral gains will evaporate. Moreover, the opposition may fear that a public initially opposed to military support will rally to the government once troops are deployed, leaving it electorally exposed.

Consider all this in light of the fact that the opposition has to decide whether to initiate a conflict with the government over military support.[43] This book assumes that the opposition (and government) takes the broader national interest—valued alliances, threats to territory, citizens, and economy, and implicated prestige—seriously, only acting counter to it when forced by almost certain future electoral consequences. The aforementioned perils of criticizing a government moving toward offering military support make the opposition reluctant to oppose the government. Under two conditions the opposition may overcome its natural reluctance to challenge the government's likely support decision. The opposition must be tempted by the prospect of election-changing electoral gains (based on the size of the majority opposed, the salience of the issue, et cetera). The opposition's history and platform must also be consistent with refusing military support.[44] If the opposition adopts a critical stance in contradiction with its history and platform, it may suffer from criticism that it is pandering to the public on issues of national security.

Combining Alliance, Threat, Prestige, and Electoral Politics

The easiest cases are those where the causal variables all point in the same direction (see Figure 2.1). If a government has low value for its alliance with

Neoclassical Realist Explanation • 21

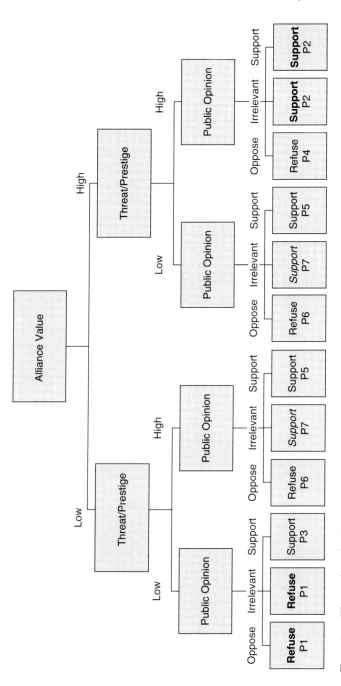

Figure 2.1 The neoclassical realist argument. Bold text indicates that the outcome is highly likely. Regular text indicates that the outcome is likely. Italics indicate that the outcome is somewhat likely.

the United States, does not see the target as a threat to its national interest (and prestige is not implicated), and public opinion opposes intervention or is irrelevant in electoral terms, it is highly likely to refuse support. If a government has high value for its alliance with the United States, sees the target of intervention as a threat (or prestige is implicated), and public opinion supports intervention or is irrelevant, it is highly likely to provide support.

When relevant in electoral terms, public opinion trumps the other factors (recall that it is rare for public opinion to be relevant). When the government has high value for its alliance with the United States and perceives the target as a threat but the public opposes support and is relevant in electoral terms, the state is unlikely to provide support. The public can also push governments to provide support that might not otherwise do so. When the government does not highly value its alliance with the United States and does not see the target as a threat to national interest but an electorally relevant public favors support, the state is likely to provide support.

Public opinion—when relevant in electoral terms—can tip the balance between split alliance value and threat/prestige. If the government attaches high value to its alliance with the United States but perceives low threat from the target (and prestige is not implicated) and public opinion favors support, then the state is likely to provide support. Similarly, if the government perceives low alliance value but high threat (or prestige is implicated) and the public favors support, then the state is likely to support. There may also be cases where the international-level factors are split but public opinion is electorally relevant and opposes support. If the government values its alliance with the United States but threat is low (and prestige is not implicated), public opposition will make the government unlikely to provide support. If the government attaches low value to its alliance with the United States but perceives a high level of threat to national interest (or prestige is implicated), public opposition will make the government unlikely to provide support.

It is most difficult to make clear claims about cases where the international factors are split and public opinion is irrelevant. High alliance value should be sufficient to lead to support even if threat is low (and prestige is not implicated). Similarly, if alliance value is low and the target threatens national interest (or prestige is implicated), the government should provide support. Several factors may complicate these causal logics, however. First, levels of alliance value and threat/prestige may be crucial: for example, extremely high alliance value will be more likely to lead to support than moderately high alliance value. Second, states might believe acting against the target will create more problems than it will solve. If alliance value is high but states perceive that the U.S.-led action is itself a threat to their national interest, the government is unlikely to provide support.

The preceding discussion of the claims resulting from the interaction of the three variables leads to the following seven propositions on transatlantic burden-sharing.

Propositions

P1: When alliance value is low, the target is not a threat, prestige is not implicated, and public opinion is opposed to intervention or irrelevant, it is highly unlikely that the government will provide support.

P2: When alliance value is high, the target is a threat or prestige is implicated, and public opinion supports or is irrelevant, it is highly likely that the government will provide support.

P3: When alliance value is low, the target is not a threat and prestige is not implicated but public opinion favors support and is relevant, it is likely that the government will provide support.

P4: When alliance value is high, the target is a threat or prestige is implicated but public opinion opposes support and is relevant, it is unlikely that the government will provide support.

P5: When alliance value is low but the target is a threat or prestige is implicated and public opinion favors support and is relevant, the government is likely to provide support. When alliance value is high but the target is not a threat and prestige is not implicated and public opinion favors support and is relevant, the government is likely to provide support.

P6: When alliance value is low but the target is a threat or prestige is implicated and public opinion opposes support and is relevant, the government is unlikely to provide support. When alliance value is high but the target is not a threat and prestige is not implicated and public opinion opposes support and is relevant, the government is unlikely to provide support.

P7: If alliance value is low and threat to national interest is high or prestige is implicated and public opinion is irrelevant, government support is somewhat likely. If alliance value is high and threat to national interest is low and prestige is not implicated and public opinion is irrelevant, support is somewhat likely.

Is the Argument (Neoclassical) Realist?

A critic might argue that the argument's realist pedigree—whether neoclassical or otherwise—is questionable.[45] Specifically, one might argue that in proposing that electoral politics can trump threat and alliance value,

24 • America's Allies and War

the argument contradicts the core realist tenet that power and security matter more than domestic factors. My response is twofold: the book's core argument is consistent with realism and it incorporates domestic factors in a way consistent with neoclassical realist scholarship.

The argument is fundamentally realist. First, the non-realist elements of the argument are less important than the realist elements.[46] There are few domestic-driven propositions relative to those where international factors dominate. Propositions three and four are only two of seven propositions. Moreover, as previously outlined, it is very rare for an electorally relevant public to oppose its government. Second, I have a realist story about how the domestic and international variables relate: government and opposition put allies, threat, and prestige ahead of electoral politics except for extreme circumstances.[47] Moreover, the cases are all instances of elective military operations where states have a choice as to whether to offer military support to an ally—these are not moments of existential crisis. Realism allows for factors other than power and security to have a role when a state's fundamental survival is not at stake.

My argument is also consistent with neoclassical realism. Neoclassical realism includes explanations of foreign policy that weigh domestic factors more heavily than traditional realist, international factors. Gideon Rose's 1998 review essay characterizes neoclassical realists as arguing that "the scope and ambition of a country's foreign policy is driven first and foremost by its place in the international system . . . " but " . . . the impact of such power capabilities on foreign policy is indirect and complex . . . " as it is filtered through unit-level variables.[48] Nowhere does Rose—or, to my knowledge, anyone else writing on the subject—say neoclassical realists eschew explanatory frameworks that include some propositions wherein domestic-level variables are in a position of superiority relative to international-level variables.[49] In fact, existing neoclassical realist scholarship includes such frameworks. Consider Randall Schweller's recent neoclassical realist explanation of underbalancing in *Unanswered Threats*: he provides four domestic-level variables that combine in four scenarios wherein domestic factors trump the international-level realist pressure to balance power.[50]

Is the Argument Constructivist? The Roots of Alliance Value and Prestige

One might argue that elements of this argument are rooted in a state's identity—stable, role-specific understandings of self and other—and, as such, that alliance value, interest, and public opinion fail to access the heart of the causal story. First, one could argue that alliance value derives from how a state sees itself relative to the United States. Perhaps Britain's high value for its alliance with the United States and France's lower value are rooted in how those countries see themselves relative to the United States. Second, one could contend that whether a state is concerned with prestige is rooted in the state's identity.[51] France and Italy may be more sensitive to cases that implicate their prestige because of how they see themselves relative to their peers.

It would be foolish to argue that identity has no effect on alliance value and prestige. However, while we know that identity is stable, alliance value and prestige concerns vary for each country over time. Moreover, the book proposes nonidentity explanations for variance in alliance value and prestige concerns. States value their alliance with the United States when they believe they will have influence in Washington. State concern with prestige varies over time on the basis of whether a government believes peer competitors underestimate its power. Prestige is implicated in particular cases when the state has ties to the target of intervention and when peer competitors agree with the use of force. The case studies include evidence to support the claims I make about the roots of the variables.

The Constructivist Alternative

Constructivist theory provides the basis for a distinct and plausible alternative framework to the previously outlined neoclassical realist one.[52] Constructivist theory stresses the ideational aspects of international politics over material factors.[53] Constructivists argue that relevant factors at the state and international levels of analysis are socially constructed (i.e., derived from social interaction). Constructivist theorists argue that identity—stable, role-specific understandings of self and other—has a significant impact on how states act and how others interpret their actions. Constructivists also argue for the importance of international-level ideational factors such as norms, which are widely shared, stable beliefs about proscribed, allowed, and required behavior in international relations.

Identity

Constructivist scholars use identity to make sense of alliance relationships.[54] As identity tells us about how a state sees itself, it would make sense for identity to influence a state's decision to provide or refuse military support to the United States. One relevant aspect of a state's identity is how consistent it is with the case of intervention; that is, a state may or may not see itself as a state that wages war, engages in peace operations, acts in

26 • America's Allies and War

support of the United Nations, etc. If the details of the case of intervention reinforce core elements of a state's identity, the state is likely to provide support. If the details of the case of intervention contradict core elements of a state's identity, the state is unlikely to provide support. The details of each case—in particular government statements about the decision—provide the best guide to which details of a state's identity are most relevant in each case. Establishing identity entails documenting widely shared elite and public notions of what a state is relative to others.

International Norms

International norms may also explain a state's action. In allowing, requiring, or proscribing particular actions, international norms attach social costs and benefits to state behavior. Constructivists argue that states comply with international norms, for example, requiring states to provide medical treatment to wounded enemy soldiers, not necessarily because it is in their national interest to do so but because they would suffer a social stigma in international relations if they failed to comply.[55] Constructivists also argue that states internalize international norms and comply with them because they see them as just. If so, international norms favoring U.S.-led intervention (i.e., norms require action) should make states likely to provide support. If norms do not clearly favor U.S.-led intervention (i.e., norms proscribe intervention or multiple norms conflict), states should be unlikely to provide support. Government statements regarding their decision are the best guides to which norms are most relevant for a particular country in a particular case. Two caveats apply. First, norms should be widely shared (although not necessarily universal) in the international system. Second, relevant actors must perceive that an international norm applies to the case of intervention.

Alternative Interaction Effects

As with the neoclassical realist explanation, the easiest claims emerge from the most radical combination of variables. When a state's identity is consistent with the case of intervention and international norms require intervention, the constructivist alternative suggests that the state should definitely provide support. Consider the special case of international norms that permit action (i.e., they allow but do not require it). While a permissive norm cannot explain a state's decision to provide support, if a state's identity is consistent with intervention, support is highly likely. Conversely, when a state's identity opposes intervention and international norms proscribe intervention or norms conflict, constructivism tells us that the state should not provide support. Mixed cases are more difficult to predict. When identity and international norms conflict, the relative intensity of the factors is likely to determine the outcome. Note: in each of the case studies I use the sources to pinpoint the most plausible aspect of identity / international norm and develop it as the alternative explanation.

Alternative Propositions

AP1: When a state's identity is consistent with the case of intervention and widely shared international norms require or permit intervention, support is highly likely.

AP2: When a state's identity is inconsistent with the case of intervention and widely shared international norms proscribe intervention or multiple norms conflict, support is highly unlikely.

AP3: When a state's identity is consistent with the case of intervention but widely shared international norms proscribe intervention or multiple norms conflict, or when a state's identity is not consistent with the case of intervention but international norms require intervention, the state's decision will be determined by the more intense factor.

Methods

The book uses congruence procedure and process-tracing methods to evaluate the neoclassical realist and constructivist explanations of the cases.[56] Congruence procedure entails assessing whether the neoclassical realist and constructivist propositions' posited combinations of causal factors and outcomes fit the actual values of factors and outcomes in the cases. For example, the following evidence would support neoclassical realist proposition two: the Blair government provided military support for the 2003 Iraq War, had a high value for its alliance relationship with the United States, believed Iraq was a threat, and the British public's opposition was irrelevant (as the Conservative Party favored support). Neoclassical realist proposition two would not have been supported had the causal factor values remained the same but the Blair government had refused to provide support.

Each case study concludes by noting the fit between the case and the relevant neoclassical realist proposition and alternative proposition (see Table 7.1 in Chapter 7). There are three case/proposition possibilities: support, not support, and minimal support. I judge the case to have supported the proposition if the causal factor values and expected outcome align and there is any

28 • America's Allies and War

evidence that one or more of the posited causal factors led to the outcome (even though the evidence may be mixed and/or convincing rebuttal points may exist). I judge the case to have not supported the proposition if the causal factor values do not align with the outcome. Finally, I judge the case to have minimally supported the proposition if the causal factors and outcome align but there is no evidence that even one of the variables led to the outcome.

Process tracing requires that the researcher uncover the links between the causal factors and outcomes. For Britain in the 2003 Iraq War, this entails establishing that value for the alliance with the United States and the perception of Iraqi weapons of mass destruction (WMD) threat were critical in the Blair government's decision to offer military support to the United States. Establishing causal effect requires the careful tracing of each causal variable from its emergence up to the moment of the outcome, revealing all points at (and ways in) which the causal variable appears to have contributed to the outcome. Congruence procedure and process-tracing methods require careful reading of secondary sources, memoirs, published documents, and contemporary news accounts.

The process-tracing method benefits from direct access to decision makers through elite interviews. From November 2008 to July 2009 I conducted fifty-nine interviews in London, Rome, and Paris with policymakers and analysts. Policymaker interviews provide a critical insider perspective whereas analysts can provide a broader, less political angle. I believe I interviewed a representative sample of government, opposition, and apolitical policymakers and analysts but I provide as much detail as possible from each interview in the cases so that readers can make their own judgments. I list roughly one-third of the interviewees as anonymous for one of two reasons: the interviewee requested anonymity because of her/his continuing career or because the interviewee declined to sign Palgrave's "Consent and Release Form." When appropriate I discuss bias as an explanation for mixed responses (e.g., government officials say one thing and the opposition says another). In most of the hour-long interviews I began with a general question about the country/case (e.g., "Why did Britain provide troops for the 2003 Iraq War?"), and then asked specific questions about the posited neoclassical realist and constructivist factors. The interviews provide the basis for alternative assessments of other sources and provide insight into the relative impact of the different causal factors.

I use process-tracing analysis to assess the causal weight of each factor in each case's outcome (see Table 7.2 in Chapter 7). For example, through process-tracing analysis I seek to assess how important alliance value was in the Blair government's decision to provide military support for the 2003 Iraq War. I classify the causal effects of each factor as follows: Opposite direction (OD) factors predict an outcome different from the one that occurred. In the case of predicted direction (PD) factors, the outcome is correct but there was no evidence of a causal role for the factor in the case. I classify factors as having provided some evidence (ED) when the analysis uncovered some policymaker or analyst assessments, including interviews, suggesting the factor affected the outcome. I classify factors as tied to the outcome by strong evidence (SE) when multiple policymaker and analyst statements, including interviews, suggest the factor was among the most important factors in explaining the outcome. For the factors I classify as ED and SE, I also note whether convincing rebuttal points cast doubt on the causal impact of the factor. Finally, I assess the causal weight of the two explanations for each case by noting the strongest individual factor for each explanation, noting any rebuttal points to that factor and any OD predictions the explanation made in that case.

Due to space constraints I developed only the most compelling of the two constructivist causal factors (identity or norms) for cases in Chapter 3, unless the sources suggested that both mattered. In the cases where I developed only one factor, I presumed that the other factor predicted the same outcome as the one I developed and based the proposition judgment on the developed factor. In the process-tracing discussion I label the factor I did not develop as N/A.

Readers may wonder how generalizable this book's findings are. Because this book is a study of three of America's transatlantic allies—Britain, France, and Italy—its findings should be generalizable first and foremost to other NATO member countries the United States asks for military support and to future instances of U.S.-led uses of force involving requests to Britain, France, and Italy. The findings may also have applicability to other advanced, industrialized post–World War II allies of the United States (e.g., Australia). Idiosyncrasies of particular allies and cases, may limit the book's generalizability, however.

Conclusion

This chapter provides a theoretical framework rooted in neoclassical realist theory to explain British, French, and Italian decisions to provide or refuse military support to the United States from Vietnam to the 2003 Iraq War. The neoclassical realist framework argues that states are highly likely to provide support when alliance value and threat are high (or prestige is implicated) and public opinion is irrelevant or supports intervention. The argument further claims that states are unlikely to provide support when alliance value and threat are low (and prestige is not implicated) and when

30 • America's Allies and War

public opinion is irrelevant or opposes intervention. When relevant, public opinion can trump alliance value and national interest. In the next four chapters, I will evaluate these claims—in the form of seven propositions—relative to British, French, and Italian decisions on seven cases from Vietnam to the 2003 Iraq War. In so doing I will be considering the evidence for these propositions relative to the aforementioned three constructivist propositions.

CHAPTER 3

Vietnam, Lebanon, Persian Gulf, and Somalia

In April 1964 Lyndon Johnson's administration created the "More Flags" program and began to put significant pressure on the United States' leading allies to contribute ground troops to the U.S.-led fight in Vietnam.[1] To the dismay of many in Washington, the allies—even the British—refused. Dean Rusk recalled with bitterness: "[a]ll we needed was a regiment. The Black Watch would have done."[2] As the prospect of war in the Persian Gulf loomed roughly three decades later, George H. W. Bush's administration again sought allies to provide a military contribution. The allies responded more favorably to American requests to contribute to the Persian Gulf War—Britain, France, and Italy all contributed, though the size of the contribution varied.

From 1964 through 1992 the United States led four significant military efforts abroad in which it asked its allies to contribute their forces. The nature of those operations and their goals varied. In the 1960s, the United States sought to defend the government of South Vietnam against the Vietcong and North Vietnamese government. In 1982, the U.S.-led Multinational Force (MNF) facilitated the evacuation of the Palestine Liberation Organization (PLO) from Lebanon and then (under MNF II) sought to aid the Lebanese government in the provision of stability. In 1991, the United States led a coalition effort to remove Iraqi forces from Kuwait. Finally, in 1992, the United States led a multinational coalition to provide sufficient security in Somalia so that famine relief could be delivered.

Allied responses to American requests varied across the cases. Britain, France, and Italy refused repeated appeals for military contributions to the Vietnam War. The three countries contributed to the MNF in Lebanon and the Persian Gulf War, though the size and timing of the contributions varied. Finally, while France and Italy contributed to U.S.-led efforts in

32 • America's Allies and War

Somalia, Britain refused the American request. How can we explain the pattern of allied responses across the four cases?

Vietnam

Britain: National Interest Trumps Alliance

American requests for allied contributions to augment the U.S.-led efforts on behalf of the government of South Vietnam date to November 1961 but they became more urgent during the Johnson administration.[3] From 1964–66 Johnson administration officials repeatedly requested that Britain—America's closest ally—provide even a small contribution of troops.[4] Yet, Harold Wilson's government did not provide British troops to fight in Vietnam.[5] Wilson's government provided political support for the United States' Vietnam policy during most of the period, though the British Prime Minister publicly criticized the U.S. bombing of North Vietnam in June 1966.[6] Finally, the Wilson government initially yielded to related U.S. requests to maintain its presence "East of Suez," though in July 1966 it announced a reduction in its Asian commitments.[7]

A variety of sources suggest that the Wilson government valued Britain's relationship with the United States. While the United States had not supported the UK in the 1956 Suez Crisis, the persistence of the Soviet threat and American power meant that the Macmillan government had to do its best to rebuild relations with Washington.[8] Specifically, the Kennedy administration agreed to sell the British the Polaris submarine-based nuclear deterrent in 1962, which made London highly dependent on the United States.[9] The British also relied on the United States for help with persistent balance of payments trouble and defense of the pound.[10] As of 1964 there were a variety of reasons for the Wilson government to value Britain's relationship with the United States and it seems that it did.[11] As Wilson told Johnson during his first visit to Washington as Prime Minister, "We regard our relationship with you not as a *special* relationship but as a *close* relationship, governed by the only things that matter, unity of purpose and unity in our objectives."[12] The Wilson government's high value for its alliance relationship explains its political support for the U.S.-led war in Vietnam, despite the fact that it thought U.S. policy was mistaken and supporting Washington was costly in domestic political terms.[13]

Johnson administration officials made clear to their Wilson government counterparts that if Britain wanted to influence American Vietnam policy, it would have to contribute troops. In a February 1965 phone call Wilson warned Johnson about the dangers of escalation in Vietnam and Johnson replied: "[a]s far as my problem in Vietnam we have asked everyone to share it with us. They were willing to share advice but not responsibility."[14] American officials made clear how important a British contribution was to them.[15] In their December 1964 meeting Johnson told Wilson that "[a] few soldiers in British uniforms in South Vietnam, for example, would have a great psychological and political significance."[16] U.S. Secretary of State Rusk would later remark, "[a]ll we needed was one regiment . . . don't expect us to save you again."[17] Given British value for the U.S. alliance, why did they choose not to provide a symbolic contribution?

The main reason why the Wilson government chose not to provide troops to the U.S.-led Vietnam War is because Vietnam was not a threat to British interests. First, the Wilson government did not view communism in Vietnam as a threat because they did not view the communist world as an ever-expanding monolith. In a May 1964 report on Vietnam, Foreign Secretary Patrick Gordon Walker noted: "[O]ur analysis of the situation differs somewhat from the Americans. We see more division amongst the Communist forces, less of a solid chain from Peking to the Viet Cong."[18] Second, the British government did not believe that the United States could succeed in attaining a military solution to the problem. A February 1964 Joint Intelligence Committee (JIC) report on Vietnam, which influenced the government, concluded that "the Southern insurgence was largely self-sustaining, that the Khanh government lacked the requisite ability and popular support to meet the challenge, that Hanoi leaders would not buckle in the face of military pressure, and that escalation across the seventeenth parallel therefore made little sense."[19] Third, the Wilson government believed that Britain's military was already overextended (including its operations in Malaysia) and, thus, it could not afford to engage in new—elective—deployments.[20] As Wilson reflected with regard to his government's first defense policy review: " . . . Britain's defence forces were over-stretched almost to breaking-point. There was an excessive strain on the troops themselves, especially unaccompanied service. Something had to give: it had to be commitments."[21] To sum up: there was no national interest reason for British troops to be engaged in Vietnam.

The British public supported the government's decision to refuse troops for the U.S.-led war in Vietnam. In May 1965, 71 percent of respondents said that Britain should focus on getting peace talks started.[22] In early 1965, the U.S. Ambassador to the UK reported that "[p]ublic opinion in Great Britain is overwhelmingly in favor of negotiations, through reconvening the 1954 Geneva conference or otherwise."[23] Over time, the British public became increasingly opposed to the Wilson government's political support for the United States' Vietnam policy.[24] The Conservative Party did not

34 • America's Allies and War

favor military support for the United States in Vietnam.[25] As such, if the Wilson government had decided to offer a symbolic contribution, voters could have retaliated by switching their vote from Labour to Conservative. It is unclear whether this factor influenced the outcome, however, as there is no evidence that the Wilson government ever considered providing a military contribution. Moreover, had electoral politics served to restrain the government, we might have seen a change (or at least a debate) in policy after Labour gained a more comfortable majority in the 1966 elections.[26] That said, it is possible that the Conservatives' stance relative to the public tipped the balance for the Wilson government between the alliance with the United States and national interest.

The constructivist alternative explanation suggests identity and norms can better make sense of the case. Wilson government officials called on their country's identity as an international mediator to explain their refusal to provide troops, citing Britain's role as cochairman of the Geneva conference.[27] In Washington on December 7, 1964, Wilson noted: " . . . [O]ur position as co-chairman of the 1954 Conference implied that we might find ourselves in a very embarrassing international position . . . " given the U.S.-led war.[28] Wilson further justified his government's position by referencing the 1954 Geneva Agreement's "ban on the introduction of fresh troops, military personnel, arms and munitions."[29] Historians have cast doubt on this explanation, however. The Geneva Conference cochair refrain, as historian Sylvia Ellis puts it, " . . . provided a convenient mask behind which Wilson could hide his own feelings of apprehension about U.S. involvement in Vietnam."[30]

The Wilson government's refusal to provide a military contribution fits proposition six (see Tables 7.1 and 7.2 in Chapter 7). Had the Wilson government been motivated primarily by alliance value, it would have offered a symbolic troop contribution.[31] While the government valued the UK's alliance relationship with the United States, its national interest was not threatened in Vietnam, and had it offered support, it would have faced negative electoral ramifications as both the public and the opposition were against providing British troops. Myriad government reports and statements by policymakers suggest that the Wilson government believed Britain's national interest was not threatened in Vietnam; in fact, it believed that the U.S.-led Vietnam War was itself a threat to British interest. The evidence also indicates that the Wilson government valued its alliance relationship with the United States and that this explains why it provided political support. Finally, the British public and opposition did not favor support. It is plausible that this factor affected the outcome but there is no direct evidence that it did. Some evidence supports the claim that Britain's decision was driven by its role as mediator, so the case provides support for alternative explanation two, but that interpretation has been rebutted by a leading scholar of the case.

France: Interest, Prestige, and Alliance

When the Johnson administration launched the April 1964 More Flags program they did not formally appeal to the French government, headed by Charles de Gaulle. Frederik Logevall writes that "[f]or obvious reasons Paris was not on the list, although the embassy did receive a copy of the cable."[32] It made sense for the Johnson administration not to appeal to Paris because de Gaulle had consistently opposed the United States' military intervention in Vietnam, dating to his May 1961 meeting with President Kennedy.[33] In fact, Dean Rusk later wrote that in 1961 de Gaulle told Kennedy that there would never be another French soldier in Southeast Asia.[34] Why was de Gaulle's government so opposed to U.S. policy that the Johnson administration refrained from asking France for military support?

De Gaulle's government did not value France's alliance relationship with the United States for myriad reasons. The United States refused to help France develop nuclear weapons, most notably with the 1954 McMahon Act and an extension of it in 1958.[35] Moreover, the 1956 Suez crisis taught the French that they could not rely on the United States in a time of crisis.[36] As historian Frédéric Bozo writes, "For French leaders the principal lesson of the Suez crisis [was] in effect Washington's 'abandonment' of its two principal allies."[37] The Cuban Missile Crisis was also significant: while De Gaulle trusted U.S. claims that the Soviets had begun placing nuclear weapons in Cuba, he was shocked that the United States did not consult with its allies in deciding on a response.[38]

Thomas Schwartz labeled de Gaulle the Western leader "most adamantly opposed to American policies."[39] Such opposition may be seen as an indication that the de Gaulle government did not value France's relationship with the United States. De Gaulle's 1963 decision to withdraw the French Channel and Atlantic fleets from NATO can be seen as a further indication that he had low value for his country's relationship with the United States.[40] Finally, the de Gaulle government valued France's alliance with the United States less because of the latter's military intervention in Vietnam.[41] In short, de Gaulle's government did not value France's relationship with the United States, so it had no reason to provide military support.[42]

De Gaulle's government also did not see communism in Vietnam as a threat to French national interests. First, de Gaulle believed the Vietnamese were nationalists first and foremost. As such, a unified Vietnam governed

36 • America's Allies and War

by Ho Chi Minh did not equal global communist expansion or a threat to French security. Frederik Lovegall writes that de Gaulle proposed "neutrality" for Vietnam knowing that "[u]ltimately, Hanoi might gain control of all of Vietnam, but it would take time and would in any event not be a big blow to the West. In the long run, de Gaulle was certain, Vietnam would be more Vietnamese than communist."[43] Moreover, de Gaulle was convinced that the threat of Soviet expansion was decreasing and bipolarity was becoming muted, thus justifying less focus on the U.S.-USSR clash.[44] De Gaulle wrote that as of 1958, "[i]t now seemed fairly unlikely that the Soviets would set out to conquer the West."[45] Second, de Gaulle drew on France's experience in Vietnam and Algeria to conclude that U.S. military intervention could not succeed in Vietnam.[46] In 1961, de Gaulle warned President Kennedy privately: " . . . [Y]ou will sink step by step into a bottomless military and political quagmire, however much you spend in men and money."[47] In April 1965, the French President told Johnson: "[i]f the United States does not decide now to withdraw from Vietnam, the war will last ten years. And the war will never end without the Americans losing face. . . . "[48] Third, de Gaulle was quite concerned that U.S. intervention in Vietnam would lead to expanded conflict and greater regional instability. De Gaulle referred to the United States as "the greatest danger in the world today to the peace" because he was concerned that the war in Vietnam would lead to regional and perhaps global conflagration.[49]

Some evidence suggests that prestige played a role in France's Vietnam policy. Scholars agree that enhancing prestige was one of de Gaulle's core foreign policy goals.[50] France had seen the social recognition of its power suffer from its quick defeat in World War II and withdrawal from colonial outposts, including Vietnam and Algeria.[51] It seems most likely that prestige tells us why de Gaulle publicly criticized America's Vietnam policy (v. why de Gaulle refused military support). Recent research by Yuko Torikata demonstrates that de Gaulle's public criticism of the United States' Vietnam policy came well after his initial assessment that the United States was unlikely to be successful.[52] Having decided against support, de Gaulle "hoped that his Vietnam stance would increase France's prestige in the Third World."[53]

The French public opposed providing military support but there is no evidence that electoral politics drove de Gaulle's decision. In a September 1966 poll 66 percent of respondents said the United States should begin withdrawing from Vietnam.[54] It is likely that a higher percentage would have opposed a French contribution. French journalists shared de Gaulle's skepticism that the U.S.-led military effort could succeed—their views were most likely an influence on public opinion and an indicator of it.[55] The

French left also opposed U.S. policy in Vietnam, disagreeing only on how France should express its disapproval.[56] As such, if de Gaulle had decided to provide military support for the U.S.-led war in Vietnam, disgruntled voters could have punished him by voting for the opposition. Perhaps de Gaulle opposed the U.S.-led war in Vietnam to maximize his electoral chances. There is no evidence, however, that de Gaulle ever considered providing military support.

Some might argue that French identity could better explain this case. Some have noted that de Gaulle saw France as a defender of humanity. As de Gaulle said: "It is a great responsibility to be France, the humanizing power par excellence."[57] Perhaps, then, French policy was driven by a desire to improve the lives of the Vietnam people. A humanitarian logic is not consistent with de Gaulle's private or public statements on Vietnam or his other significant policies, however. De Gaulle did not mention the suffering of the Vietnamese people in public or private discussions about the U.S.-led war. Moreover, de Gaulle took little issue with the French military's brutal repression of the *Front de libération nationale* (FLN) in Algeria or with the human suffering French policies caused; he agreed to Algeria's independence because he believed military operations would not succeed.[58]

The de Gaulle government's decision to refuse support for the Vietnam War provides support for proposition one. De Gaulle's early private assessment was that Vietnamese communism was not a threat to French interests and that military action in Vietnam would not succeed. He also did not value France's alliance with the United States. Thus, he had no difficulty criticizing the United States publicly to enhance France's prestige. While the French public and opposition might have punished de Gaulle had he provided support, there is no evidence that he considered doing so. French humanitarianism is a plausible explanation but no evidence supports it, thus, this case provides only minimal support for alternative proposition two.

Italy: Interest Trumps Alliance

In July 1964, President Johnson instructed the U.S. Ambassador in Rome (along with the ambassadors of ten other allies) to press the Italian government to provide a military contribution to the Vietnam War.[59] Italy provided political support for the U.S. effort and "abstention from direct criticism" but it did not make any military contribution.[60] Finally, the Italian government engaged in or supported a number of attempts from 1965 to 1968 to spur peace negotiations regarding Vietnam.[61] Why did Italy refuse to provide military support despite a specific request from President Johnson to do so?

38 • America's Allies and War

The Italian government, headed by Prime Minister Aldo Moro, valued Italy's alliance relationship with the United States. Italy was a founding member of NATO, was host to U.S. air and naval bases, and its alliance with the United States was popular, with the exception of the Italian Communist Party (PCI) and its followers.[62] Soviet threat and Italy's proximity to the Soviet bloc and its inability to provide for its own defense made it dependent on the United States for its security.[63] While the Italian government did not welcome the perceived "international declassification" that came with the U.S. withdrawal of Jupiter medium range nuclear missiles from Italy in 1963, a substantial American military presence (including nuclear weapons) remained in Italy.[64] The U.S. government frequently demonstrated how much it appreciated Italy as an ally, such as in its billion-dollar loan of spring 1964.[65]

In 1958, Prime Minister Amintore Fanfani (Foreign Minister in 1965 and 1966–68) said: "Today, as yesterday, the guiding star of Italian foreign policy is the fullest and most effective Atlantic solidarity."[66] In 1962, Giuseppe Saragat, who would serve as Italian Foreign Minister (1963–64) and President (from 1964–71), said he hoped Italy would never have to choose between Europe and America "[b]ut if it should come to this, I would choose America and so would the overwhelming majority of my countrymen, with the only exception of the Communists and of the Neo-Fascists. America, the alliance with America are essential for our security and for our freedom. . . . "[67] The December 1963 "opening" to the left, wherein the Christian Democrats formed a coalition with the Socialists, did not change the alliance value calculus as the Socialists made clear their full support for Italy's relationship with the United States.[68]

Vietnam did not pose a threat to Italy's national interest, however. In the 1960s, Italian officials believed Italy's interests to extend to Europe, perhaps the Mediterranean but not Asia. In 1965, Moro responded to criticisms that Italy should be more engaged in seeking peace in Vietnam by saying "Italy is a power that does not have direct interests beyond Europe, neither does it have international commitments that allow or oblige it to engage in concrete action in non-European areas."[69] Italy's President Giuseppe Saragat agreed, saying Moro had "taken into account both Italy's solidarity with the U.S. and the fact that we have no specific commitments in that area, but are interested in peace and progress toward international *detente*."[70] Simply put, " . . . the war in Vietnam ended up representing for Italy a concrete fact far away from its own immediate interests. . . . "[71]

Italian officials like Giorgio La Pira, former Mayor of Florence and friend of Foreign Minister Fanfani, held the view that a political solution (leaving Ho Chi Minh in power) was a much better outcome than the

U.S.-led war.[72] Others, such as Vice Premier Pietro Nenni, worried that the Vietnam War could ignite new East-West conflict and would hurt America's image in Europe.[73] As U.S. involvement grew, Italy's Ambassador to Saigon, Giovanni D'Orlandi, reported that he did not believe the U.S.-led war would succeed.[74] With no threat to national interest in Vietnam and a growing perception that U.S. policy would not succeed, it made sense for the Moro government to refuse military support.

Conditions were ripe for electoral politics to be a decisive factor in this case. First, the Italian public was opposed to the U.S.-led war in Vietnam. The PCI perceived such a swell of public opposition to the Vietnam War that it chose to use the war as a "theme of mass mobilization."[75] Mario Sica, a diplomat at the Italian embassy in Saigon, stressed the importance of the media in cultivating the Italian public's opposition to the war.[76] Second, as mentioned previously, the PCI was very critical of the Moro government's political support. PCI leader Palmiro Togliatti had already criticized the Christian Democrats for being so allied to Washington as to not have a foreign policy—with the government's support for the United States in Vietnam the criticism only mounted.[77] One might imagine that the government would have considered providing a symbolic contribution if they had not been restrained by public opinion.

The problem with this logic is that the PCI was not a credible threat to govern Italy. While its share of the vote had been increasing since the end of World War II, it had garnered only 25 percent of the vote in 1963 relative to the Christian Democrats' 38 percent, and other parties were loath to form a governing coalition with the PCI.[78] It is hard to imagine a small Italian contribution to Vietnam leading to a sufficiently large shift of votes to the PCI that would make up the vote gap. Moreover, while the Moro government expressed "understanding" for the U.S. position in Vietnam, I have seen no evidence that it considered providing a military contribution.

Italy emerged from World War II with an image of itself as a force for peace, working to make the world a better place through the United Nations. In discussions with UN Secretary General U Thant, Aldo Moro affirmed Italy's "solidarity with the United Nations, as well as complete adhesion to the ideals and principles of its Charter, represent the anchor of Italian foreign policy."[79] In September 1965, Fanfani was elected President of the UN General Assembly, thus cementing the peace identity logic. While Italy's peace image and the lack of a United Nations Security Council (UNSC) resolution endorsing intervention in Vietnam may have contributed to the Moro government's policy, it does not seem like this factor was the principle one. First, policymakers or analysts did not cite this factor to explain the outcome. Second, if the Moro government had been driven

40 • America's Allies and War

primarily by its peace image, why did it express "comprehension" with the United States rather than firmly criticizing American escalation of the war in Vietnam and the resulting massive loss of life (often in brutal fashion)? Third, the Moro government's peace efforts were limited—as established previously, by the fact that Italy's national interest was not implicated—and the negotiation efforts were cleared with the United States in advance.

The Moro government's decision to refuse support for the Vietnam War did not provide support for proposition seven. Policymaker statements and analysts' assessments provide strong evidence that the Moro government believed Italy's national interests would be negatively affected by U.S. military action in Vietnam and that assessment overrode the government's high value for Italy's alliance with the United States.[80] While the public and opposition favored refusing the Johnson administration's request, the opposition was not a credible electoral threat. No policymakers or analysts suggest Italy's peace image explains its decision to refuse support so the case provides only minimal support for alternative proposition two.

Lebanon

Britain

Britain's contribution to the MNF in Lebanon was anemic. In August 1982 the United States, France, and Italy contributed troops to make up the MNF, which sought to facilitate the PLO's evacuation from Beirut. Upon accomplishing its task, the MNF withdrew and dissolved itself. Shortly thereafter, Christian Falangist (and pro-Israel) President Bashir Gemayel was assassinated. From September 16 to 18, Israeli forces stood by as Falange militias massacred Palestinian civilians in the Sabra and Shatila refugee camps. In the wake of the massacre the United States, France, and Italy agreed to Lebanese government requests to create MNF II. Within days 3,500 MNF troops were in Beirut.[81] On December 20, Britain's Foreign Secretary, Francis Pym, told the House of Commons that Britain would contribute eighty troops to MNF II. Ultimately, the British contribution grew to 120 troops, observing and reporting cease-fire violations, patrolling, and guarding cease-fire committee meetings.[82] Why did Britain contribute? Why, given that it contributed, did it take so long to make its contribution and why was the contribution so small?

The Thatcher government valued Britain's alliance with the United States. In a fall 1982 parliamentary debate on nuclear disarmament, for example, she said, "It is not for us to tell the United States what to do about their strategic nuclear force. It is for us to recognize that their strategic nuclear force is the final guarantor of Europe's liberty."[83] Britain also valued its alliance with the United States because it meant Britain had influence with the world's most powerful country. Ronald Reagan's advisers saw Thatcher as "potentially decisive" on issues she cared about.[84] Of course, Thatcher did not always get what she wanted but she often shaped unfavorable policies in Britain's favor. Perhaps the greatest irritant in the U.S.-UK relationship as of summer 1982 was the Reagan administration's sanctions on foreign subsidiaries of American firms that were building a Soviet gas pipeline. By September 1982, Reagan's new Secretary of State, George Shultz, had begun talks with the relevant parties that would ultimately lead to a significant rollback of the sanctions.[85] Undoubtedly, the Falklands War was the most significant instance where the alliance with the United States bore fruit. While the United States was not as supportive as Thatcher would have liked, the United States went against its own regional interests and shared critical intelligence with the UK and allowed Britain to use its base on Ascension Island.[86]

Some evidence links the Thatcher government's high value for Britain's alliance with the United States to its decision to provide support. Journalists writing for *The Times* wrote that the United States wanted Britain to contribute and that U.S. desires were important in explaining the outcome. An article published on November 8, 1982 noted that the United States had been urging countries to contribute troops to the MNF.[87] On November 16, *The Times*' diplomatic correspondent Henry Stanhope noted that "Britain was to give a positive response to President Gemayel, especially as the United States would like it to."[88] John Dumbrell characterized Britain's contribution as "Joint U.S.-UK military action."[89] David Sanders argues that Britain's contribution to the MNF is an example of the UK providing "support to U.S. efforts to protect the presumed world-wide interests of the Western capitalist powers. . . ."[90]

Middle Eastern instability was a moderate threat to British national interests. A chapter on the British contribution notes that there was a " . . . wider British interest in promoting the peace process in the Middle East. . . ."[91] As Sir Percy Cradock, who would serve as Thatcher's Foreign Policy Adviser starting in 1984, wrote with regard to the Middle East, "British interests were now of a more general kind and shared with European Community partners: ensuring the continued supply of oil; doing what could be done to mitigate the effects of the Arab-Israeli feud and preserve regional stability."[92] *The Times* put it this way in arguing for a British contribution: "It is very much in the interest of the West to help that part of the world find peace and stability."[93]

Two characteristics of the case relating to Britain's national interest explain why the contribution was so tardy and small. The Thatcher

42 • America's Allies and War

government did not believe MNF II would resolve the threat to Britain's interest and the threat was not so great as to justify a large contribution. First, Thatcher was apparently skeptical about the MNF's ability to achieve its objectives. As she wrote in her memoirs with regard to the MNF, "it is unwise to intervene in such situations unless you have a clear, agreed objective and are prepared and able to commit the means to secure it."[94] If it were not likely to be effective, then it would not resolve a threat to Britain's interest. Second, Thatcher government officials argued that their ability to contribute was limited because they were overstretched (the Falklands War ended in mid-June). Francis Pym and other officials stressed Britain's overcommitment in *The Times*.[95] When asked in June 1982 about whether the government was considering a contribution Thatcher replied: "[we] are already playing a part in the multinational force in Sinai. It would be unwise to make further promises in view of our already extended commitment."[96]

Of course, both points indicate limits on the threat to Britain's national interest. If threat had been higher, Thatcher would have argued for a more robust force and clearer objectives and would have made the sacrifices necessary to make them happen. *The Times* reported on November 11 that Britain was capable of contributing a battalion (over eight hundred troops) to the MNF but doing so would disrupt existing plans for troop rotation.[97] Thatcher made the logic even more explicit when she answered an American television interviewer's question about the MNF, "[o]ne musn't get too overstretched. And we always have to remember, both the United States and ourselves, that the main potential aggressor is the Soviet Union and the Warsaw Pact because they are really hitting at our total way of life. We must never lose sight of that."[98] In other words, Britain could not best prepare for defense against the USSR if it made large contributions to address only moderate threats to its national interest.

Margaret Thatcher came to office concerned about the state of Britain's power and prestige. As she said a few months before the 1979 general election, "[t]wenty years ago Britain stood really high in the world. . . . Britain is now seventh out of nine nations of Europe. . . . And this is no place for Britain."[99] Many saw the 1982 Argentine invasion of the Falkland Islands as an indicator of how low Britain's prestige had fallen and as a challenge to it.[100] The British military's success in retaking the islands led to an upward adjustment in assessments of British prestige. Conservative MP Alan Clark said, " . . . our standing in the world has been totally altered by this. It has made every other member of NATO say 'My God, the British are tough'."[101] Prestige may have contributed to the decision to contribute troops to the MNF, though I know of no evidence to this effect.

Public opinion was not a significant factor in this case. It seems that the British public favored support. *The Times* argued on October 22 that "Lebanon Needs Help" and that Britain should be among the countries contributing.[102] A December 8 article argued that the Sabra and Chatila massacre led public opinion in Britain to support a contribution.[103] The opposition Labour Party also appears to have favored military support. A book chapter on Britain and the MNF by J. A. Kenny and Peter Woolley notes that "assistance in the restoration of stability in Lebanon seemed a vital step which the British government should be ready to take. There was certainly a general British political consensus to this effect when the decision to participate was taken."[104] There is no evidence that this factor pushed the government to choose to make a contribution, however. In the immediate wake of the victory in the Falklands, the Conservatives had opened a massive lead against Labour, especially on foreign policy.[105] It is extremely unlikely that public opinion on such a peripheral issue would have been decisive in upcoming general elections.

Margaret Thatcher saw Britain was a force for good in the world and a country that upheld international law.[106] The MNF was reconstituted in an environment of moral outrage at the Sabra and Shatila massacres.[107] It does not appear that moral revulsion drove Britain's contribution to the MNF, however. If it had been a critical factor in this case, moral revulsion should have been highest immediately after the massacres on September 16–18. Yet, Britain chose to intervene in December. It is also possible that the Thatcher government chose to intervene to uphold an international norm. The difficulty here is that the MNF did not flow from international norms—such as contributing to UN peace operations—in existence at the time. The operation was not conducted under UN auspices because Israel and Lebanon preferred otherwise.[108] Identity and norms do not provide an effective explanation of this case.

The Thatcher government's decision to provide a contribution to the MNF in Lebanon provides support for proposition seven. Thatcher put high value on the UK-U.S. relationship and there is some evidence that this influenced her decision to provide support. Thatcher's government did not believe MNF II would resolve the low-level threat to Britain's national interests. Because the issue was relatively low profile it was unlikely that a refusal to contribute would have been electorally relevant. Britain's tardy intervention undercuts the claim that moral revulsion at the Sabra and Shattila massacres explains the decision to provide support. The Thatcher government's decision defied an international norm in favor of UN-endorsed peace operations. There is no evidence in favor of the moral

44 • America's Allies and War

revulsion explanation so this case provides no support for alternative proposition three.

France

Ronald Reagan's administration wanted France to participate in the MNF to enhance the force's legitimacy and to better share the burden. France chose to join the force after the United States and it did so at the request of President Reagan.[109] France announced that it would participate in the MNF on August 6, whereas the Reagan administration had approved a U.S. contribution on July 3.[110] Hubert Védrine, François Mitterrand's Foreign Policy Adviser, quoted the President as saying: "[i]t was at Reagan's personal request that I accepted the creation of the Multinational Force. . . . "[111] The French contributed roughly eight hundred troops to the MNF.[112]

François Mitterrand's government had a sophisticated sense of France's relationship with the United States. Mitterrand believed that the American commitment to Europe was in France's core strategic interest. In 1986, the French President wrote that "[t]he worst danger for us, as for our neighbors in Western Europe, would be . . . that America move away from our continent's shores."[113] This basic strategic value of France's alliance with the United States may explain the Mitterrand government's support for the deployment of Pershing II and cruise missiles to Europe.[114] Of course, Mitterrand and his advisers disagreed with some U.S. policies. They were firmly opposed to the Reagan administration's attempt to get its allies to adopt economic sanctions on the Soviet Union.[115] The Mitterrand government was particularly concerned with the Reagan administration's lack of interest in the European perspective on the issue. As Claude Cheysson, Mitterrand's Foreign Minister, said in a Senate debate about the gas pipeline, "[i]t's the Washington Treaty that we have signed, not the Warsaw Pact!"[116] The Mitterrand government also criticized the Reagan administrations' policies in Latin America.[117] Third, Mitterrand agreed with the Gaullist notion that France's prestige was best guaranteed by maintaining a degree of independence from the United States.[118]

There is little evidence that alliance value played a causal role in this case, however. While Mitterrand's government valued the strategic benefits of France's alliance with the United States, he did not have reason to believe that his decision on Lebanon would impact the alliance. Cheysson noted "serious divergences" with the United States over Lebanon—the United States refused to give the French a role in the peace negotiations and it was far too tolerant of Israel.[119] Moreover, France continued to fight for its independence relative to the United States.[120] Specifically, France refused to allow its troops to fall under U.S. command.[121] Finally, there is some evidence that—as will be seen in the next section—the Mitterrand government intervened because of concern that its interests would be adversely affected if the United States acted alone.

Much evidence links the Mitterrand government's decision to provide troops to a desire to resolve a threat to French interests and prestige. France's postwar *politique Arabe* is an indicator of the country's interest in the region.[122] Claude Cheysson later recalled that "[d]uring the first years of the first *septennat* [the seven year presidential term], problems of stability in the Near and Middle East and North Africa were at the forefront of the president's preoccupations."[123] Hubert Védrine recalled that Mitterrand's general interest in equilibrium provided a central reason behind French policy in the Middle East during his presidency.[124]

The Mitterrand government believed that if they did not provide troops, the instability threat to French interests would not be resolved. First, the Mitterrand government was concerned that if the United States sent troops but France did not, regional stability would suffer. Mitterrand later recalled to his Council of Ministers that they "went to protect the Muslims; because of the American attitude, it could have been an anti-Muslim operation."[125] McDermott and Skjelsbaek note that "[w]hen Claude Cheysson emphasized at the time that the Palestinians' problem had to be solved, he expressed fears of an American solution."[126] Second, the Mitterrand government believed that only France could guarantee that Yasser Arafat would continue to lead the Palestinians and that peace was more likely with Arafat alive.[127] In short, the Mitterrand government contributed troops because it sought to resolve a threat to stability in the region and because it believed only French troops could resolve it.

Mitterrand, like many of his predecessors, was concerned with France's prestige. In 1989, he told *The Economist* that "[t]he role of France is to protect its rank."[128] France's *politique Arabe* was also a means to preserve its prestige by preserving historical ties to and influence in the Middle East.[129] Because France's prestige was implicated in Lebanon, it had no choice but to participate or lose prestige relative to its peers. Pia Christina Wood notes that France's prestige in the region clashed with the fact that it knew the United States would dominate the MNF. Yet, she argues, "[i]n the French view, playing an active role in the region to protect its status and interests took precedence. . . . "[130] France's historical ties and ties to Lebanon at the time meant that its prestige was at stake.[131] If France had not contributed, its absence would have been conspicuous.

France's prestige played out in a number of more specific ways in the Lebanon case. Mitterrand had tried and failed to prevent Israel from

46 • America's Allies and War

invading Lebanon in June 1982.[132] One way to counter the view that France could not influence outcomes in the Middle East was to intervene in the MNF. In fact, the Mitterrand government insisted that French troops be the first of the MNF to enter Beirut.[133] On August 20 *The New York Times* noted that "[i]n a rare television interview Tuesday night, President Francois Mitterrand proudly emphasized that the French would be the first foreign forces to enter Beirut."[134] The successful withdrawal of MNF I might have led to an increase in French prestige had it not been for the Sabra and Shatila massacres shortly thereafter. Mitterrand warned that he would not accept an "Oradour" (a 1944 Nazi massacre of civilians in a French village) in Beirut: subsequent inaction would have hurt France's prestige.[135] As George Shultz wrote: " . . . the French and Italians felt that we all had taken a black eye by having pulled out the MNF just before the massacre."[136] The only way to make the black eye go away was with another French contribution to the reconstituted MNF in September 1982.

Public opinion does not appear to have played a significant role in this case. The French public supported a military contribution. John Vincour of *The New York Times* explained that "France and the French Army have been historically involved in Lebanon, and many people in France feel there is a kind of unstated legitimacy in their role there, rather like their view of the French presence in France's former colonies in West Africa."[137] The only opposition of note to the Mitterrand government's decision to contribute troops to the MNF came from the French Communist Party, which was within the governing coalition led by Mitterrand's Socialist Party.[138] Was the government pushed by public opinion to intervene? I have come across no evidence that the government was pushed by the public into making a contribution. While the Gaullist center-right supported the deployment, they were critical of the subservient role they claimed Mitterrand was playing relative to the United States.[139] Thus, it is unclear whether they would have criticized the government had it chosen not to participate in MNF I or MNF II.

Some evidence supports the claim that France's identity—in the form of its historical ties to Lebanon—explains the Mitterrand government's decision to contribute troops to the MNF. For example, Védrine wrote of France's responsibility in Lebanon that "I do not recall having heard it justified otherwise than by general allusions to France's mission and its history."[140] There are two main shortcomings of the identity explanation in this case, however. First, the identity explanation refers to France as a defender of the Christian Maronite community—a role that it did not play in this case. Bassma Kodmani-Darwish quoted Mitterrand as saying that in participating in the MNF France was continuing with a "mission it felt itself invested with since the nineteenth century, that of consolidating Christianity in the country."[141] Kodmani-Darwish—as well as McDermott and Skjelsbaek—followed that quote by noting that it is completely at odds with France's role in the crisis, as also outlined previously.[142] Mitterrand and Cheysson focused primarily on the Palestinian aspect of this story.[143] Second, in policymaker and analyst statements about identity, prestige actually appears to be the underlying factor. Mitterrand explained that France's policy of presence in the Middle East was necessary because " . . . for centuries France has had privileged relations in this region of the world, because our country is one of the five permanent members in the UN Security Council, and is rich with a great history and special duties which I intend to perpetuate."[144] Prestige entailed continuing privileged relations and maintaining France's UNSC seat. Consider what U.S. Secretary of State Shultz had to say: "I knew that France wanted its troops in the MNF as a way to reassert its traditional influence in the Levant."[145]

The extent to which widely diffused norms apply to this case, they would suggest that countries should contribute to a UN-approved peace force. This explanation is half right for this case. McDermott and Skjelsbaek note the importance of "France's belief that the UN should be the foremost international vehicle for intervention in regional crises."[146] On June 26, 1982, France proposed a UNSC resolution that would have created a UN force. France's draft resolution and the idea of a UN authorized force suffered from a U.S. veto and Israeli opposition.[147] Faced with the reality of U.S. and Israeli opposition, France chose to contribute to a force that was not authorized by the United Nations. Why? McDermott and Skjelsbaek note that " . . . France does not always put the UN first when its own interests are involved."[148]

The Mitterrand government's decision to provide support for the MNF in Lebanon provides support for proposition two. The Mitterrand government had a high value for France's relationship with the United States but there is no evidence that it affected the outcome in this case. Policymaker and analyst statements indicate that the Mitterrand government chose to send French troops to Lebanon because of a view that France's national interest would be served by a more stable Middle East and France's prestige was implicated because of its *politique Arabe* and history in the Levant. The French public and opposition favored support but there is no evidence that this factor drove Mitterrand's decision. French identity provides a plausible explanation of this case but it is undermined by the fact that France's historical tie was to the Maronite Christian community in Lebanon whereas Mitterrand was focused on the Palestinians and the identity evidence seems to reveal prestige concerns. The international norm of UN endorsement of

48 • America's Allies and War

peace operations cannot explain this case. There is no evidence that France's identity outweighed its concern with international norms, so this case provides minimal support for alternative proposition three.

Italy

On August 26, 1982, 575 Italian troops joined the French and American contingents of the MNF.[149] On September 26, an Italian contingent of 1,400 troops joined those of France and the United States to constitute MNF II.[150] The Italian government was responding to a U.S. request. As Giuseppe Mammarella and Paolo Cacace state in their survey of Italy's foreign policy: "[t]he United States decided to intervene militarily to facilitate the evacuation of Palestinians from Beirut and they asked France and Italy to participate in a 'Multinational Force'."[151]

In the postwar period Italy's security was fundamentally dependent on its relationship with the United States.[152] In December 1979 Francesco Cossiga's government made the domestically controversial decision to host American nuclear-tipped Jupiter missiles in Sicily.[153] The "euromissile" decision indicates that the Italian government valued its relationship with the United States.[154] While Italy and the United States had policy disagreements (e.g., over economic sanctions against the Soviets), the fundamentals of the relationship were strong.[155] Luigi Vittorio Ferraris' volume noted that Italian foreign policy in the early 1980s emphasized "Atlantic reinforcement" and a commitment to global détente.[156] Mammarella and Cacace wrote that their "country's Atlanticism found strong reference points . . . " with Foreign Minister Emilio Colombo and Prime Minister Giovanni Spadolini.[157]

Evidence suggests that alliance value played a significant role in the Spadolini government's decision to provide troops. As mentioned earlier, the Italian decision followed an American request and some believe Italy's relationship with the United States was crucial. Ferraris' study says that sympathy with the Maronite Christians and Palestinians was important but "[f]urthermore, with military participation [Italy] intended to support—and Prime Minister Spadolini was very sensitive to this—a request from the United States. . . . "[158] Valter Coralluzzo wrote of the decision to offer a contribution: "[D]eterminant in this phase was a reference to Washington's choices, which with Reagan's ascendance to the presidency turned increasingly toward the militarization of the West's Middle East policy."[159] How important was the Italy-U.S. alliance relative to national interest or prestige in the form of a special role for Italy in the Middle East? Italy's Defense Minister at the time made clear that " . . . no political military role could be envisioned for Italy if not in the context of the alliance and the treaties that tie it to the West. . . . "[160] Therefore, alliance was more important in this case because it was a means to pursue the ends of prestige and interest. Finally, Italy's contribution had a positive effect on the relationship. As the Ferraris volume notes, "Italian participation in the multilateral mission in Lebanon, from summer 1982, consolidated relations with the Reagan administration. . . . "[161]

Since the mid-1970s Italy had been moving toward a " . . . greater commitment to an active role in the Mediterranean and North Africa."[162] There are three reasons for Italy's increasing engagement in the Mediterranean, including the Middle East. First, Italy became more engaged politically to defend its growing economic interests in the region. For example, as of the 1980s Italy was the leading Organization of Economic Cooperation and Development (OECD) provider of export credits to Mediterranean countries.[163] Second, Italy chose engagement in the Mediterranean and Middle East because of their proximity, which meant instability there could affect Italy.[164] On August 30, 1982, Spadolini argued that Italy's security was tied not only to the U.S.-Soviet struggle but also to " . . . Third World areas, until yesterday marginal and today the center of dangerous conflicts. . . . "[165] Carlo Santoro explained with regard to Italian deployments in the 1980s (including the MNF): "[t]hese were the result of focused attention to the geopolitical theater of Italy's strategic interests, above all in the Mediterranean. . . . "[166] Spadolini said of Italy's peacemaking and stabilizing role in the Mediterranean: "It is focused, first of all, on favoring the resolution of conflicts that, being close, interest our country."[167] Third, by raising its profile in the Mediterranean and Middle East, Italy was making an effort to increase its prestige. The Ferraris book argues that in the early 1980s Italy had " . . . an 'emerging profile' in the Arab-Islamic geopolitical context."[168] For Franco Angioni and Maurizio Cremasco, Italy's contribution to the MNF in Lebanon was "the culmination of a developing trend" of greater engagement in the region.[169] The *New York Times* reported that Italy's contribution was " . . . in keeping with the emphasis in Italy's foreign policy of a more aggressive role in Mediterranean affairs."[170]

One can also make sense of Italy's contribution to the MNF by stressing its interest in stability in the Middle East. Italy's aforementioned economic ties to the region meant that it had a real national interest in regional stability, including stability in Lebanon and the prospect of peace between Israel and the Palestinians.[171] In a July 7, 1981, speech launching his government, Spadolini stressed Italy's role in the Mediterranean and argued for maximum effort to maintain stability in Lebanon.[172] For Angioni and Cremasco the Spadolini government's decision to join the MNF should be seen in the context of its belief that " . . . the PLO should not be 'dismantled' because it was a necessary element in any future peace process."[173] The Ferraris

50 • America's Allies and War

volume stresses regional stability concerns, saying that humanitarian concerns " . . . flanked strategic-political objectives, to safeguard an area of Western influence, to secure minimum conditions of stability, which one needs to preserve Lebanon."[174]

There is also evidence that prestige was a factor. The Ferraris book stresses Italy's growing "self confidence" in the early 1980s and will to deploy troops abroad "to confront the anxiety in the definition of its rank," which became especially acute as Germany became a global economic power.[175] Italians were concerned with incidents like the early 1979 Guadalupe Summit France had organized, excluding Italy from a meeting between the United States and leading states.[176] Mammarella and Cacace refer to the U.S. request for Italy to contribute to the MNF alongside France as "[a] recognition for our government as unforeseen as it was welcome."[177] In responding to the American request and in performing well in the difficult situation of the MNF, the Spadolini government passed "an important test for the country's image, a significant redemption for our armed forces."[178] Analysts believed that the fact that the U.S. request singled out Italy explains the mission's popularity there.[179] Finally, it may be useful to recall George Shultz's phrase that the Sabra and Shatila massacres had given the United States, France, and Italy a "black eye."[180] Only by participating in MNF II could Italy maximize the likelihood that the social recognition of its power would not suffer.

Electoral politics almost certainly did not have a decisive impact on this case. First, the Italian public supported the Spadolini government's decisions to contribute to the MNF. On August 20, 1982, *The New York Times* reported that "[f]ar from being controversial, the Italian decision to send troops seems to be sweeping the country up in a sense of pride . . . "[181] Valter Coralluzzo notes that announcement that Italy would participate in MNF II " . . . was favorably received by the parties (except for the Radicals and the PDUP) and Italian public opinion. . . . "[182] Second, the leading opposition party—the PCI—supported both deployments, at least initially. While the opposition was driven by different motives (more humanitarian than pro-U.S.), their support for the deployments was clear.[183] There is some evidence that the opposition's support provided cover for the government. According to Carlo Santoro, "without the comfort of some form of implicit bipartisanship, no Italian government would have had the daring to send, for example, an expeditionary force to Lebanon in 1982. . . . "[184] That said, the PCI was not an electoral threat, and given how radical it was for an Italian government to deploy troops abroad it is highly unlikely that the Spadolini government would have been removed from office had they refused to send Italian troops.

Constructivist factors provide plausible explanations of parts of this story. There is evidence that humanitarianism, consistent with Italy's aforementioned identity as a force for peace, explains the Spadolini government's decision to contribute. Angioni and Cremasco note "the widespread emotional reaction" to the Sabra and Shatila massacres in explaining the decision to contribute to MNF II.[185] This explanation cannot make sense of the Italian contribution to the first MNF, however. This explanation has further difficulty explaining Italy's actions. Valter Coralluzzo notes that in setting up and implementing MNF II, humanitarian goals played "a secondary role" relative to political goals, such as reestablishing the sovereignty of the Christian Maronite government.[186] For example, MNF II engagement rules allowed for the use of force only in self-defense (i.e., for each nation's contingent to defend itself—not in defense of Palestinian or Lebanese civilians).[187]

Foreign Minister Colombo stated that Italy's contribution was motivated by a desire to uphold the international legal ban on territorial aggression violated by Israel's invasion of Lebanon on June 6, 1982.[188] This explanation is problematic because the initial MNF was undertaken with Israel's consent and it withdrew from Lebanon while Israel continued to occupy Beirut.[189] While the second MNF sought to facilitate an Israeli withdrawal from Beirut, it did not seek an Israeli withdrawal from Lebanon—in fact, Israel's occupation continued until 2000.[190] To sum up: neither humanitarianism nor international law provides an adequate explanation of the Spadolini government's decision.

The Spadolini government's decision to provide a contribution to the MNF in Lebanon provides support for proposition two. Evidence from policymakers and analysts suggests that the Spadolini government valued Italy's relationship with the United States and that its decision was designed to uphold the relationship. Numerous analyst statements suggest that Italy's national interest in the Middle East and its prestige played a critical role in the Spadolini government's decision. Some evidence supports the humanitarian identity logic and international legal norms' explanations, so the case provides support for alternative proposition one. There are important rebuttals to both factors, however. The humanitarian logic for a contribution is not consistent with the MNF's goals or its engagement rules. The international legal norm explanation fails to explain the Spadolini government's lack of concern with the international legal anomalies of the MNF.

Persian Gulf

Britain

Margaret Thatcher was in the United States when Saddam Hussein invaded Kuwait on August 2, 1990. She coordinated her opposition to the invasion

52 • America's Allies and War

with President Bush, ordering an armored brigade to the region to contribute to the U.S.-led defense of Saudi Arabia in early September. On November 28, 1990 (just before John Major replaced her as Prime Minister), Thatcher approved the deployment of an additional brigade, bringing the total to 45,000 British troops.[191] Britain made the second-largest contribution after the United States and even allowed their troops to fall under the direct command of U.S. General Norman Schwarzkopf.

Some have argued that Thatcher pushed Bush into firm action against Iraq, warning him "this is no time to go wobbly."[192] Perhaps the United States was pushed to contribute to a U.K.-led war and, thus, this case is not appropriate for the study? In fact, Bush set the stage for the ultimate showdown with Iraq with his August 5 statement, "This will not stand, this aggression against Kuwait."[193] While he and Thatcher were reluctant to focus on force, by saying Iraq's attack on Kuwait would not stand, Bush was pledging the United States to military action if other means failed.[194] Thatcher made the "wobbly" statement weeks later and it had to do with the point at which the United States and allies should use their ships to enforce the embargo against Iraq.[195]

The Thatcher government had the highest value for Britain's alliance relationship with the United States. Thatcher's Foreign Policy Adviser Sir Percy Cradock (who also advised John Major) explained that the United States " . . . provided the fundamental guarantee of [Britain's] security. Over wide areas British and American policies naturally coincided."[196] When the UK and United States disagreed, he went on, London had to be cognizant " . . . that the Americans held the preponderant power and responsibility."[197] Specifically, Percy Cradock also served as Chairman of the JIC, and in that capacity his stress on the value of Britain's intelligence sharing with the United States is noteworthy.[198] While the Thatcher government took issue with the Bush administration's arms control positions and with its emphasis on the U.S. relationship with Germany, it remained convinced of the need to preserve the valuable U.S.-UK relationship.[199]

There is some evidence that the Thatcher government's value for the UK-U.S. alliance affected the decision to provide support. First, the Thatcher government knew that it had influence with the United States and that if it made a significant contribution it would have more. Thatcher recalls that shortly after the invasion of Kuwait she traveled from Colorado to Washington at Bush's invitation and "[f]or all the friendship and co-operation I had had from President Reagan, I was never taken into the Americans' confidence more than I was during the two hours or so I spent that afternoon at the White House."[200] British government officials almost certainly expected to get more influence over the war in exchange for the

September armored brigade deployment.[201] More broadly, contributing troops to the U.S.-led war was likely to cement Britain's role as the United States' closest, most dependable ally. John Campbell's biography of Thatcher states with regard to the Persian Gulf War that " . . . she was delighted to have the chance to demonstrate once again that Britain was still America's best friend in a crisis."[202] British policymakers believed that their country's military contribution had demonstrated to the United States that it was an "indispensable ally."[203]

The Thatcher government also believed Iraq's invasion threatened Britain's national interest. First, in occupying and annexing Kuwait, Iraq controlled roughly 20 percent of the world's oil supply, which gave Saddam Hussein a powerful tool of statecraft he could use against Britain in the future. British Foreign Secretary Douglas Hurd wrote at the time that if Hussein's Iraq controlled Kuwait's oil, he could disrupt the world economy and Britain would suffer.[204] Second, Iraq's invasion of Kuwait upset the balance of power in the Middle East, which might have led to further arms races and war (including the potential for an Iraqi attack on Saudi Arabia's large oil reserves), which would adversely affect Britain's political and economic interests in the region. Thatcher wrote in her memoirs that in her first conversation with Bush after the invasion she stressed to him that " . . . if Saddam Hussein were to cross the border into Saudi Arabia he could go right down the Gulf in a matter of days. He would then control 65 percent of the world's oil reserves and could blackmail us all."[205] Percy Cradock wrote that the invasion "... posed a direct threat to regional, and world, stability."[206] Thatcher later recalled her concern that Hussein would be a fundamental threat had he remained in control of Kuwait's oil and a threat to Saudi Arabia's oil.[207]

The Thatcher government was particularly concerned about Britain's prestige—perceptions of its power in the world.[208] The Thatcher government's firm response to the Argentinean seizure of the Falklands can be seen in this light.[209] Some have suggested that during the Thatcher years Britain's prestige was intertwined with its alliance relationship with the United States. For example, Foreign Secretary Hurd argued that Britain's relationship with the United States allowed it to "punch above its weight."[210] Prestige and Britain's relationship with the United States combine to provide a nice explanation of the size of the Thatcher government's contribution.[211] Overall, Joseph Lepgold wrote, Thatcher " . . . was eager to show that the Anglo-American 'special relationship' still gave her country prestige and a coherent world role after the Cold War."[212]

The British public was highly supportive of the 1991 Persian Gulf War. As of mid-October 1990, 86 percent of those polled said they approved of

54 • America's Allies and War

the government's aims and strategy on Iraq.[213] On the eve of the war, polls found between 60 and 75 percent of respondents in favor of using force after the January 15 deadline set by the UNSC.[214] The opposition Labour Party leadership expressed its preference for more time for economic sanctions to work but ultimately supported the government's decision to deploy British troops.[215] Was the Thatcher government pushed by a hawkish public to provide a military contribution? There is no evidence that Thatcher considered withholding military support when it became clear that sanctions would not work within a time frame acceptable to the allies. Moreover, Labour's ultimate support for government action does not necessarily tell us how they might have acted had the Conservatives refused to provide support.[216]

Some have suggested that the defense of international law is a core element of Britain's self image.[217] The Thatcher government's public statements stressed Iraq's violation of international law as the primary reason for the U.S.-led war and Britain's contribution to it. As the Prime Minister declared shortly after the invasion, "[w]hat has happened is a total violation of international law. You cannot have a situation where one country marches in and takes over another country which is a member of the United Nations."[218] Foreign Secretary Hurd later wrote that the U.S.-led war had been a "campaign of principle" in defense of the international legal ban on aggression.[219]

The international law logic poses a number of questions, however. First, it is unclear why the enforcement of international law required the urgency with which the Thatcher government confronted Iraq's actions. While many believed economic sanctions held the potential to be effective in the medium to long term, as Sir Percy Cradock noted, they " . . . would take a long time to bite and would not be able to force the policy changes on the part of Iraq that we needed *in a time-frame we would find tolerable.*"[220] In her memoirs, Thatcher recorded—as outlined previously—her first post-invasion discussion with Bush in which she stressed British and American national interest in keeping Iraq from invading Saudi Arabia and the blackmail potential it contained. She concluded her summary of the conversation by stating: "[n]ot only did we have to move to stop the aggression, therefore, we had to stop it quickly."[221] Iraq's threat to Saudi Arabia—and with it British interests—explains why force had to be used rather than economic sanctions whereas international law cannot explain the choice of force.

Second, Thatcher's view that a UNSC resolution explicitly authorizing the use of force was not necessary clashes with the claim that she was motivated primarily by a desire to uphold international law. In her memoirs Thatcher writes, " . . . although I am a strong believer in international law,

Vietnam, Lebanon, Persian Gulf, and Somalia • 55

I did not like unnecessary resort to the UN, because it suggested that sovereign states lacked the moral authority to act on their own behalf."[222] While the UN Charter recognizes the right to self-defense, it also says this right " . . . shall not in any way affect the authority and responsibility of the Security Council under the present Charter to take at any time such action as it deems necessary in order to maintain or restore international peace and security."[223] Security Council members may have believed that international peace and security was best preserved by continued economic sanctions against Iraq. A government driven by a desire to uphold international law would have insisted on attaining explicit UNSC authorization for the use of force.

Iraq's violation of international law in invading Kuwait played an important role in the British decision. Was it more or less important than Britain's national interest? Thatcher biographer John Campbell wrote that while Bush and Thatcher talked publicly about international law, " . . . their real concern was that—having annexed the Kuwaiti oil fields—Saddam might, if not prevented, go on to seize the even more important Saudi reserves."[224] While public statements about the defense of international law played well with the British public and those in the Labour Party disinclined to favor the use of force, threat appears to have been the dominant logic in private analysis and discussion. Days before Iraq's invasion of Kuwait the JIC warned that Iraq would probably take action and advised that " . . . the emergence of a successful predator in that part of the world would be extremely dangerous for Western interests."[225] In Thatcher's summary of her private discussions with Bush she mentions oil but not international law.[226] Campbell puts it this way: "[h]er outrage about Iraq's violation of Kuwaiti sovereignty, though perfectly sincere as far as it went, was at the same time a convenient cover for deeper national and western interests."[227]

The Thatcher government's decision to provide military support for the Persian Gulf War supports proposition two. Thatcher's government highly valued its alliance relationship with the United States but there are no policymaker statements and there is little analysis suggesting this factor was critical in the decision to provide support. Multiple private and public policymaker statements serve as evidence that the U.S.-led war against Iraq would eliminate a serious threat to Britain's national interest and that this factor played a critical role in the outcome. The British public and opposition Labour Party favored support but there is no evidence that electoral politics affected the government's decision. Policymaker statements provide evidence that the Thatcher government provided support to uphold international law and, as such, provide support for alternative proposition one. The government's lack of interest in a UNSC resolution and impatience

56 • America's Allies and War

with economic sanctions casts doubt on this factor, however. Analyst and policymaker statements serve as a further rebuttal.

France

The Bush administration sought military contributions from allies to share the burden of the Gulf War and to enhance domestic and international legitimacy.[228] François Mitterrand's government provided political support for the U.S.-led efforts to defend Saudi Arabia, sanction Iraq, and forcibly remove Iraqi forces from Kuwait. Mitterrand's government also pursued diplomatic solutions to the crisis, however, that American decision makers did not welcome.[229] When war came the Mitterrand government contributed roughly 10,000 troops and air and naval forces.[230] Lawrence Freedman and Efraim Karsh argued that France's military contribution was of great value to the legitimacy of the U.S.-led effort because "it was a country that could not be accused of being an American puppet and had enjoyed close links with Iraq in the past."[231]

The Mitterrand government valued France's relationship with the United States, though this was not always evident. On the one hand, the French were not as afraid as the British of an American withdrawal from Western Europe.[232] In addition, the Mitterrand government increased its cooperation with NATO while making clear that it would work to strengthen security and defense cooperation in the European Community.[233] On the other hand, the government valued its alliance with the United States because of American primacy and the potential for resurgent threat.[234] In April 1990 Mitterrand and Bush met in Key Largo and the French President said that while the risk of war had decreased with Soviet decline, "[n]evertheless, a threat remains. Gorbachev may have to make dangerous postures if he is forced by necessity, so we must retain our security arrangements . . . a great power in a weakened condition is dangerous. The United States should have a say in all issues that affect the equilibrium in Europe."[235] Moreover, Bush consulted Mitterrand frequently prior to and during the Iraq crisis giving the French leader influence in Washington worth preserving.[236] For example, Secretary of State Baker recounts how Mitterrand suggested an important change in Bush's January 1991 letter to Saddam Hussein.[237]

The evidence suggests that the Mitterrand government's value for France's relationship with the United States led it to make a military contribution. One analyst says of this case, " . . . one could not take the risk of angering its principal potential allies in the world if the European ensemble continued to be so uncertain."[238] Mitterrand explained that France offered a military contribution to the Gulf War because "[w]e are content to have the Americans in certain circumstances. We are their allies . . . in the present case one needs clarity and solidarity. If it is necessary to choose, I believe we must fight against Saddam Hussein, whatever the consequences may be. If we do not do so, we will be the false brother of the West."[239]

The Mitterrand government also believed Iraq's invasion of Kuwait threatened France's national interest. Of course, France's economic ties with Iraq at the time were extensive and contributing to the war stood to put such ties at risk.[240] Some analysts have further noted that French officials' public statements did not focus on oil prices.[241] There is evidence, however, that the Mitterrand government saw military action as resolving a threat to France's national interest. Hubert Védrine recalled that "[i]t seemed impossible to George Bush as to François Mitterrand to let a Saddam Hussein control at the same time the petroleum reserves of Iraq and Kuwait, that is 20% of world reserves, and waiting on those of Saudi Arabia and the Emirates."[242] The French were concerned with Hussein's control of Kuwaiti oil because he might have used it to blackmail France and its allies, hurting the French economy in the process.[243] Védrine also recalled a concern that the conflict might spread. He wrote of Mitterrand's reaction to the invasion of Kuwait that "[f]rom the first days, it was him that judged that 'one' could not allow this annexation; that it was necessary to stamp out all the contagion. . . . "[244] In annexing Kuwait, Hussein's Iraq had become more powerful: what was to stop it from continuing? Claude Cheysson (Mitterrand's Foreign Minister from 1981–84) believed that "[t]he decisive argument for Mitterrand was the risk of a disruption of the balance in the Middle East. We contributed to maintain that balance."[245] George Bush recalled that in his first conversation with the French President after Iraq's invasion, Mitterrand stressed that to accept the status quo "would allow Saddam to secure his hegemony over the Arab world."[246]

François Mitterrand seems to have been conscious that the hierarchy of international prestige would be reshuffled by the Persian Gulf War and that France stood to gain prestige by providing military support.[247] Germany and Japan had been pressing for UNSC reform to reflect their rising economic power. France's military contribution to the Gulf War demonstrated that it had greater military power and willingness to act than countries of greater wealth.[248] Increasing prestige by contributing to the Gulf War was also important to convince France's European partners to move forward with further integration on security policy. According to Védrine, the choice facing the Mitterrrand government was to "[b]e in the Gulf or lose [their] leadership in Europe."[249] By participating in the Persian Gulf War France could avoid any downgrading of its rank that otherwise might occur.[250]

58 • America's Allies and War

The Mitterrand government's concern with France's prestige elucidates a number of the characteristics of France's behavior. First, in mid-September 1990, Iraqi officials chose to storm the French Ambassador to Kuwait's residence and kidnap four French citizens, including the military attaché. One could see Iraq's actions as a challenge to France's prestige. Analysts agree that the mistreatment of French officials in Kuwait led directly to the deployment of 6,000 French troops to the region (though deployment did not commit France to war).[251] Second, the size of France's contribution seems to have—at least in part—been driven by the desire to make a favorable comparison with its peer competitor, Britain.[252] Finally, the Mitterrand government insisted on an autonomous mission for French troops: it agreed to "coordinate" with the American command but refused to "integrate" with it so as to better distinguish the French contribution.[253] As Denis Lacorne wrote with regard to the Persian Gulf War, "France's prestige, the reaffirmation of its rank among the great powers, demanded that it distinguish itself."[254] As war loomed, Mitterrand justified France's participation this way: "France is present. It must remain present. France is not a small country. It has a say. . . . "[255] Hubert Védrine remarked that Mitterrand "was not angry to find a field where [France] could engage itself militarily and recall its rank as a permanent member of the Security Council."[256]

The French public's view of their country's role in the Iraq War varied in the period preceding it. As late as December 1990, 76 percent approved of France's military response to the Gulf crisis.[257] As of January 9, 1991, however, 57 percent said they were opposed to French participation.[258] Védrine suggests that Mitterrand followed public opinion closely and that he tried hard to shape it.[259] It would have made perfect sense to ignore the early January public opposition to the French contribution, however. Such a large swing in a short period of time indicates that it would have been unlikely for public opposition to stay high (and, thus, it was unlikely to impact future electoral contests).[260] Moreover, the fact that the center-right opposition supported the Mitterrand government's decision to participate meant that voters would have had to vote for the far-right National Front or far-left French Communist Party to express their frustration with government policy and neither provided a credible electoral threat.[261]

The Mitterrand government may also have been motivated by a desire to uphold the international legal ban on aggression and territorial conquest.[262] While this factor may have contributed to the outcome, there is little evidence that it was the primary factor driving the Mitterrand government's decision. If Mitterrand had been motivated by a desire to uphold the international legal ban on aggression, why would he—as outlined above—propose that Iraq avoid the use of force with the mere declaration of its intent to withdraw from Kuwait? Denis Lacorne notes that French peace proposals like Mitterrand's made clear that the French were not "hardliners, blindly aligned with the American positions," which also meant that they were not committed to a defense of international law.[263]

The Mitterrand government's decision to deploy French troops to aid the United States in the Persian Gulf War provides support for proposition two. Policymaker statements demonstrate that the French valued their relationship with the United States but there is little evidence that this factor was critical in the Mitterrand government's decision. Numerous policymaker statements support the claim that the Mitterrand government believed that a U.S.-led war would resolve a threat to France's national interest and enhance its prestige and that these factors were critical in its decision. Prestige was probably the most significant factor in this story. Védrine wrote that international law and oil were important but then went on to say that he thought Mitterrand's "true motivation" was his calculation that " . . . if France did not participate, she would be morally, militarily, and diplomatically discredited on European and Euro-Atlantic terrain, where at the same time her credibility and future role were at play."[264] The French public opposed the use of force on the eve of the Persian Gulf War but the center-right opposition supported the government and there is no evidence public opinion affected the decision. Statements that the government sought to defend the international legal ban on aggression provide support for alternative proposition one. The Mitterrand government's proposal to defer the use of force in case of an Iraqi declaration of its intent to withdraw from Kuwait serves as a rebuttal, however.

Italy

On September 14, 1990, James Baker visited Rome, requesting the Italian government to provide military support for the U.S.-led protection of Saudi Arabia.[265] Giuliano Andreotti's centrist government responded to Baker's request by adding one frigate to the two frigates and fueling ship already in the Gulf and deployed eight Tornado fighter-bombers to the region.[266] The Andreotti government further allowed Italian planes and ships to participate in the U.S.-led war against Iraq—the Tornadoes engaged in thirty-two bombing missions against Iraqi targets.[267] Some in the United States valued Italy's contribution and were impressed by its first participation in a war since World War II.[268] While the Andreotti government provided a military contribution, it also supported attempts to negotiate a settlement to the conflict.[269] Why did the Andreotti government make the difficult decision to contribute its ships and planes to the U.S.-led war?

60 • America's Allies and War

There is evidence that the Andreotti government's high value for Italy's alliance with the United States led it to provide a military contribution. The Andreotti government seems to have seen the potential for gains for Italy from a relationship with the world's only superpower, especially as European integration on foreign and security policy faced setbacks.[270] Moreover, the United States had acted in ways beneficial to Italy in the years preceding the Iraq crisis. Secretary of State Baker was responsible for expanding the G-5 to G-7 to include Italy.[271] Moreover, Andreotti was "enthusiastic" about Bush administration proposals to adapt NATO to the post–Cold War environment.[272]

Additional evidence ties alliance value to the outcome. Political scientist Valter Corralluzzo's study of cases in Italian foreign policy concluded with regard to the Andreotti government's decision to participate that "[d]eterminant in this [precrisis] phase was the reference to the choices of the White House. . . . "[273] In the January 17 parliamentary debate, Prime Minister Andreotti stressed the American role in World War II, suggesting that the United States was an ally worth keeping.[274] Parliamentary opponents of the Italian contribution to the war clearly thought the Italy-U.S. relationship motivated the Andreotti government—they criticized the government's "pavlovian reflex" to follow the United States.[275] Finally, an interview with a high-ranking official at the U.S. embassy in Rome stressed the U.S.-Italy relationship to explain the Andreotti government's decision. In his words, "[t]hey were keen to participate because they knew what it meant to the U.S."[276]

There is also evidence that the Andreotti government believed that the removal of Iraqi forces from Kuwait would resolve a threat to Italy's national interest. Roughly 80 percent of Italy's oil consumption consists of imports, so Italy would have been negatively impacted had Iraq attempted to use its control of Kuwaiti oil reserves to blackmail the West.[277] Italy's other concern was stability in the Middle East as it might affect Italy's interests in the region. Andreotti government officials emphasized stability as they discussed the crisis and Italy's contribution. Italian Foreign Minister Gianni De Michelis warned that Iraq's invasion of Kuwait was "an initiative which does not end in Kuwait but aims to destabilize the Middle East, using military pressure to change political situations, means of communication, and the use of strategic resources like oil from outside."[278] De Michelis also noted that " . . . this way could develop elements of instability that could project themselves beyond the Gulf region and the Middle East."[279] During the war Andreotti noted that Hussein's Iraq posed a future security threat that the U.S.-led coalition was addressing.[280]

Postwar Italian governments increasingly sought more prestige for their country. The Andreotti government sought to participate in major international institutions and other venues to increase Italy's prestige.[281] Consider also that Italy's regional prestige competitors—Britain, France, and Germany—supported the Persian Gulf War. True, Italy could not match Britain's contribution of 45,000 troops or France's 10,000 troops and it did not have the financial resources to match Germany's estimated $11 billion financial contribution.[282] Italy could differentiate itself from Germany, however, by providing a small military contribution. The Andreotti government knew others were making assessments about power based on countries' contributions in the Gulf. Secretary Baker recalled that in visiting Milan on January 9 the Italians " . . . were sensitive that we sometimes paid more attention to the British, French, and Germans."[283] On January 18 De Michelis directly used the prestige logic, noting that when the war was over Italy could have "a different weight at the international level."[284] While it might have been unreasonable to expect Italy's status to increase, given that it did not commit ground troops, at least it could avoid losing prestige relative to its peers. Prestige concerns may have led to Italy's decision to commit the Tornado fighter-bombers to the U.S.-led war. Valter Coralluzzo argues that concern with appearing "tepid, reticent, and ambiguous" in the eyes of its allies led the Andreotti government to send the Tornadoes.[285]

Some evidence suggests electoral politics played a role in the nature of the contribution the Andreotti government chose to make to the Persian Gulf War. While 59 percent of Italians supported the use of force in the Gulf as of mid-October 1990, by the eve of the war a majority of Italians opposed a military contribution.[286] By the date of the UNSC ultimatum—January 15—62 percent of respondents opposed Italian military participation in the war.[287] A leading survey of Italian foreign policy notes that in sending the Tornadoes, the Andreotti government " . . . reignited the internal contraposition between those that supported the necessity of the intervention and an ample pacifist front—supported by the Church—that fought for an immediate withdrawal of our contingent."[288]

The opposition PCI opposed Italian participation in the Persian Gulf War.[289] The Andreotti government could expect the electoral fallout from Italy's participation to be limited because the opposition was not a credible threat, however. First, as of late 1990 and early 1991 the PCI was undergoing a wrenching internal struggle over the collapse of the USSR (which would lead the party to split shortly thereafter), whereas the DC and its allies were relatively cohesive.[290] As such, the PCI—which had only won 26 percent of the vote as a united party in 1987—did not provide a credible threat of challenging the DC for control of the government.[291] Second, the PCI was divided on the war: the party leadership directed parliamentarians to abstain from the initial deployment vote (whereas they urged opposition to the January 17 vote).[292]

62 • America's Allies and War

Italy's identity and international norms clashed in this case. The repository of Italy's identity on the use of force can be found in Article 11 of the Italian constitution, which proclaims "Italy rejects war as an instrument of aggression against the freedom of other peoples and as a means for the settlement of international disputes."[293] The government's argument that its actions were consistent with the sentence in the article noting that Italy "promotes and encourages" international organizations is problematic. Article 11 firmly and emphatically rejects war and it does not specify that Italy may wage war when an international organization permits it. As such, Article 11 cannot be used to justify the waging of war. Andreotti government officials seem to recognize this problem when they insisted on referring to the war as an "international policing operation."[294] Moreover, it is not clear why or how providing a military contribution to the Persian Gulf War was the only/primary means for Italy to promote and encourage the UN.

The government asserted that it was motivated by a desire to support the United Nations. De Michelis argued that the government's intention was to " . . . anchor ourselves strictly and rigorously, even if naturally in a positive and active mode, to the actions of the United Nations."[295] There are a number of problems with this logic as a cause for the Andreotti government's decision aside from the fact that it clashes with Article 11. First, UNSC resolution 678 authorized states to use "all necessary means" to remove Iraqi forces from Kuwait but it *did not require* any state to do so. While Italy's contribution was permitted under international law, nothing required Italy to provide military support, so a desire to further the UN cannot explain the outcome. Second, Italian officials were aware (as will be discussed below) that their contribution would not determine the outcome of the Persian Gulf War and, as such, would not make or break the UN.

There was a complex array of causal factors on display in this case. While national interest pointed toward contribution, Italian officials knew that their contribution was so small relative to the fighting force that they could free ride off the U.S.-led coalition. A U.S. General even stated that the withdrawal of Italy's contribution would not influence the outcome of the war.[296] While public opposition did not keep the Andreotti government from offering an Italian contingent to support the U.S.-led war, it does seem to have impacted the nature of the contribution. Valter Coralluzzo suggests that public opinion kept the Andreotti government from providing ground troops.[297] Public opinion may also have led Andreotti to support a negotiated settlement even though doing so hurt Italy's relations with the United States.[298]

The Andreotti government's decision to provide ships and planes for the Persian Gulf War provides support for proposition two. Numerous policymaker and analyst statements make clear that the Andreotti government's high value for Italy's relationship with the United States was a critical factor in its decision. Policymaker and analyst statements also provide strong support for the claim that Italy's national interest was threatened and its prestige implicated in this case. Public opposition to the war did not affect the government's decision because the opposition Communist Party was not a significant electoral threat. Italy's contribution to the Persian Gulf War was a complete contradiction of its peace image. The Andreotti government's claim that it was supporting the UN is plausible but supporting the UN did not require a contribution in this case and Italy's contribution was so small that it could not have impacted the outcome. Because there is no evidence that the intensity of the international normative obligation overrode Italy's identity, this case provides minimal support for alternative proposition three.

Somalia

Britain

In the summer of 1992, severe famine gripped Somalia. Warring factions crippled attempts by the United Nations and private groups to provide relief by looting supplies as they arrived on Somalia's docks and airports. The United Nations Operation in Somalia force (UNOSOM), created in August 1992, proved unable to guarantee the effective delivery of relief supplies to those in need. On December 4, 1992, U.S. President George H. W. Bush ordered 28,000 American troops to deploy to Somalia to lead a UN-sanctioned task force, UNITAF, with the goal of providing the stability and security necessary for the relief effort.[299] President Bush phoned Prime Minister Major on December 2 and asked Britain to contribute troops to UNITAF.[300] Aside from being a leading American ally, many felt that as a colonial power in Somalia Britain had a special responsibility to intervene.[301] Major refused to contribute to UNITAF, however, agreeing only to provide two transport planes under Operation Provide Relief.[302] As John Hirsch and Robert Oakley write, the British refusal stands out: "President Bush made personal telephone calls to a number of heads of state asking for participation in or support for the proposed operation. All but British Prime Minister John Major pledged to send troops or provide other assistance."[303]

64 • America's Allies and War

There is some evidence that low alliance value explains this case. First, John Major's government had made initial moves to distinguish itself from the Thatcher government through closer ties to Europe and more independence relative to the United States. In April 1991, Major announced an initiative to provide "safe havens" for Kurds in Iraq. Major made the announcement at a European Community summit and had not coordinated the move with Washington prior.[304] Second, there was reason for the Major government to fear that they would have limited influence with the incoming Clinton administration, which would take office in January 1993. Figures in the Conservative Party aided Bush's presidential campaign and British officials searched Home Office records for evidence of Bill Clinton's anti-Vietnam activities while he was a student at Oxford.[305] Analysts have warned against overstating the long-term effects of the election issue.[306] That said, it is plausible that the Major government did not see alliance value as a great incentive to contribute to UNITAF and did not expect an extremely high degree of influence with the incoming Clinton administration. Raymond Seitz, the U.S. Ambassador to London, wrote of Clinton that " . . . as far as he was concerned, the Tory Party had done its best to prevent his election. His coterie of score-keeping advisers was even more embittered. . . ."[307] It is also possible that the Major government believed their decision would not have a significant impact on alliance value because Somalia was not central to U.S. interests and the operation was much smaller than the Gulf War.

I have come across no evidence that instability in Somalia was a threat to Britain's national interest. Because of the strong humanitarian logic in favor of intervention (which I address later) it is not surprising that politicians and analysts were reluctant to state publicly that Britain was not contributing because its interests were not at stake. Yet, the Major government's stated reason for not contributing only makes sense in national interest terms. On December 4, 1992, *The Times* reported: "John Major has told Mr. Bush that, while he backs military intervention in Somalia, Britain would not participate in the operation because of its commitment of troops in Bosnia-Herzegovina and elsewhere."[308] Douglas Hogg, Minister of State at the Foreign and Commonwealth Office, offered existing "obligations" to explain Britain's lack of contribution to UNITAF in the only extended House of Commons debate on the subject, which was held on December 4.[309] Major and Hogg's statements imply a critical role for national interest. As of late 1992, Britain had roughly 2,300 troops in Bosnia (where regional instability threatened British interests).[310] In 1990 Britain had sent 45,000 troops to join the U.S.-led coalition against Iraq. It borders on the ridiculous to suggest that as of December 1992 the British

Armed Forces were incapable of deploying a few thousand troops to Somalia, which would have brought the total to less than one-tenth of the force it had deployed only two years prior.[311] If one views UNITAF as in no way addressing a threat to Britain's national interest, however, then Major and Hogg's logic makes sense.

The Major government does not appear to have believed Britain's prestige was implicated in Somalia. This is somewhat puzzling because factors that often lead states to feel their prestige is at stake were at play here. There was widespread international consensus in favor of UNITAF, including a UNSC resolution. France—one of Britain's historic peer competitors—announced that it would contribute 2,000 troops.[312] Moreover, the fact that Britain had ruled part of Somalia as a colony meant that others saw it as obligated to intervene.[313] How can one explain the Major government's lack of concern with the prestige consequences of refusing support? First, as Thatcher had successfully increased Britain's prestige, the Major government may have decided that her efforts had taken the country as far as it could go.[314] Second, Major and his advisers may have believed that Thatcher succeeded in enhancing Britain's prestige because she committed Britain to participate in high-profile, successful wars (the Falklands and the Persian Gulf War), not small peace operations.

There is little evidence that electoral politics affected the Major government's decision. Attempts to persuade the British public and policymakers to intervene in Somalia indicate that the public was not clamoring for a British contribution to UNITAF. *The Times*, for example, published a number of editorials arguing for action to alleviate the suffering in Somalia.[315] Diplomat David Owen noted that if the British public could not get indignant about Bosnia, it was unlikely to do so over Somalia.[316] As the public was not focused on Somalia, neither was the parliament. The House of Commons featured only one debate on Somalia during the period—it occurred within a broader debate on the UN, did not feature high-ranking government or opposition officials, and none of those participating explicitly and vigorously pressed for a British contribution.[317] The opposition Labour Party was hardly a threat to the government as Major's Conservatives had just defeated it in March 1992. The Labour Party was generally cautious and confused on foreign and defense policy at the time.[318] Labour's stance on Somalia was characteristically timid: it pushed for engagement but it did not explicitly advocate the contribution of British troops to UNITAF.[319]

The international normative logic in this case was quite clear and the Major government's policy was in complete contradiction with it. There was little doubt that an extraordinary humanitarian disaster was underway, one

66 • America's Allies and War

that UNITAF could alleviate. As of the early 1990s, a norm had emerged that countries should intervene to stop humanitarian crises, especially when authorized by the UNSC to do so. Lynda Chalker, Minister for Overseas Development, recognized the dimensions of the crisis and Britain's obligation. On August 5, 1992, the *Financial Times* published a letter in which she acknowledged the "desperate and harrowing conditions," but also noted that "Britain has not forgotten Somalia. The government is deeply concerned about what is happening there. For months, we have been in the forefront of efforts to alleviate the suffering."[320] Chalker was referring to the relief aid the UK had contributed to that point but in so doing she made clear that the humanitarian intervention norm bound Britain to contribute to UNITAF. On October 13 Chalker was even more explicit, stating: "[w]e have a duty to the starving to make clear to those who are using violence to frustrate the relief effort that the international community will no longer stand by and see the poor and sick held to ransom."[321] Mark Lennox-Boyd, Parliamentary Undersecretary in the Foreign and Commonwealth Office, also made clear the government's view that UNITAF would be effective in providing the security necessary to enable the relief effort.[322] An explanation stressing international norms cannot explain this case.

The Major government's refusal to provide support for U.S.-led efforts in Somalia provides further support for proposition one. The Major government anticipated lower influence with the incoming Clinton administration and, as such, may not have thought it had much to lose by refusing to contribute. The available evidence suggests that the Major government chose to refuse support because it believed doing so would not enhance Britain's national interest. Neither the public nor the opposition was clamoring for intervention, making refusal an electorally safe choice. The Major government's refusal to provide support contradicted the emerging norm of humanitarian intervention. As a result, this case does not provide support for alternative proposition one.

France

On December 2 *The New York Times* reported that the United States government asked the French to contribute to UNITAF.[323] Presumably, Bush telephoned François Mitterrand on or just prior to December 1 and requested French participation.[324] On December 4 Mitterrand announced that France would deploy between 1,500 and 2,000 troops to Somalia to join the U.S.-led, UN authorized relief force.[325]

There is some evidence that alliance value played a role in this case. As outlined in the Persian Gulf War case, Mitterrand and his advisers placed high value on France's alliance with the United States because of American power in the uncertain post–Cold War world.[326] Mitterrand also had access to Bush and a reasonable expectation that he could influence U.S. policy.[327] The Mitterrand government's level of influence with the Bush administration may explain why it had less of a problem with U.S. leadership than its critics (as I discuss later). Mitterrand and his advisers must have believed that France would have a high level of influence with Bill Clinton's administration, though because the latter had no foreign policy experience it was difficult to be sure.[328] Defense Minister Pierre Joxe, who had opposed a French contribution to UNITAF, felt that the Mitterrand government's value for France's alliance with the United States was the critical factor in this case. Joxe recalled that when he made the case against intervention the President replied, "[y]ou may be right, but we cannot refuse it to the Americans. They are engaged."[329]

There is no evidence that a threat to France's national interest led the Mitterrand government to deploy troops to Somalia. While some in France suggested, for example, that the United States intervened in Somalia because of its geostrategic significance relative to the Middle East, there is no record of claims of a threat to France's national interest in Somalia.[330] In fact, French government efforts to keep the costs of UNITAF to an absolute minimum indicate that its national interest was not threatened. As an adviser to Mitterrand, Bruno Delhaye, said on December 12, "[w]ith luck, it shouldn't last more than three-four months and in the meantime we will try our best not to do anything foolish."[331] Limited national interest in Somalia also tells us about where the French were deployed. French Admiral Jacques Lanxade asked for an area where "nothing was likely to happen."[332] The French ultimately deployed to Bakool Province (to the north of Mogadishu), choosing it because of French intelligence reports on the internal situation in Somalia.[333]

There is a significant amount of evidence that prestige concerns spurred the Mitterrand government to contribute to UNITAF. The Mitterrand government, like those before it, believed in defending France's global rank. As Daniel Vernet wrote in late 1992, "France remains obsessed with its 'position' in the world, in the name of which Mitterrand justified its participation in the Gulf War."[334] France's prestige was implicated in Somalia primarily because of France's special role and status in Africa. As of the early 1990s, France had a high degree of political, economic, and social ties in Africa, mainly with—but not limited to—its former colonies.[335] While

68 • America's Allies and War

France did not have historical or current ties with Somalia (Djibouti, to Somalia's north had been a French colony), a refusal to contribute French troops to UNITAF would have reflected poorly on its status throughout Africa, which is a component of France's global prestige. As Guy Martin wrote in 1995, "[t]oday, Africa remains the only area of the world where France retains enough power and influence to support its claim to medium-power status in the international system."[336]

When the United States—definitively less engaged in Africa than France—announced that it would lead UNITAF, France's prestige was implicated. Analysts and government officials have stressed the critical role of prestige in the Mitterrand government's decision to send troops. On December 12, Jean-Marie Colombani of *Le Monde* analyzed the Mitterrand government's decision this way:

> . . . [I]t's the first time for many years that American troops have intervened in Africa, which is a European, principally French, zone of influence. While the Americans are 'leaders' in the Persian Gulf, it is for us an acceptable situation, given the historical Anglo-American influence in the region. But that they disembark in Somalia, which adjoins Djibouti, could not but be interpreted in certain political and military circles as a defeat of the ancient guardian country. . . . [337]

In fact, opposition figures criticized the Mitterrand government for an insufficient defense of France's prestige in this case. Former French President Valéry Giscard d'Estaing argued that Europe's ties to Africa meant that European countries should have led the force.[338] Alain Juppé, Secretary General of the center-right RPR *(Rassemblement pour la République)* Party, criticized the government for following rather than leading in the Somalia crisis because "France has specific interests to defend in Africa."[339] Finally, Mitterrand adviser Bruno Delhaye noted that he initially favored intervention for domestic political reasons (to be outlined below) but "[t]hen I also phoned some of our African friends. . . . They all agreed: as francophone Heads of State, they would look ridiculous in Africa if the Americans went and we stayed home."[340]

There is some evidence that electoral politics affected the Mitterrand government's decision to contribute to UNITAF. The French public supported a contribution. Of the respondents to a December 10, 1992, CSA poll, 82 percent said that they approved of the military action that France, the United States, and others had launched to assure the delivery of aid to Somalia.[341] Leading figures in the opposition RPR also favored a contribution, such as Alain Juppé and Jacques Chirac, then a former Prime

Minister.[342] In addition, the RPR was at the head of a center-right coalition that was a credible threat to take control of the parliament in the upcoming 1993 National Assembly elections.[343] Finally, we know that a serious debate was waged within the Mitterrand government regarding the decision with Defense Minister Alain Joxe arguing against a contribution and Minister of Health and Humanitarian Action Bernard Kouchner in favor.[344] It is possible, then, that Mitterrand and his advisers decided in favor of a contribution because of a fear that angry voters would flee the Socialist Party in favor of the RPR in the next election. When Gérard Prunier asked Mitterrand adviser Delhaye why France was contributing to UNITAF, he replied, "[y]ou see, it is soon going to be Christmas and it would be unthinkable to have the French public eat its Christmas dinner while seeing on TV all those starving kids. It would be politically disastrous."[345]

One should offer a few caveats regarding the causal impact of electoral politics, however. The opposition RPR was not fully unified on the issue. François Fillon, designated RPR spokesperson for defense, criticized the Mitterrand government for surrendering its autonomy to the United States and labeled the French contribution "useless."[346] In addition, the RPR does not appear to have made its position on Somalia known prior to the Mitterrand government's decision.[347] Thus, Mitterrand could not have been certain that if he refused support he would lose votes to the center-right opposition.

The Mitterrand government's publicly stated reason for contributing to UNITAF was the humanitarian intervention norm, referred to as the "right to intervene" or even the "obligation to intervene."[348] In December Prime Minister Pierre Bérégovoy stated: "What is going on in Somalia is a challenge to humanity. It is essential to react. France was one of the first countries to estimate that we could not let it be."[349] He went on to say that there exists "an obligation to intervene when lives are threatened."[350] Bernard Kouchner and France's Ambassador to the UN, Jean-Bernard Mérimée, offered similar justifications.[351] Finally, respected external observers such as the UN Secretary General, Boutros Boutros-Ghali, and the editor of *Le Monde* were also calling for humanitarian intervention in normative terms.[352]

A number of aspects of the case cast doubt on the importance of the humanitarian intervention norm, however. First, the available evidence indicates that the United States was alone in calling for a UN force and creating it. The prestigious French daily *Le Monde* recorded the U.S. decision to lead the force on November 28.[353] I am not aware of any evidence that French officials lobbied for military intervention in Somalia prior to (or after) that point. As noted above, it appears that Bush phoned

70 • America's Allies and War

Mitterrand on December 1 and Mitterrand announced France would contribute on December 4. That is hardly the urgency one would expect from a country seized by the human suffering of the Somali people. Second, critics note that the Mitterrand government ignored many other, worse cases of human suffering and it was not clear UNITAF would improve the lives of the Somali people.[354] Third, the previously discussed French desire for a quick, low-risk engagement—as reflected by its decision on where to deploy—does not seem to fit with a concern for the well-being of Somalis.

It is possible—and consistent with the previously stated critical points—that the Mitterrand government was motivated at least in part by public opinion, which was reacting to the human suffering on display in Somalia. As adviser Delhaye said, " . . . don't worry: as soon as this stuff blows over and TV cameras are trained in another direction, we will quietly tip-toe out."[355] Had Mitterrand government officials been truly motivated primarily by the suffering of the Somali people it would not have had to contribute at all. As François Fillon said at the time, UNITAF would succeed or fail based on America's large contribution—France's was simply too small to be crucial.[356]

The Mitterrand government's decision to provide troops for the U.S.-led intervention in Somalia provides support for proposition two. Mitterrand placed high value on France's relationship with the United States and there is some evidence that this factor affected the outcome. Myriad analyst and policymaker statements bolster the claim that France's prestige—implicated because the United States initiated an intervention in a region where France enjoyed elevated status—was the critical factor in the Mitterrand government's decision. The French public and center-right opposition favored support and some evidence supports electoral politics as a significant factor in this case. The Mitterrand government's decision to contribute to UNITAF provides support for alternative proposition one because the humanitarian intervention norm was consistent with the outcome of support. The fact that the United States—not France—pushed for and created UNITAF and France's force-protection logic detract from the policymaker claims that humanitarian concerns led to French support.

Italy

According to the *Corriere della Sera* George Bush phoned Giuliano Amato on November 28 and requested an Italian contribution to UNITAF.[357] There were accounts at the time of " . . . American contrariness to an Italian participation . . . " and the U.S. special envoy to Somalia, Robert Oakley, said that it was better for Italy to wait to deploy to Somalia "because they had left a pretty bad image."[358] On the other hand, the *Financial Times* reported that "the U.S. is said to have sought Italy's military presence given its colonial links with Somalia and knowledge of the factions in the civil war."[359] A high-ranking official in the U.S. Embassy in Rome at the time clarified this episode for me. While President Bush extended the request for support and desired Italian participation, U.S. military officials opposed Italy's participation. Of course, the President's preference overruled skepticism among the American Generals.[360] On December 4 Foreign Minister Colombo and Defense Minister Andó formally announced that Italy would contribute roughly 2,500 troops.[361]

Alliance value may have contributed to the outcome in this case but there is little evidence that it played a critical role in the Amato government's decision. On the one hand, the Amato government valued Italy's alliance with the United States. American power—on display in the Persian Gulf War—stood out in the post–Cold War world. Italians also believed that the end of the Cold War made it necessary for allies to prove their value to the United States.[362] On the other hand, there is little evidence that alliance value was critical in the Amato government's decision. There is only one way that the alliance with the United States appears in the narrative accounts or analysis. The Amato government was sincerely concerned that American officials did not want an Italian contribution. If the Bush administration had not favored an Italian contribution, it is unlikely that Italy would have pressed to make one. Once, however, the Bush administration publicly clarified the U.S. government desire for an Italian contribution, the Amato government confirmed it would contribute.[363]

Italy's national interest was not threatened in Somalia. While certain Italian politicians—such as former Prime Minister Bettino Craxi—had profited from kickbacks from Italian aid to Somalia, there was no sizable Italian business involvement in Somalia as of the early 1990s.[364]

Much evidence supports the claim that prestige concerns played a critical role in the Amato government's decision to contribute. Many in Rome believed that with the end of the Cold War, "Italy has had to raise the profile of its foreign policy. . . . "[365] Italian General Bruno Loi, who commanded Italian forces in Somalia, later recalled that "Italy viewed this particular moment with enthusiasm, hoping for itself a role more appropriate for its rank as a great economic power."[366] At the time Franco Venturini of the *Corriere della Sera* wrote that Italy should deploy troops to Somalia

72 • America's Allies and War

because " . . . in our world today the credibility of a country is won on the field and [once one has it], if one wants to, one can make use of it in all manner of negotiations that involve national interest."[367]

Italy's prestige was implicated in this case because Somalia had been an Italian colony and Italy had remained engaged in Somalia after the country's independence in 1960.[368] John Hirsch and Robert Oakley wrote that " . . . politicians in Rome [were] anxious to see more publicity for a prominent Italian role in the former colony."[369] In 1994, Defense Minister Fabio Fabbri said Italy's historical and recent ties meant that it could not refuse to participate.[370] Finally, Italy's domestic turmoil made it reasonable for its peer competitors to question whether it was willing and able to act in the global arena. Sergio Romano argues that one of two reasons why Italy participated was "[g]oing to Somalia we would demonstrate to the world that we were still capable of conducting foreign policy and to 'show the flag.'"[371] Osvaldo Croci notes that Senate Foreign Affairs Committee Vice President Gian Giacomo Migone stressed *presenzialismo*" (the imperative of being present), saying that " . . . it fully explains the Italian government's decision to intervene in Somalia."[372]

Electoral politics do not appear to have played a critical role in this case. The Italian decision appears to have initially been popular.[373] The Pope supported the deployment and the parliament overwhelmingly approved it.[374] As of September 1993, 59 percent of Italians were in favor of the intervention in Somalia.[375] In December 1992, the Italian political system was undergoing a major corruption scandal that implicated the main political parties in the Amato government (the Italian Socialist Party and the Christian Democrats). The opposition Refounded Communists voted against the deployment, while the more centrist PDS and Verdi abstained on the vote.[376] As such, had the government chosen not to contribute, angry voters could not have vented their frustration by voting for the left. It is possible, however, that given the extreme flux of the Italian political system, the Amato government chose to address a public concern as an insurance policy against future electoral uncertainty. Fabio Fabbri, who was Amato's Undersecretary at the time, recalled in 1994 that " . . . the government made itself the interpreter of our population's humanitarian sentiment, traumatized by the extermination by hunger that had struck that part of the Horn of Africa."[377]

The humanitarian logic also appears in the narrative and in analysts' summaries of the Amato government decision. Sergio Romano reminds us that " . . . images of a desperate and starving Somalia seemed intolerable."[378] In addition, one might see Italy's colonial and recent ties to Somalia—especially Italian support for the Siad Barre regime—as making it morally responsible for ending the human suffering there.[379] Concern with the suffering of the Somali people no doubt played a role in the Amato government's decision but two points cast doubt on whether it was critical in determining the outcome.

First, most references to the humanitarian factor emphasize the Italian *public's* perception of the humanitarian situation. In addition to the previously cited quote from Fabio Fabbri, Sergio Romano begins the paragraph about a "desperate and starving Somalia" by stating that "[p]ublic opinion was moved."[380] It seems likely that if humanitarian concerns were significant it was because of their potential electoral consequences. Second, the humanitarian logic cannot explain why the Italian government did not plan to engage its military or call for others to do so as the situation worsened in Somalia in the year prior to the creation of UNITAF. As of the summer of 1992, the UN's Special Representative reported that between 4,000 and 5,000 Somali children were dying every day from the famine.[381] While the Italian government offered to increase aid and mediate between the warring factions, it refused Somali calls to deploy Italian troops—until the United States announced that it would lead UNITAF.[382] If the Amato government's December 1992 decision to contribute was motivated primarily by humanitarian concerns, why did those concerns not lead it to—as critics put it—have the "courage" to push for action to improve the situation in Somalia prior to this?[383]

The Amato government's contribution of Italian troops to UNITAF supports proposition two. While the government valued Italy's relationship with the United States there is little evidence that this factor explains the outcome. Italy's historical ties to Somalia meant that its prestige was implicated and a host of policymaker and analyst statements point toward this as a critical factor in the Amato government's decision to contribute. The Italian public favored support but the opposition opposed it, so the government would probably not have suffered electoral consequences had it refused to contribute. Some evidence supports the humanitarian logic and, thus, provides support for alternative proposition one. Rebuttal points cast doubt on the humanitarian logic explanation, however: Italy did not push for action but responded to the U.S. initiative and the Amato government seems to have been driven by public concern with Somali suffering rather than from its own convictions.

Conclusion

Some patterns emerge from the preceding analysis. First, alliance value varied positively with contribution most of the time but it was rarely a critical factor. Second, strong evidence often suggested threat to national interest and/or implicated prestige were critical factors in a government's decision. Third, electoral politics accurately predicted the outcome but they were rarely a significant factor in the causal process. Finally, while strong evidence did not support a constructivist explanation as often as it supported threat/prestige, evidence suggested that norms or identity played a role in some of the cases.

CHAPTER 4

Kosovo

As the 1990s drew to a close, it was not obvious that the U.S. government—led by President Bill Clinton—would decide to use force against Serbia (formally the Federal Republic of Yugoslavia). By February 1999, however, the White House believed that an air campaign was the only way to achieve American and NATO goals.[1] The Serbs—led by President Slobodan Milosevic—had refused to sign the February 1999 Rambouillet Agreement, which would have granted autonomy to the Kosovar Albanians. The Clinton administration was convinced that force was the only way to degrade the Serbs' ability to engage in ethnic cleansing, bring them to agree to terms like those in the Rambouillet Agreement, and preserve NATO's credibility. On March 24, 1999, American planes led NATO into war for the first time in the alliance's history.

Burden-sharing played a critical role in this story. Milosevic knew that NATO had him outgunned by a massive margin. If the leading NATO member countries committed their capabilities and kept them engaged, Serbia would have to accept NATO's terms or be destroyed. Milosevic's only hope was that one or more of the leading countries would refuse to participate, leading the alliance to weaken itself by internal squabbling. Unfortunately for Milosevic, Britain, France, and Italy contributed aircraft to Operation Allied Force (OAF). As the air campaign wore on, the allies maintained their contributions even as the voices of domestic critics rose. In early June 1999, Milosevic agreed to accept NATO's terms. Analysts suspect the Serb leader's surprise at NATO's unity played an important role in his decision to accept terms very similar to those he had refused earlier.[2]

A reader with prior knowledge of this case might ask whether Kosovo is appropriate for this study. One might ask whether European pressure on the United States to stand firm against the Serbs disqualifies this case. OAF fits the parameters of the book for three reasons. First, while the British

76 • America's Allies and War

favored an air war earlier than the United States, the Clinton administration decided that an air war would be necessary if negotiations with the Serbs failed. Second, it is critical to distinguish British pressure to threaten and use force against Serbia from the question of which countries would contribute to the air war and how much they would contribute. While Britain pushed harder than any other country for the use of force, it contributed far fewer aircraft than France or Italy. Third, the United States was the clear and undisputed leader of the air war with seven hundred planes—almost ten times the next largest allied contributor, France. The United States had an interest in getting as many allies to contribute as much as possible and the allies knew this.

The United Kingdom: Threat

Britain provided a respectable contribution to OAF. Britain contributed thirty-nine aircraft to allied operations, which put it fourth after the United States, France, and Italy.[3] The British air contingent in OAF was particularly active in dangerous, high-demand strike sorties: 62 percent of British sorties were strike sorties whereas only 28 percent of NATO sorties were strike sorties.[4] Moreover, Britain took an important role early on in making the case for a tough line with Serbia, and Prime Minister Tony Blair became the most high-profile advocate of a land invasion as the war dragged on.[5]

Alliance

Tony Blair was convinced that Britain's relationship with the United States was of extraordinary value and must be maintained. When Clinton visited 10 Downing Street in May 1997, he noted: " . . . our unbreakable alliance has helped to bring unparalleled peace and prosperity and security."[6] In a December 1998 speech, Blair made clear his view that Britain benefitted from its relationship with the United States, saying, "Britain's relationship with the United States has been fundamental to our foreign policy throughout this century."[7] He cited American contributions to World War I and World War II, cooperation on foreign economic policy, shared values, and American power as reasons why Britain should be as close as possible to the United States.[8]

The Blair government valued Britain's relationship with the United States because it was convinced it had a special degree of influence with the world's only superpower. Peter Riddell, Assistant Editor of *The Times*, writes that Blair had a "hug them close" transatlantic strategy driven by a desire to influence the American President (first Clinton, then Bush) and, thus, American policy.[9] Blair experienced the influence the UK-U.S. alliance yielded roughly a year after becoming Prime Minister. On September 14, 1998, Britain and the United States suspended planned air strikes due to a last-minute statement by Saddam Hussein that he would resume cooperation with UN inspectors. The next day Clinton—reacting to renewed Iraqi resistance on the inspectors—was strongly inclined to reorder the strikes but Blair persuaded the President to give Hussein an intermediate period to comply.[10]

Some evidence suggests that Britain's alliance with the United States explains the decision to contribute. Dana Allin of the International Institute for Strategic Studies (IISS) told me he thought there was a real fear in the British government that the United States might disengage from Europe so the British contributed to OAF in part to keep the United States engaged.[11] Louise Richardson argued, however, that the UK-U.S. relationship could not explain Britain's Kosovo policy because Blair pushed Clinton to agree to the use of force (and later he pushed for ground troops), even to the point of annoying the American President.[12] If one bears in mind the distinction between lobbying for action versus contributing to it, value for the UK-U.S. relationship may explain the decision to contribute.

The British value for NATO was also relevant in this case. Blair's government valued the North Atlantic Treaty as the principal means by which the United States was tied to Europe. While Blair embraced European integration on defense, he always envisioned doing so in a way that did not threaten NATO or jeopardize relations with Washington.[13] Britain's 1998 *Strategic Defence Review* substantiates this claim, stating, " . . . NATO has been reinvigorated and has shown its continuing value by its role in Bosnia and its response to events in Kosovo."[14] The *Strategic Defence Review* cited NATO's enlargement to its East and the resulting regional stability as further evidence of the alliance's value.[15]

Some evidence supports the claim that the Blair government provided support because NATO's credibility was at stake. Because NATO officials and leading allies had threatened Milosevic to change his behavior or suffer the alliance's military wrath, anything other than a unified air campaign would have undermined NATO's credibility—especially as the alliance neared its fiftieth anniversary. NATO's credibility emerged as a reason for Britain's contribution to OAF in the House of Commons deliberations on Kosovo and in the House of Commons Foreign Affairs Select Committee's postwar report on Kosovo.[16] Some of those I interviewed said NATO credibility was an important factor in Blair's decision.[17] Finally, Louise Richardson concludes that "[t]he importance of maintaining the credibility of NATO is an adequate explanation for British involvement in the air campaign. . . . "[18]

78 • America's Allies and War

The NATO credibility argument has limits, however. As the House of Commons Foreign Affairs Committee's report on Kosovo noted, "reference to NATO's credibility begs the question of why NATO had got itself into the position of being forced to bomb Yugoslavia to defend its credibility."[19] The Blair government—like any member of the alliance—could have kept NATO from threatening Milosevic. A member of the Shadow government with responsibility for the issue told me that while credibility was important, "one has to look elsewhere" for why the alliance put its credibility on the line in this case.[20] In short, Britain's alliance with the United States and its value for NATO does not sufficiently explain the Blair government's decision.

Threat

More evidence suggests that the Blair government saw instability in the Balkans as a threat to Britain's national interest and that this was a critical factor in the decision to contribute. Many believed that if the conflict between Serbia and the Kosovar Albanians were not halted, it would spread to other countries in the Balkans.[21] Moreover, the Kosovo conflict was geographically close to the United Kingdom, making it likely that British interests would be adversely affected if the conflict spread. The July 1998 *Strategic Defence Review* emphasized that while Britain did not face a direct military threat, "[i]nstability inside Europe as in Bosnia, and now Kosovo threatens our security."[22] As John Kampfner wrote, "Britain's national interest was engaged, as this was Europe's back yard. . . . "[23] Blair and his advisers were particularly likely to see Kosovo in this light as they believed in the importance of interdependence: problems in one area could spread across space and issue area.[24]

Public statements, British action, and evidence from interviews tie regional stability concerns to the British decision to provide its aircraft for OAF. The *Strategic Defence Review* followed a discussion of Bosnia as a classic case of conflict threatening regional instability by noting that "[e]vents in Kosovo emphasise the continuing dangers and the need to be able to mount a military response rapidly to contain crises before they get out of hand."[25] In the January 18, 1999, debate on Kosovo in the House of Commons, Robin Cook, Britain's Foreign Secretary, pointed out that "Kosovo is part of the European continent. Europe itself cannot have any pride or any rest while there is such instability and such atrocity immediately over the borders of the European Union."[26] Blair and his advisers were concerned that violence might spread to Macedonia (with its Slav majority and Albanian minority), Albania, Bosnia, and even Greece.

Kosovo • 79

On March 23, 1999, Tony Blair explained the reasoning behind Britain's contribution to the Kosovo War to the House of Commons. He said:

> [W]e know from bitter experience throughout this century, most recently in Bosnia, that instability and civil war in one part of the Balkans inevitably spills over into the whole of it, and affects the rest of Europe, too. I remind the House that there are now more than 1 million refugees from the former Yugoslavia in the European Union. *If Kosovo was left to the mercy of Serbian repression, there is not merely a risk, but the probability of re-igniting unrest in Albania, of a destabilised Macedonia, of almost certain knock on effects in Bosnia, and of further tension between Greece and Turkey.* Strategic interests for the whole of Europe are at stake. We cannot contemplate, on the doorstep of the EU, a disintegration into chaos and disorder.[27]

Blair's concern with regional stability recurred after his formal introductory statement. During the debate Opposition Leader William Hague asked whether Britain would sustain its commitment to the air war, and Blair replied that he was sure Britain would because "[w]e know from bitter experience that we cannot afford such instability on the borders of Europe."[28]

Most of those I interviewed believed regional stability was an important part of Blair's calculus. Tim Judah, journalist and author of *Kosovo: War and Revenge*, told me that the regional instability the Serb campaign against Kosovar Albanians was expected to create "was a common fear and was a factor in the British decision."[29] The anonymous Shadow Secretary told me that Britain's interests were implicated because in the absence of NATO action lawlessness would reign in Kosovo and with it a haven might emerge where illegal drugs trade, human trafficking, and other activities antithetical to British interests would hold sway.[30] Another interviewee agreed that Blair believed British interests would be served by an end to Serbia's ethnic cleansing campaign even as he questioned Blair's assessment of British interests in this case.[31] One anonymous interviewee expressed the view that regional stability was an important factor in the government's decision and pointed out that British forces in Bosnia were at risk if the conflict spread.[32] Only the IISS' Dana Allin took issue with this argument, stating, "It seems like the conflict could have been contained and wasn't terribly troubling in security terms. It wasn't like Milosevic was going to march on Paris. . . ."[33] Allin's point raises a critical question, however: must one face a threat to invade Paris to engage in a relatively low-cost air war?

Why does the free-riding rebuttal to national interest arguments not apply in this case? Because, as noted in the introduction to the chapter, alliance cohesion was critical to getting Milosevic to sue for peace.

80 • America's Allies and War

OAF could only succeed if NATO's most important members contributed, thus sending a signal to Milosevic that the alliance was united. While Britain's contribution may not have been necessary in pure military terms, it was necessary in political terms.

Analyst and policymaker statements support the view that the Blair government cared about Britain's prestige. For example, prestige provides an excellent rationale for British retention of its own nuclear weapons, especially when there is little practical need to do so (given that in any calculus Britain would be under the American nuclear umbrella).[34] Foreign Secretary Cook returned repeatedly to the theme of Britain's prestige in the House of Commons debates on Kosovo. On October 19, 1998, Cook drew attention to the "leading part" Britain played in bringing Milosevic to accept an Organization for Security and Co-operation in Europe (OSCE) verification meeting and that it was "among the first nations" to participate in overseeing the implementation of the agreement.[35] On February 16, Cook deflected skepticism as to whether Britain could provide a substantial contribution to a peace force (if Serbia had signed the Rambouillet Agreement) by noting that noncontribution " . . . would gravely undermine our standing in NATO."[36] Finally, Cook appealed to colleagues in a January 18 debate: "We cannot expect to retain our position as a permanent member of that council—and the respect that goes with it—and as a major member of the North Atlantic alliance if we are not willing to take part in actions when mounting such actions is deemed necessary."[37] Two of those I interviewed believed the Blair government's view that Britain's prestige was implicated played an important role in its decision to contribute.[38]

Electoral Politics

The domestic political environment was quite favorable to a British contribution to OAF. The British public favored their country's contribution to NATO's air war. Of the respondents to a March 26–27 MORI poll, 55 percent said Britain was right to have joined in the NATO bombing of Yugoslavia whereas 27 percent said it was wrong.[39] In an ICM poll of March 26, 56 percent said the involvement of British troops in NATO's bombing campaign was right (as compared to 28 percent who said it was wrong).[40] Blair's government was aware that the opposition Conservative Party would support its decision to provide military support for OAF. During the October 19, 1998, Commons debate, Shadow Foreign Secretary Howard criticized the government for not threatening Milosevic with airstrikes sooner.[41] The Conservatives continued to urge the government to take a firm line with the Serb leader during the January 18 and February 1 debates and they expressed support for the government decision to participate in OAF on March 23.[42] Even the Liberal Democrats made clear well in advance that they would support British participation in an air war if it became necessary.[43]

Did the domestic climate affect the policy process? Given the state of public opinion and the stance of the opposition parties, the only logical possibility is that the public and opposition pushed Blair's government to provide support whereas it preferred not to. There is almost no evidence to support this claim. First, there is no evidence that Blair opposed providing troops but changed his mind as it became clear the opposition and public were in favor. Second, there is little evidence that public opinion or the opposition was a factor in the Blair government's decision. None of those I interviewed on Britain and Kosovo believed public opinion pushed Blair to provide support.[44] Finally, as the war began in March 1999, Blair commanded a large majority in the House of Commons and was quite popular in the country.[45] As such, even if he had felt pushed by the public and opposition, Blair almost certainly could have resisted the pressure without the risk of significant future electoral setbacks.

Humanitarian Intervention and International Law

Some evidence supports the constructivist alternative explanation that humanitarian intervention consistent with British identity drove Blair's government to provide a military contribution to OAF. Robin Cook called for an ethical dimension to British foreign policy, saying that Britain should be a "force for good" in the world.[46] Central to this argument is the idea that rising violence—especially the January 15, 1999, Raçak massacre—was a spur to government action.[47] In his March 23 speech to the Commons, Blair made the case in explicit humanitarian terms: "We do so primarily to avert what would otherwise be a humanitarian disaster in Kosovo."[48] Many stress Blair's "doctrine of the international community" speech in Chicago as a critical element in explaining British participation.[49] In the Chicago speech Blair said of Kosovo: "This is a just war, based not on any territorial ambitions but on values. We cannot let the evil of ethnic cleansing stand."[50] On this basis, the Independent International Commission on Kosovo (IICK) referred to the war as "illegal but legitimate" and the House of Commons Foreign Affairs Select Committee concluded the war was "illegal but moral."[51] Dana Allin and an anonymous interviewee stressed the humanitarian imperative as the primary reason for the Blair government's contribution.[52]

82 • America's Allies and War

While the humanitarian logic is undoubtedly an important part of the story, it has some important shortcomings. There is little evidence that Blair was committed to a more moral British foreign policy until about halfway through the Kosovo War. Robin Cook was very much on his own in developing the "force for good" notion of British foreign policy; when Blair's Chief of Staff Jonathan Powell heard of Cook's idea he responded: "What a load of crap!"[53] In fact, Blair initially devoted little time to international relations and one of the few early foreign policy speeches he gave—the November 1998 Lord Mayor's banquet speech—followed the "traditional foreign office line."[54] The 1998 *Strategic Defence Review* provided an expansive list of British interests worldwide but only mentioned the "force for good" logic briefly and paired it with immediate qualifications.[55]

Moreover, one cannot use the Chicago speech to explain Blair's Kosovo policy given that he delivered it on April 24 and the war began on March 24. By the third week of April, Blair faced serious criticism over the lack of clear progress in the air campaign and civilian deaths from NATO airstrikes, confiding to an aide, "[t]his could be the end of me."[56] Seldon wrote that in the environment of rising criticism, "Blair thus intensified the propaganda war in Britain to ensure the humanitarian case was being made."[57] It made sense for Blair to provide a rhetorical justification for the war that targeted his most strident critics—those who focused on civilian bombing deaths.[58] As Oliver Daddow, who has written on Blair's Kosovo policy, told me, "It's true, this was a justification and it was retrospective, taken at the moment that the media was focused on civilian casualties and many were saying NATO was losing."[59]

Other aspects of the humanitarian explanation are potentially problematic. Some—including those debating British policy in the Commons— asked whether the Blair government believed there was a strong likelihood that NATO airstrikes would lead to a net improvement in the lives of the region's inhabitants (considering the damage the war would cause and the increase in ethnic cleansing it would allow).[60] What if the air campaign had not succeeded in getting Milosevic to grant Kosovo autonomy? In that case, only a land invasion—which appeared highly unlikely when the war began—could possibly even the humanitarian scales.[61] If Blair's government had been driven primarily by a desire to reduce human suffering, why did it not take issue with the use of cluster bombs and depleted uranium-tipped shells, and why was it so reluctant to accept Kosovar refugees on British soil?[62] Finally, the timing of Blair's rhetoric and policy focus is not fully consistent with a primary humanitarian motive. The IICK's report shows that Serb violence against Kosovar Albanians was "considerably lower" in late 1998 and early 1999 than it had been in summer and fall of 1998.[63]

It is fair to expect a lag between the peak of the violence and NATO action because it takes time to mobilize and coordinate an allied response. There is little record, however, that Blair and his advisers (with the exception of Robin Cook) were preoccupied by the suffering of the Kosovar Albanians in summer and fall of 1998.[64] In numerous private conversations and correspondence with Liberal Democrat leader Paddy Ashdown preceding the war, Ashdown almost always raised the subject and Blair did not articulate humanitarian concerns.[65]

International legal norms on the use of force cannot explain the Blair government's decision to provide military support. International law prohibits the use of force for anything other than self-defense in the absence of explicit authorization from the Security Council.[66] While an emerging humanitarian intervention norm exists, international law does not permit humanitarian intervention in the absence of UNSC authorization.[67] Moreover, while the UNSC had passed resolutions 1199 and 1203 that urged Serbia to change its behavior, it did not authorize the use of force.[68] It is true that Russia and China would have vetoed a resolution explicitly authorizing the use of force against Serbia but this does not make NATO's air war legal.[69] Blair privately told Ashdown in September 1998 that he would commit Britain to war even if what was to become resolution 1199 did not pass.[70] The IICK's *Kosovo Report* notes there was a general lack of international support for NATO's air war against Kosovo, which may explain why Britain and others did not attempt to attain UN General Assembly authorization through the "Uniting for Peace" mechanism.[71]

The Blair government knew that it was defying international law in providing aircraft to Allied Force. A number of speakers in the House of Commons debates laid out the consensus view that war without explicit UNSC authorization would violate international law.[72] While Blair government officials publicly claimed existing UNSC resolutions provided sufficient legal cover, they admitted otherwise in private. In her memoirs, U.S. Secretary of State Madeleine Albright recalls that in late spring of 1998, "I called Robin Cook, who said his lawyers had told him a council mandate would be needed if NATO were to act. I told him he should get himself new lawyers."[73] Cook knew NATO's air war would violate international law but still supported a British contribution. Analysis since the war supports the view that the war violated international law. As noted, the IICK's *Kosovo Report* labeled the war "illegal but legitimate."[74] The House of Commons' Foreign Affairs Committee report judged the case this way: "Our conclusion is that *Operation Allied Force* was contrary to the specific terms of what might be termed the basic law of the international community—the UN Charter. . . ."[75] When I asked about international law the anonymous

84 • America's Allies and War

Shadow Secretary said the legal status of the war was "ambiguous" but it was justified in moral terms.[76]

Case Conclusion: Regional Stability and Humanitarian Intervention

Britain—like other countries—must decide which cases of humanitarian crisis it will incur costs to try to stop. One central criterion is a threat to national interest. As Blair said in his Chicago speech, it was critical to ask "And finally, do we have national interests involved? The mass expulsion of ethnic Albanians from Kosovo demanded the notice of the rest of the world. But it does make a difference that this is taking place in such a combustible part of Europe."[77] When asked after leaving office about the Kosovo and the Chicago speech, Blair stressed that the core point he sought to make was that, as a result of interdependence " . . . it then became in our self-interest, not as simply part of some moral cause, but in our self-interest to regard ourselves as affected by what was happening in another part of the world."[78] When I asked the anonymous Shadow Secretary about human suffering in this case he said it was "important, but not decisive." I asked what he thought was decisive and he responded "[r]egional stability. Consider the classic distinction between Iraq and Zimbabwe. Both of which were equally nasty to their people. Only in the prior case were British national interests implicated. No matter how moved one is in these cases one has to be quite hard headed."[79] The anonymous Shadow Secretary added that he thought the government shared his view.

The Blair government's decision to contribute aircraft to the 1999 Kosovo War offers additional confirmation of proposition two. Britain valued its alliance with the United States and NATO, and interviews provide some evidence that alliance value was central to the outcome. However, the Blair government also took steps—such as pressing for ground troops—that angered the United States, and its concern for NATO's credibility poses the critical prior question of why it and others allowed the alliance's credibility to be pledged in this case. Myriad statements by policymakers and analysts strongly support the claim that the threat regional instability posed to Britain's national interest was a critical factor in this case. While the British public and opposition favored support, there is no evidence that this factor affected the outcome.

Numerous policymaker statements provide evidence that humanitarianism drove the Blair government's decision. That Blair did not press for action when the violence against Kosovar Albanians was at its highest and did not stress the humanitarian rhetoric until a month into the war (and the left of the Labour Party started to oppose it) cast doubt on this factor's importance. The Blair government's decision directly contradicts international legal norms requiring UNSC authorization. While plausible, I know of no evidence that the intensity of the Blair government's desire to improve the lives of Kosovar Albanians overrode the international legal imperative to attain explicit UNSC authorization, so this case provides minimal support for alternative proposition three.

France: Threat and Prestige

One would have been foolish to take French participation in OAF for granted. France had a history of supporting the Serbs in Balkan conflicts. In addition, leading French officials publicly argued that explicit UNSC authorization was necessary prior to war. Finally, the French Communist Party (PCF) opposed the use of force and it was a critical member of the center-left coalition in control of France's National Assembly. Given these factors, it is not surprising that French Foreign Minister Hubert Védrine expressed initial skepticism for NATO military action except as a peace-keeping force in the event of a negotiated settlement. In the end, Védrine, President Jacques Chirac, and Prime Minister Lionel Jospin agreed that NATO should engage in airstrikes against Serbia, with France providing military support. France provided eighty-four planes to OAF, making it the largest non-U.S. contributor.[80] Moreover, while the French clashed with the United States on the move to "Phase 3" of the air war and demanded "greater insight" into targets, U.S. Deputy Secretary of State Strobe Talbott says the French were "unshakeable on the need to keep bombing."[81]

Alliance

In the years preceding the Kosovo War, the Chirac/Jospin government valued France's relationship with the United States and NATO and there is some evidence that alliance value influenced the outcome. True, France and the United States clashed on a variety of issues prior to the war, including U.S. and UK air strikes against Iraq in December 1998.[82] More fundamentally, in February 1998 Foreign Minister Védrine—building on previous statements—told an interviewer that the United States was a "hyperpower" (*hyperpuissance*).[83] Védrine was most concerned that the United States would abandon the multilateral approach characteristic of the Bush and Clinton years in favor of unbridled unilateralism.[84] Védrine realized that American primacy meant that France must engage the United States and push it in the right direction, however. As Chirac said in an address to the U.S. Congress, "Today, as in the past, the world needs the United States.

86 • America's Allies and War

Your engagement is necessary to build up the uncertain post–Cold War world and advance peace, democracy, and development."[85]

Chirac's experience with the Clinton White House was a critical factor in his government's value for France's relationship with the United States. Chirac had a high degree of access to Clinton and it appears he had a high degree of influence. For example, Chirac contributed to the firming up of U.S. and NATO policy on Bosnia in 1995.[86] Journalists Gilles Delafon and Thomas Sancton argue that Clinton granted Chirac access and influence because he saw France as speaking for Europe.[87] They conclude that "the new Franco-American relationship that Chirac and Clinton put in place characterizes itself precisely by a fierce will to overcome disagreements and to act together on important problems."[88]

There is some evidence that the Chirac/Jospin government chose to make a large contribution to OAF to maximize its influence with the United States. The French influenced the United States' Kosovo policy in the period leading up to the war. According to Craig Whitney of *The New York Times*, the Clinton administration preferred to issue an ultimatum to Serbia on January 28 but agreed to wait after pressure from the French.[89] Louis Gautier, Lionel Jospin's adviser for defense and security told me that the United States was quite willing to consult with France in the period preceding the war—he recalled frequent tripartite phone calls among Albright, Védrine, and German Foreign Minister Joschka Fischer.[90] The French government believed that a large contribution would lead to influence over the United States. A relevant French Government Minister told me, "[o]ne of the motivations shared by Jospin, Védrine, and myself was that the larger the contribution France made the more influence it would have over the United States. We were especially worried that the United States would be too liberal with bombing targets."[91] This assessment turned out to be correct. As a senior Foreign Ministry official said after the war, "Despite everything, we did exert a moderating influence."[92]

The French started to reevaluate their relationship with NATO with the end of the Cold War. The Chirac government took various steps in the 1990s to move closer to NATO. While France did not rejoin the alliance's military command, it ended the decade more integrated and committed to NATO than when the decade began.[93] The Chirac/Jospin government's value for NATO appears to have affected its decision to contribute to OAF. First, the Chirac/Jospin government was convinced that France had influence in NATO worth preserving. As Louis Gautier explained to me, " . . . we have a greater weight [than the United Kingdom] because we are not in NATO and can't be taken for granted. France, in contrast, was able in Kosovo to impose itself in the decision making process and affect strategy."[94] Similarly, the Chirac/Jospin government knew that NATO's rules meant that France would have the ability to influence future NATO decisions to threaten and use force.[95]

Second, as NATO had made increasingly serious threats to Milosevic, its credibility was on the line. Because France valued NATO, it had to provide support or the alliance would suffer. Gilles Andréani, Head of Policy Planning (*Centre d'analyse et de prevision*) at the French Foreign Ministry in the period leading up to the war, wrote, " . . . the threat NATO brandished since October . . . put in play its credibility in the region and that of the principle allied countries."[96] A postwar report prepared by Paul Quilès and François Lamy for the National Assembly's Defense and Armed Forces Commission concluded that " . . . NATO had implicated itself to such an extent that it would have been impossible to not act without putting its credibility in doubt."[97] Thus, it seems likely that French value for NATO contributed to its decision to provide military support for OAF.[98]

Threat and Prestige

The Kosovo crisis was a threat to France's national interest given the conflict's geographic proximity to France and its potential to spread. Gilles Andréani wrote that Kosovo differed from other humanitarian crisis cases because of its historical and geographical characteristics including " . . . proximity and the risks of an extension of the conflict that made it a direct security question for NATO countries."[99] An editorial in the prestigious daily *Le Monde* on March 25 similarly stated, "the longer NATO waits, the more the Kosovo conflict will be heavy with massacres and the more regional destabilization will be exacerbated."[100] The aforementioned Quilès and Lamy report concluded that "[t]o allow President Milosevic to impose a radical and violent solution would have entailed a humanitarian and geopolitical danger because *the stability of the entire Balkan region was threatened*."[101] The Quilès and Lamy report included an entire section titled "The Stability of South-eastern Europe in Danger," emphasizing that the conflict might spread to Albania, Montenegro, and Bosnia-Herzegovina.[102]

Jacques Chirac cited regional stability concerns in explaining his government's decision to provide French aircraft for NATO's air war. In February Chirac warned: "[w]e will not accept that the cycle of violence threatens, bit by bit, the stability of all of south-east Europe. We want peace on our continent."[103] Similarly, in justifying France's contribution to NATO's air war as it began on March 24, Chirac said, "That which is at issue today is peace on our soil, peace in Europe and also here at home, human rights."[104] While he stressed the human suffering logic in his March 26 address to the

88 • America's Allies and War

National Assembly, Jospin stated: "[t]his action also has as a goal the prevention of the risk of an extension or intensification of fighting and the troubles that arise from it."[105] Foreign Minister Védrine argued that regional stability concerns justified a French contribution to OAF.[106] Defense Minister Alain Richard explained to the National Assembly's Defense Commission that " . . . the risks of NATO inaction were superior to those of the current intervention, notably owing to instability in Macedonia, a country without military potential, with very contrasting communities and which counts on the solidarity of allies."[107]

Interviews provide further support for the claim that regional stability was a critical factor in explaining the French decision to contribute.[108] Jean-Pierre Maulny, who was Chargé de Mission for the President of the National Assembly's Defense and Armed Services Committee, told me the geographic proximity of the conflict was one of two reasons why France provided aircraft (the other was that diplomatic means had been exhausted), explaining, "[t]he public might have thought 'Well, the Balkans are a long way away, why do I care?' On the other hand, Kosovo had the potential to turn into something analogous to the Israeli-Palestinian conflict. That would not have been good for France."[109] When asked about regional stability Jospin's adviser Gautier responded that if Serbia had been left to its own devices, " . . . the counter blows [reverberations] would impact us: the arms traffic, immigration, and prostitution were just some of the related destabilizing factors. This view was almost unanimous in the government."[110]

Policymaker and analyst statements suggest the Chirac/Jospin government was committed to preserving or enhancing France's prestige. Interestingly, both Chirac and Jospin uttered the same phrase about French power: "France is a country that matters."[111] Védrine wrote and spoke much about France's rank, saying that France was not a "great power" along the lines of the United States but was a "power" among the top twenty in the world.[112] Prestige also motivated French policy. Delafon and Sancton argue, for example, that France favored a firm stance against the Serbs in 1995 because France's participation in the ineffectual UN force in Bosnia cast doubt on France's prestige.[113] When Isabelle Lasserre asked French diplomats about the principles guiding French diplomacy they stressed "France's past" and its *grandeur*.[114] Similarly, Alex Macleod wrote (in a chapter about France and Kosovo): "[a]t the heart of French foreign policy lies the pursuit of France's place among the major players of the international system, or its *rang* (rank)."[115]

France's prestige was implicated in three ways in the Kosovo case. First, French prestige would suffer if it did not offer its aircraft to Allied Force because it had so implicated itself in the threats to Milosevic. In the March

26 National Assembly debate, Jospin noted with pride that "France played a catalytic role at the heart of the contact group to define the terms of reference for a political solution. . . . "[116] France's catalytic role peaked as it hosted the Rambouillet Conference. As host, France would have suffered considerable loss of prestige had it responded to a Serb refusal to sign and ratify the peace agreement by not providing French planes for NATO's air war. Thus, while some analysts have stressed the importance of NATO's credibility, others such as Gilles Andréani have noted that "lead allied countries" such as France had also put their credibility on the line.[117] Consistent with this logic, one sees a hardening of the French position as the Rambouillet Conference drew to a close and Serb intransigence became apparent.[118] This discussion poses the question of why the Chirac/Jospin government would allow its prestige to be implicated in this case.

France could not stand aside a conflict so close to it and avoid damage to its prestige. As Louis Gautier told me, "[g]iven that Kosovo was much closer to France and its interests than the Persian Gulf War, it was reasonable for France to want to show that it was capable to act, to play a leadership role in the effort."[119] As in Bosnia, France would have to get involved in some way, and contributing to a forceful response was superior to the "humiliation" France suffered as part of the United Nations Protection Force (UNPROFOR).[120] As France led the OSCE observer mission in Kosovo, it risked a repeat of Bosnia and the doubt such a failure would cast on France's power and position in international relations.[121] Given that two of France's closest power competitors—Britain and Germany—were likely to contribute to the air war, France had to provide support. As one senior Foreign Ministry official said, " . . . we had no choice. The alternative was to go down in splendid isolation." Another high-ranking diplomat posed the hypothetical of a French refusal to provide a military contribution: "What did we stand to gain except applause from Russia, China and possibly India?"[122]

Finally, there is some evidence that the Chirac/Jospin government contributed to OAF to enhance French prestige with a specific goal in mind: to demonstrate that France and Europe could make a meaningful contribution to solving a regional security problem, thus building support for the move toward greater European security and defense integration. Jean-Pierre Maulny told me the move toward common foreign and security policy was a "major factor" in the Chirac-Jospin decision to provide military support, stating that "[a]s France and Germany were the two motors of this initiative France had to be a major military and diplomatic contributor to the Kosovo war."[123] Jacques Chirac similarly declared: "[be] assured that France, as it has done since the beginning of the conflict in the former Yugoslavia, will

90 • America's Allies and War

fulfill all of its responsibilities. It owes it to its European ambition."[124] Defense Minister Richard noted that if European countries did not demonstrate their ability to contribute to such a war in the heart of Europe, "European integration would know a grave reversal."[125]

Electoral Politics

One might think public opinion can explain this case. Given that French citizens were exposed to television images of suffering Kosovar Albanians, it is plausible that they pushed the Chirac/Jospin government to contribute troops. In an interview conducted before he became Foreign Minister, Védrine expressed concern that foreign policy might become too driven by "the suffering of television viewers."[126] A March 26, 1999, IPSOS poll found 59 percent of respondents supported French participation while 57 percent approved of NATO's air war against Yugoslavia.[127] Some believed the French public was particularly concerned with civilian casualties from NATO's bombing but as of the third week of May, 67 percent continued to favor French participation.[128]

The most fundamental problem with this argument is in locating any decisive future electoral impact. The Chirac/Jospin government was an instance of cohabitation (i.e., a center-right President and center-left Prime Minister and National Assembly) so the government could not win or lose by distinguishing itself from its likely main electoral competitor. Had the government chosen to refuse military support, unhappy voters would have had nowhere to take their protest vote. The French Communist Party and the far-right National Front were the only political parties to oppose the government.[129] Finally, while the French position on the air war hardened in the period leading up to war, I have seen no evidence that public opinion drove this development. Interviewees confirmed the view that public opinion was not significant in this case. Louis Gautier (adviser to Lionel Jospin at the time) told me that the government played a "pedagogical" role with public opinion.[130] France"s Ambassador to the United States, François Bujon de l'Estang, told me that public opinion did not drive French policy whereas Jean-Pierre Maulny said that at the time parliamentarians were concerned that the public would turn against the war as casualties mounted. As such, it is highly unlikely that the public forced the government to provide support.[131]

Human Suffering and International Law

Evidence from a variety of sources supports the view that the Chirac/Jospin government provided a military contribution to OAF because they were concerned with the suffering of Kosovar Albanians and alleviating such suffering was consistent with French identity. For example, Jacques Chirac said, "France's destiny was never to withdraw within its hexagon. On the contrary, it is to project itself abroad and share its values and make them come alive."[132] Védrine offered a view of the humanitarian crisis in terms of European identity, saying, "The root reaction—'never again in Europe'—was as much a European reaction as an American one."[133] The Foreign Minister also said that the Raçak massacre of 15 January "accelerated everything."[134] In making the case for the war in the National Assembly, Jospin said that inaction would entail accepting " . . . the return of barbarity on our continent. . . . "[135]

A couple of interviewees stressed the humanitarian factor above all others. François Bujon de l'Estang said, "I may be mistaken but in my view the humanitarian factor was the number one concern, but there was also concern that the conflict would spread to other areas, including other Albanian majority countries."[136] Louis Gautier said that while key decision makers had decided in favor of force—if it became necessary—as of summer of 1998, Raçak was the tipping point. Gautier also said that human suffering was more important than regional stability in the calculus of Chirac and Jospin.[137]

Yet other evidence casts doubt on the humanitarian logic. In the wake of the Raçak massacre, French government officials continued to be reluctant to use force. Journalist Claire Trean wrote on January 18 that when she asked about NATO's threats of air strikes against Serbia: "'But we are not there yet!' Exclaims an official at the Foreign Affairs Ministry in Paris—that will not resolve anything."[138] The French also frequently expressed a view on the moral complexity of the conflict at odds with making the humanitarian logic a central role in French decision making. When atrocities such as Raçak occurred, the French often suspected that the Kosovo Liberation Army (KLA) might have provoked or even caused them.[139] By the end of February, *Le Monde* had published an essay highly critical of Védrine for not addressing the humanitarian situation with any real urgency.[140] It seems unlikely that Védrine only became struck by the human suffering of Kosovo's Albanians as the Rambouillet Conference ended. It is more likely that having put French prestige on the line (for the reasons outlined above) the Chirac/Jospin government knew that it had to follow through.

In pledging its planes to Allied Force, France threw international law to the wind. French officials at the highest levels admitted as much. As of the summer of 1997, Védrine said that the UNSC's authorization—as provided in the 1991 Gulf War—provided the "only admissible" right for a country

92 • America's Allies and War

to intervene militarily in the sovereign affairs of another.[141] Chirac reacted to the U.S. and UK's 1998 decision to launch 1998 strikes on Iraq without explicit UNSC authorization by warning that "[t]he principle lesson of this crisis is: nothing should weaken the Security Council because it is irreplaceable."[142] Later Chirac tried to claim that because UNSC resolution 1199 on Kosovo was under Chapter VII of the UN Charter it "opened the way" for military action.[143] Jospin said that because the UNSC "wasn't in a position to act" NATO had to take it upon itself.[144] Such a position has no basis in international law.

French critics of the war stressed that it violated the UN Charter, which allows the use of force only when the Security Council explicitly authorizes it.[145] Interviews confirmed this interpretation of the international legal aspects of the case. Jean-Pierre Maulny admitted that the French government's legal case was somewhat far-fetched *"tiré par les cheveux."*[146] Another interviewee agreed that Kosovo demonstrates that France violates international law when doing so is in its interest.[147] In interviews where time did not permit me to pose a question about international law, no interviewee raised it unprompted as an important causal factor.[148]

Case Conclusion: Threat and Prestige

The evidence presented in this case study suggests that the Chirac/Jospin government was motivated to stake French credibility on a Rambouillet-like settlement because of regional stability concerns, to further its aims on European security and defense integration, and to maximize its influence over the United States. Once French credibility was implicated, France's prestige would have suffered had it not provided a military contribution.

Were the realist factors or the humanitarian logic more important? When I asked the French Government Minister about the relative importance of regional stability and the humanitarian logic, he favored the latter, saying, "If it had just been regional stability, we would have pushed for a diplomatic solution."[149] While the Minister's statement should be taken seriously, it does not explain why France switched from supporting diplomacy to force only as the humanitarian situation improved.[150] Moreover, it is unlikely that Chirac was insincere in offering the regional stability logic, as it is difficult to imagine how he would have gained in so doing as the government faced very little criticism from the Gaullist/nationalist camp. In contrast, humanitarian rhetoric was most likely to convince numerous skeptics on the center-left. Louis Gautier said human rights were more important than regional stability but admitted that Jospin referred to human rights more than Chirac because he was speaking to his left-wing base.[151] Jean-Pierre Maulny posited that realist factors were more important than humanitarianism: "Human rights were more a consequence than a cause of OAF [and France's decision to participate]. Remember that Védrine thought in terms of realpolitik. He was concerned by stability in the region, not by human rights."[152] As a recent survey of France-U.S. relations states, "[o]verall, the Kosovo initiative encapsulated the diverse strands of French attitudes toward advancing its own national aspirations, contending with a domineering United States, and exploiting the utility of international organizations."[153]

The Chirac/Jospin government's decision to provide aircraft for the Kosovo War provides support for proposition two. The government highly valued France's relationship with the United States and myriad sources suggest that a desire to maintain influence over the United States contributed, albeit was not critical, to the outcome in this case. Numerous policymaker and analyst statements suggest that the Chirac/Jospin government was motivated primarily by a desire to resolve a threat to France's interest in regional stability and preserve French prestige. While the French public supported the war, it was irrelevant because the cohabitation government meant there was no credible political opposition. Prestige concerns, not humanitarianism better explain the timing of the Chirac/Jospin government's decision (well after the peak in violence against the Kosovar Albanians). While some evidence supported a role for humanitarianism, I found no direct evidence that it *overrode* international legal norms so the case provided minimal support for alternative proposition three.

Italy: Alliance and Prestige

There were several reasons to expect Italy not to participate in a NATO air war over Kosovo.[154] Italy's public was opposed to the use of force and far-left parties in Massimo D'Alema's government opposed the war. Moreover, war over Kosovo was likely to hurt Italy's economy and some even feared that in the case of war the Serbs might launch missile attacks against Italian territory. Yet, in the end D'Alema's government chose to make a significant military contribution to NATO's OAF. According to a RAND study headed by John E. Peters, Italy contributed fifty-eight aircraft (mostly Tornado fighter-bombers), which was the third-largest contribution (the United States' was first and France's was second).[155] Italy's planes flew the fourth-highest number of sorties and allowed the alliance the full use of its air bases—critical in waging the air war given Italy's proximity to the war.[156]

What if one looks a little deeper? On the eve of the air war, Italian Defense Minister Carlo Scognamiglio announced that Italian planes would

94 • America's Allies and War

not bomb Serb targets; instead they would "defend our air space."[157] In the war's third week, Italian fighter-bombers began engaging in strikes; the government said they were necessary for "integrated" defense activities.[158] Italy's Prime Minister Massimo D'Alema subsequently explained that the only limitation on Italy's planes was " . . . not to go beyond the 40th parallel; that is, in concrete terms, not to bomb Serb cities."[159] This meant that Italian fighter-bombers could strike Serb targets elsewhere—and they did. The aforementioned RAND study shows that Italy ranked fourth in number of strike sorties (after the United States, France, and the UK).[160] In fact, Italy's restriction on the use of its planes seems to have generated little attention outside of Italy.[161]

Italy might have adopted a role like Greece's, wherein it would not veto NATO action but also would not directly participate in the war.[162] Italy could have modeled itself after Germany, which provided planes but did not engage in any strike sorties.[163] Instead, the D'Alema government took the costly step to participate in NATO's air war over Kosovo. Why?

Alliance

One might doubt whether the D'Alema government valued Italy's alliance with the United States and NATO in the period prior to the Kosovo war. Italy and the United States struggled to reach consensus on numerous issues in late 1998 and early 1999.[164] Italy criticized the American and British air strikes against Iraq in December 1998.[165] Italy also clashed with the United States over the Kurdish leader Abdullah Ocalan and the "Cermis" ski lift incident, wherein an American pilot caused nineteen deaths.[166] When the government's critics called for the closure of U.S. bases in Italy, Foreign Minister Lamberto Dini responded: "[t]he alliance with the United States and Italy's loyalty to NATO are not in question."[167] The Ocalan and Cermis cases indicate alliance value because Italian policy was characterized by a sensitivity to the American position and a willingness to compromise that would have been lacking had Italy not valued the relationship.

In the years preceding the Kosovo War, Italy became increasingly influential in allied decision making regarding the Balkans. In April 1994 when a Contact Group on Bosnia was created to facilitate dialogue on Bosnia between Russia and key NATO allies (the United States, UK, France, and Germany), Italy found itself excluded. Italian officials resented their exclusion, feeling that their interest in the region and contribution to Balkan peace operations justified a seat at the table.[168] In September 1995, Italian Foreign Minister Susanna Agnelli announced that Italy would refuse the use of its air bases to F-117 stealth bombers flying missions over Bosnia until it was admitted.[169] Italy finally attained entry to the Contact Group after the November 1995 Dayton Accords. In a 1997 letter to the Foreign Affairs Committee of the Chamber of Deputies Foreign Minister Dini stated that with Italy's entry into the Contact Group, "[o]ur country has so far succeeded in placing itself at the core of decision-making mechanisms on security in Europe, thus ensuring protection against its geo-strategically exposed position."[170] An Italian Foreign Ministry official I interviewed stressed Italy's participation in the Contact Group as proof that Italy was not just "a payer" but also "a player" in the decision-making process.[171]

D'Alema's statements indicate that Italy valued its alliance relationship with the United States and NATO. First, D'Alema made clear that he believed that Italy stood to benefit greatly from NATO's new post–Cold War mission of projecting stability in Europe. In January 1999, D'Alema wrote, "Italy is particularly exposed to the risks of instability and conflict from the very areas where NATO's functions have been consistently growing in scope and duration in the 1990s. In other words, in the 'new NATO' Italy is, more than in the past, a front-line state with vital interests on the immediate periphery of the alliance's core area."[172] Second, D'Alema recognized that during the Cold War Italy had been a "consumer" of the security goods produced by NATO but he argued that in the post–Cold War era Italy should become a security "producer" through NATO.[173] Clearly, Italy would not seek to become a security producer in NATO if it did not value the alliance.

Statements on the eve of the war provide strong evidence that high alliance value drove the D'Alema government's decision.[174] In the March 26 Italian Senate debate, D'Alema stressed the importance of Italy's "loyal support" to the Atlantic alliance.[175] D'Alema also contended that Italy benefitted from the alliance because it was an arena where Italy mattered, saying, " . . . in this alliance and in this unified Europe Italy is a country that can and wants to have its say, that wants to have its voice heard."[176] D'Alema reiterated the importance of the Atlantic alliance to Italy as the war progressed.[177]

Analysts and those I interviewed cited Italy's value for the Atlantic alliance as a key factor in explaining its contribution. Analyst Roberto Menotti wrote of Italy's decision to participate in the Kosovo War: "In sum, Italy's primary interest was encompassed in the goal of cultivating traditional links with the United States. . . . "[178] Stefano Folli of the *Corriere della Sera* explained D'Alema's Kosovo policy by reference to the Atlantic alliance.[179] Osvaldo Croci listed Italy's "duty toward NATO" as one of two imperatives driving Italy's participation in OAF.[180] An Italian Foreign Ministry official I interviewed who had responsibility for Kosovo policy

96 • America's Allies and War

offered—unprompted—Italy's solidarity with NATO as the most important factor explaining Italy's contribution.[181] I spoke with three members of the government at the time all of whom agreed that Italy had to contribute to attain influence over the air war and U.S. and NATO policy.[182] As Defense Minister Scognamiglio told me, " . . . if you don't participate actively, you don't have influence."[183] Other interviewees stressed the importance of Italy's alliance relationship with the United States and NATO as an important factor in the D'Alema government's decision.[184]

One might ask whether it was important that Massimo D'Alema was an ex-member of the Italian Communist Party (PCI) and, hence, had to prove himself to Washington.[185] When I asked D'Alema whether his prior membership in the PCI played a role in his government's decision, he said (perhaps predictably) that it was not particularly important.[186] Interestingly, though, he added, "The United States is an absolutely necessary partner for Italy. The U.S. is especially important for Italy because Europeans have a tendency to marginalize us whereas we can use our relationship with the U.S. to matter more in Europe."[187]

Threat and Prestige

The Kosovo War stood to resolve a threat to Italy's national interest but it also entailed costs and risks. Undoubtedly, as many critics noted, the war was costly to Italy in national interest terms.[188] For example, the war caused economic disruption.[189] Moreover, the Serbs responded to NATO air strikes by heightening their ethnic cleansing campaign, which led to a short-term increase in Kosovar Albanian refugees arriving at Italy's borders. Critics argued that these refugee flows were bad for Italy because they brought with them drugs, crime, and other social ills.[190] Finally, some voiced concerns that the Serbs might respond to Italian participation in OAF by launching attacks against Italian territory.[191]

D'Alema and his advisers recognized that the war would be costly but they believed that a resolution of the Kosovo conflict—which required the use of force—would end the fundamental medium- to long-term threat to Italy's national interest.[192] The government believed that only a resolution of the Kosovo conflict could solve the refugee problem. The Kosovo conflict had caused refugee flows to Italy for years preceding the war. The *Corriere della Sera* published a steady stream of articles on Kosovar refugees from the last months of 1998 to the first months of 1999.[193] D'Alema, Scognamiglio, and Interior Minister Rosa Russo Jervolino expressed concern about Kosovar refugees in the period leading up to the war.[194] As Renato Mannheimer wrote a few days into the war, "In reality, the military episode did nothing but augment the intensity of a phenomenon that had occurred for some time and became still more remarkable in the three months preceding."[195]

Government officials also believed a successful war would increase regional stability, thus resolving another threat to Italy's national interest. Stability in the Balkans in the medium term would be best for Italy's economy, and for the safety of its citizens. As Angelo Panebianco wrote, " . . . we in the West (and we Italians more than others, given our geographic position) have a vital strategic interest in an outcome wherein the Balkan blaze is, if not spent, at least limited."[196] Only a successful resolution of the conflict through OAF had the potential to provide durable stability.

A number of government statements tied the threat to Italy's national interest—especially the concern with refugee flows—directly to the decision to provide military support. When asked about Italy's decision to support the October 1998 "Actord" (authorizing NATO airstrikes against Serbia), D'Alema explained that "Italy felt the emergency more profoundly than any other country, being on the front lines of the exodus of refugees."[197] As of January 1999 the *Corriere della Sera* reported that "[t]he crackle of guns from the other side of the Adriatic has become 'the principle preoccupation' at Palazzo Chigi [the Prime Minister's residence]. And above all else for one reason: if things get worse, people will flee from Kosovo. Thousands of fleeing wretches will show up on our coasts. 'A true exodus—fears the head of government—would be difficult to control from our country.'"[198] Finally, on March 30 D'Alema explained his decision this way to the Italian people: "We want peace in that land that is so close to us, that we know also because we know the faces of the refugees, the displaced persons by now for many years."[199] If OAF succeeded, Italians would be much less likely to see the faces of Kosovar refugees in the future.

Analysts suggested the key to the D'Alema government's decision to provide support was the threat to Italy's national interest. Ernesto Galli della Loggia wrote that while there seemed to be a taboo on saying so publicly, Italy's national interest (refugees and regional stability) could explain its participation much better than humanitarian motives.[200] The Istituto Affari Internazionali's Ettore Greco explained that "[i]t was essential for the government in particular to prevent a new massive and disorganized wave of refugees from the areas populated by Albanians."[201] Greco made clear that he believed Italy also sought to increase Balkan stability and to "reinforce its international status."[202] Stefano Folli and Franco Venturini of the *Corriere della Sera* also made the case that Italy's national interests provided an excellent reason for Italy to provide military support.[203]

Interviews suggest the threat to national interest played an important role in the D'Alema government's decision. Most of those I spoke with said

98 • America's Allies and War

they thought Italy's national interest—in regional stability and limits on refugee flows—was a central factor in the D'Alema government's decision.[204] A high-level Ministry of Foreign Affairs official told me without prompting that "Italy's interests were at stake. Italy's interest was in a stable Balkan region."[205] Defense Minister Scognamiglio acknowledged that the airstrikes had led to a short-term increase in refugee flows but added "had there been no OAF not only would the flows have been greater but there would have been no way to repatriate the refugees."[206] D'Alema offered a definitive statement: "[i]t was in our national interest: consider the large influx of refugees that had been heading toward Italy's shores during the 1990s as a result of the Balkan wars. It would have been foolish to risk destabilization of the region."[207] In contrast, a couple of interviewees expressed skepticism that Italy's national interest was among the most important factors in this case.[208]

In the period preceding the Kosovo War, Italy made clear that it cared about its prestige. For example, Italy was a leading proponent of a UNSC reform plan that would have resulted in a European seat on the council, which policymakers believed would elevate Italy to a "*Serie A*" (i.e., major league or first rank) country.[209] Italian policymakers also felt their leadership of Operation Alba, the 1997 peace and stability operation in Albania, enhanced their country's prestige. In January 1999, D'Alema reminded his parliamentary colleagues that the prestige Italy had won needed to be defended, stating, "Operation Alba demonstrated very clearly, however, that Italy could be a country willing and able to take on direct responsibility."[210]

As the Rambouillet Conference opened, D'Alema made clear his government's view that if NATO chose to use force, Italy would have to participate if it wanted to be among the leading powers: "[w]e are aware of our dimensions, but all the same we know how to participate in *Serie A*."[211] Umberto Ranieri, Undersecretary at the Ministry of Foreign Affairs, told the *Corriere della Sera* that "Italy is a serious country, when necessary we know how to assume our responsibilities."[212] Italy's prestige was on the line also because the countries it measures itself against in the international security context (Britain, France, and Germany) were contributing.

Italy's prestige was also on the line because of Kosovo's proximity to Italy. In January 1999 D'Alema noted that "We are not a great power, but here we are speaking of our backyard (*le porte di casa nostra*): I believe that Italy must be present every time international military contingents are deployed to the Balkans."[213] The Prime Minister offered similar logic when explaining Italian participation to the Chamber of Deputies.[214] Senator Cesare Marini agreed with D'Alema, warning that if Italy were not to participate in OAF, it would "weaken Italy's image in Europe."[215] Not long after the war D'Alema explained his decision: "It was completely clear to me that we could not suffer a new crisis in the Balkans delegating to others the responsibility that awaited us. We would have finished by weakening the international prestige Italy had just gained with Operation Alba."[216] In an interview to mark the ten-year anniversary of the war, D'Alema recalled that Clinton had given him the option of providing bases but no aircraft. D'Alema responded: "Mr. President, Italy is not an aircraft carrier. If we take this action together, we will assume our responsibilities like the other members of the alliance."[217] D'Alema then recounted the recognition Italy had gained from its contribution to OAF.[218]

Analysts referred to prestige in their explanations of Italy's contribution to the Kosovo War. Maurizio Cremasco argued that "Massimo D'Alema wanted Italy to have a significant role in postwar Kosovo and become one of the principal actors in the efforts toward stability in the region."[219] Osvaldo Croci said that Italy could have chosen not to provide support but "the price of evading such a responsibility would be a loss of prestige and, even more importantly, missing an opportunity to become a permanent member of the 'noble circle of Great Powers.'"[220]

Interviews similarly supported the importance of prestige in this case.[221] A Foreign Ministry official I interviewed said the attention that Britain, France, and Germany get relative to Italy "creates a certain unease" in Rome. He stressed that Italian officials were aware that given Kosovo's proximity to Italy, a decision not to provide military support would have resulted in a loss of prestige for Italy.[222] Marta Dassù explained that Italy's regional proximity to Kosovo meant that its prestige and its interests were implicated.[223] She also noted that Italy often pursues a *politica della sedia* whereby it seeks to be seen as having a seat at the table even if it does not have specific interests it intends to pursue.[224] To assume the role of a leading European power Italy had to—as an anonymous official told me—be willing to pay "in gold or blood. And you can't only pay in gold—it is almost never enough."[225] In his initial response as to why his government chose to provide support, D'Alema said, "[a]ctive participation was key in finding a role for Italy. It would have been a humiliating situation to not participate actively."[226] I asked him whether Italy's prestige might explain its willingness to engage in bombing and he responded: "[t]hat was the game. It was that. We couldn't do it halfway."[227]

Electoral Politics

While a potential factor of influence, public opinion cannot explain Italy's decision to provide military support for the Kosovo War. In a poll published

100 • America's Allies and War

on March 27 in the *Corriere della Sera*, Renato Mannheimer reported that just under 50 percent of respondents found the air war unjustified, with only 25 percent finding it justified (the other 25 percent chose not to express an opinion).[228] Almost 50 percent of respondents said Italy should support the war politically but not militarily, while only just over 30 percent said Italy should provide military support.[229] The critical factor was the center-right opposition's support for the D'Alema government's decision. As D'Alema clarified later: " . . . the right supported the operation with a sense of responsibility and, as such, the war never became an object of the electoral campaign."[230] Public opinion was not likely to have devastating electoral consequences because the center-right supported the government's decision. While parties within the governing coalition (the Italian Communist Party and the Greens) were not in favor of the air war, they remained within the government.[231] Interviews supported the preceding analysis. None of those I interviewed stressed public opinion or electoral politics as among the most important factors in explaining the D'Alema government's decision to participate. Ettore Greco argued, however, that public opinion could explain the government's restrictions on where Italian planes could bomb.[232]

Human Rights and International Law

Fabrizio Coticchia and Giampiero Giacomello note that there is a strong bipartisan consensus in Italy that the country is a force for peace.[233] As D'Alema said in his address on Kosovo, "Italy will fulfill its responsibilities; we are a people that loves peace. . . . "[234] During the March 26 Senate debate, D'Alema stressed that Italy was the fourth-largest contributor to UN peace operations (after the United States, UK, and France).[235] Article 11 of the Italian constitution is an important repository of the country's identity in international relations; it states that "Italy repudiates war as an instrument that offends the liberty of other peoples and as a means to resolve international conflicts."[236] Not all agree that Article 11 provides a total ban on Italy participating in war; those with a looser interpretation have argued that it proscribes war unless the UNSC explicitly authorizes it.[237]

In providing aircraft to NATO's war over Kosovo, the Italian government contradicted core elements of its identity and international law on the use of force. Italy joined with others to wage war against another state to force it to change its behavior within its borders.[238] Moreover, while the UNSC passed numerous resolutions criticizing Serb treatment of the Kosovar Albanians, it did not explicitly authorize the use of force to enforce those resolutions. Critics noted that the D'Alema government's support for the Kosovo War entailed a violation of Article 11.[239] For example, Aldo Tortorella (who resigned from D'Alema's party after thirty years in the Italian parliament) explained that " . . . the entire operation is illegitimate, peppered with a long series of irregularities; in order, the following were violated: the UN Charter, international law, the North Atlantic Treaty, and, finally, the Italian Constitution."[240] On the other side of the political spectrum, the right-wing Northern League's Luciano Gasperini argued that Italy was participating in war and quoted Article 11 to support his criticisms.[241]

D'Alema provided two responses to these critiques. First, he argued that Italy was promoting peace, as true peace was only possible with Milosevic's acceptance of NATO's aims.[242] Second, the Prime Minister argued that the Italian constitution allows for an exception to Article 11 when fulfilling treaty obligations.[243] Both points are problematical. The problem with saying one is willing to wage war to achieve peace is that it provides little to distinguish Italy from some of history's worst aggressors who also often preferred peace on their terms. Post–World War II international law dictates that the UNSC determines whether a threat to the peace exists and the measures that are appropriate to address it. A significant problem with arguing that the D'Alema government was exempt from Article 11 is that nothing in the North Atlantic Treaty requires members to provide military support when the alliance acts. Greece provided no military support for OAF and did not violate the North Atlantic Treaty. Finally, even if the D'Alema government's attempt to make its actions consistent with Italy's identity and Article 11 were compelling, it would not explain Italy's decision to engage in bombing. If the D'Alema government truly believed Italy was a force for peace, why would it choose to engage in bombing (unlike Germany, which participated in the air campaign but refused to bomb)?

The D'Alema government argued that it was providing military support to OAF to end the suffering of Kosovar Albanians. Foreign Affairs Undersecretary Ranieri responded to the Raçak massacre by stating, "The brutal murder of tens of Albanian civilians, whose bodies were found by international observers, takes us back to scenes of barbarism which we did not ever want to witness in the heart of Europe. The international community will not allow new atrocities to repeat themselves."[244] D'Alema made similar statements. In his televised March 30 address he said, "Italy had to and has to do its part to stop the genocide under way. . . . "[245] D'Alema continued to stress the suffering of the Kosovar Albanians during the war, especially after his Easter visit to a refugee camp—which he recounted frequently.[246] Foreign Minister Dini later reflected that OAF was justified by a need to stop a "possible genocide."[247]

102 • America's Allies and War

One weakness of the normative explanation is that it does not illuminate why Italy was willing to put its aircraft and pilots at risk in Kosovo but not in other cases where states mistreated their citizens. As Fausto Bertinotti said, "Why then does NATO not bomb Turkey to defend the Kurds?"[248] Another Italian politician stated: "If one wants to apply international justice, then we must have absolute determination and punish all the guilty of transgressions, of violations of human rights."[249] That politician was Massimo D'Alema, expressing his criticism of American and British airstrikes against Iraq in December 1998. His language provides an excellent critique of the humanitarian explanation for contributions to the Kosovo War. Finally, in the interviews that I have conducted no interviewee offered human rights or international legal norms as among the primary factors explaining Italian support. One interviewee suggested that the repeated references to human rights were designed to sell the war to the center-left's electorate.[250] Other interviewees suggested that the suffering of Kosovar Albanians explained NATO's decision to wage an air war, which was distinct from whether Italy should contribute its aircraft to the air war.[251]

Case Conclusion: Alliance and Prestige

It is difficult to determine the relative importance of the realist factors in this case. There is some evidence that threat to national interest affected the outcome but there is less evidence to support it than there is for the other factors. True, Italy had much to gain from resolving the conflict in the Balkans. That said, the D'Alema government could have contributed aircraft but not allowed them to engage in bombing (i.e., Italy's strike sorties did not make NATO more likely to succeed). Participating fully in OAF would help preserve Italy's alliance relationship with the United States through NATO and would help maintain or improve Italy's prestige. Alliance and prestige figure in elite statements, in the writings of analysts, and were leading factors in the interviews. Italy's peace identity and international legal norms cannot explain the outcome because in this case Italy waged war and did so without explicit UNSC authorization. When I asked Defense Minister Scognamiglio whether political factors such as the alliance, threat, and prestige were more important than the suffering of Kosovar Albanians in explaining Italy's decision, he replied, "Yes, Italy's contribution is better explained by political factors. The humanitarian solution would not have changed with or without the sixty Italian planes. Yet, there would have been political consequences had Italy not participated actively."[252]

The D'Alema government's decision to provide aircraft for the Kosovo War provides support for proposition two. A multiplicity of policymaker and analyst statements—including interviews—suggest Italy's high value for its alliance with the United States and NATO was a critical factor in the decision. Policymakers and analysts also made clear that Italy's prestige was tied to the Kosovo War and that this factor was critical in the D'Alema government's decision (there was also some evidence the government strove to resolve a threat to its national interest). While the Italian public opposed support, the center-right favored it so the government knew it would not face electoral punishment for its decision. Italy's peace image and international legal norms predict the exact opposite outcome in this case, providing no support for alternative proposition two.

Conclusion

Defense of NATO's credibility played a role in each country's decision to provide its aircraft to support the U.S.-led war against Serbia. This explanation is unsatisfying alone, however, as it poses the question of why each country agreed to allow NATO's credibility to be pledged in this case. Each of the three countries sought to resolve a threat to its national interest in the form of instability in the Balkans (though the Italians were more sensitive to the destabilizing effects of war). France and Italy were motivated to contribute to maintain their prestige in Europe and while it would have been plausible for Britain to have been similarly motivated, there is little evidence that it was. While humanitarian concerns may have motivated the British, French, and Italian governments, there is also evidence that they used humanitarian rhetoric to appeal to left-wing critics of the air war.

CHAPTER 5

Afghanistan

In the wake of the terrorist attacks of September 11, 2001, the United States' leading European allies offered and provided military support for the U.S.-led military effort in Afghanistan. The United States initiated Operation Enduring Freedom (OEF) against the Taliban and Al-Qaeda in Afghanistan on October 7, 2001. OEF drew on allied airpower and Special Forces combined with the local knowledge and support of indigenous Afghan groups, including the Northern Alliance. Britain and France contributed Special Forces and aircraft to OEF and Italy contributed an air and naval contingent. On December 20, 2001, the United Nations Security Council (UNSC) authorized the creation of the International Security Assistance Force (ISAF) for Afghanistan, which initially was restricted to providing security to Kabul and surrounding areas. Britain, France, and Italy contributed ground troops to ISAF as well. As a highly motivated global hegemon, it was clear to all that the United States could have achieved the fall of Kabul with no allied support. Given the ease of free riding in this case, why did Britain, France, and Italy contribute to OEF? The chapter does not seek to explain allies' contributions to ISAF but draws on some public statements about ISAF for their insight into the prior decision to contribute to OEF.

Some might question whether Afghanistan should be included in this book. In the days and weeks after the 9/11 attacks, U.S. Secretary of Defense Donald Rumsfeld and his advisers stated that they did not want their war against the Taliban to resemble the war by coalition NATO waged over Kosovo in 1999.[1] True, the United States did not seek large contributions of allied ground troops because it did not plan to fight a large ground war. It is also true that the United States gave allies little or no input into the planning and implementation of OEF. As the following pages will document, however, the U.S. government extended requests for military support for OEF to France and Italy and President Bush's desire for British support in OEF is implied in what we know of that case.

106 • America's Allies and War

The United Kingdom: Alliance

Upon hearing of British interest in participating in U.S.-led efforts against the Taliban regime, Bush reportedly told Secretary of Defense Rumsfeld: "[g]ive them a role."[2] The British provided two royal navy submarines, which launched cruise missile attacks against Taliban targets. In addition, its Special Forces joined with their American counterparts in aiding indigenous elements against the Taliban and Al-Qaeda in Afghanistan and surrounding areas.[3] As OEF began to bear fruit, British Prime Minister Tony Blair and his government made the case for a peace force and offered to lead it.[4] By early January Britain had committed 1,500 troops to ISAF, which had an initial mission of providing security to Kabul.[5] Britain's contribution to OEF made it the first and most high-profile ally providing military support for the U.S.-led Global War on Terror.

Alliance

Britain's alliance relationship with the United States tells us much about its willingness to provide military support for OEF. As documented in the previous chapter, Blair's experience with Bill Clinton led him to believe that Britain had a unique level of access and influence with the United States as a result of the "special relationship." At the first meeting between Blair and George W. Bush in February 2001, the American President told the press that Britain is "our strongest friend and closest ally."[6] In private Blair extracted Bush's support for European integration on defense in exchange for British support for the United States' National Missile Defense program.[7] The British Ambassador to Washington, Christopher Meyer, advised Blair before the latter met Bush that there was a special opportunity for influence, saying, "[t]he risk is to be seen as American bag-carriers, a story which the British press is already starting to write. The opportunity is to be able to influence American policy before it has formed."[8] Fundamentally, Blair was convinced that—without regard to any specific American President—a close alliance with the United States was in Britain's vital strategic interest.[9]

The terrorist attacks of September 11, 2001, led Blair's government to attach an even greater importance to its alliance with the United States than it had up to that day. In the immediate wake of the attacks Blair's spokesperson and confidant Alastair Campbell recorded in his diary that the Prime Minister was convinced he could influence Bush's response to the attacks.[10] The British were concerned with the Bush administration's propensity for unilateralism.[11] According to the *Financial Times'* Philip Stephens, Blair felt he needed to try even harder to bind Britain to the United States because of the Bush administration's tendency to unilateralism.[12] Specifically, Blair's government would not publicly take issue with the more controversial statements emerging from Washington so as to maximize its influence on issues of greater importance.[13] Analysts agree that Blair was the United States' most influential ally during George W. Bush's administration.[14] Bush told a joint session of the U.S. Congress on September 20, 2001, with Blair the only foreign leader invited to attend, that the United States "has no truer friend than Great Britain."[15] Ambassador Meyer wrote that after the speech Blair's " . . . relationship with Bush had been transported to a new and higher level of trust and friendship."[16] It was fair for the Prime Minister to believe that Britain would be influential in U.S. decision making. On October 11 Campbell wrote in his diary that Blair " . . . felt he was getting somewhere with Bush. . . . "[17] When I asked Sir Lawrence Freedman why Blair did not, as French leaders had, make a public statement that Britain's contribution to OEF would be contingent on influence over strategy and operations, he responded: "I think Blair's view was 'If you have to ask, you don't have it.' It is natural to Britain's relationship with the U.S. to have that level of influence."[18]

Britain's value for its alliance with the United States emerged as a key factor as the Blair government decided to provide military support. On October 6, 2001, Foreign Secretary Straw told the House of Commons that " . . . the truest test of friendship is in the hour of need. Twice during the last century, the United States came to Britain's aid; today, we have to come to the United States' aid."[19] Interviews provide further support for the importance of Britain's alliance with the United States in the Blair government's decisions. A senior British intelligence official told me that his government valued the benefits from its relationship with the United States (e.g., intelligence) too much to do anything other than provide support and that contributing was key because "Britain has always aimed for the lead position of influence relative to any other U.S. ally."[20] Theo Farrell, a specialist in British security affairs, told me that the Blair government believed it would have greater influence than other allies and that its alliance with the United States would yield prestige.[21] He went on to say that had Al-Qaeda not attacked or threatened the United States, the British government would have embraced nonmilitary means to respond.[22] In short, the Blair government valued its country's alliance relationship with the United States and wanted to preserve it, so it provided military support for the U.S. efforts in Afghanistan.

Threat

The Blair government also believed toppling the Taliban regime and stabilizing Afghanistan would resolve a significant threat to Britain's national

108 • America's Allies and War

interest. The British government initially believed hundreds of its citizens were killed in the 9/11 attacks and, as such, that its national interests were directly implicated.[23] Blair told the House of Commons on September 14, 2001, "Murder of British people in New York is no different in nature from their murder in the heart of Britain itself."[24] More fundamentally, Blair and his advisers believed Al-Qaeda would not limit future attacks to the United States. In the days following the attacks Blair made clear his view that the terrorist network was a threat to the entire "civilized world."[25] A House of Commons Library Research Paper released on October 3, 2001, agreed that Al-Qaeda worked to coordinate and support *anti-Western* groups (v. strictly anti-American ones).[26] The Prime Minister warned that Al-Qaeda was potentially even more threatening than it appeared on 9/11 because it had the will and the potential to acquire weapons of mass destruction.[27] The Blair government took care to assure British citizens that it had no evidence Al-Qaeda would strike at a particular place and time. Nonetheless, its extensive domestic security measures demonstrated that it took Al-Qaeda's threat to the UK seriously.[28] As the *Times'* Peter Riddell put it, "[a]t this stage, no one knew whether similar attacks might not be about to happen in Britain."[29] In responding to the 9/11 attacks, the Blair government recalled Al-Qaeda's failed attempt to attack the UK in 2000.[30] By mid-October 2001, eliminating the threat from Islamic radical terrorism had become the primary objective of British foreign policy.[31] As a survey of Blair's second-term foreign policy puts it, "[n]o doubt the British—and indeed the common European—interest was clear enough at this time: preventing a terrorist attack on our own cities, while helping the United States to realise that a considered response was much preferable to a spasm of immediate violence."[32] Finally, the Blair government was also convinced that Al-Qaeda's ability to threaten major terrorist attacks was significantly enhanced by the group's safe haven in the Taliban regime's Afghanistan.[33]

Public statements from key policymakers about Britain's contribution provide further evidence that their view of the threat from Al-Qaeda played a fundamental role in Britain's decision. Blair offered the following rationale as he announced Britain's contribution to OEF (which the British termed Operation Veritas) on October 7, 2001: "[w]e know the al-Qaeda network threaten Europe, including Britain . . . [s]o we have a direct interest in acting in our own self defence to protect British lives."[34] On the next day in the House of Commons the Prime Minister said, "We in Britain have the most direct interest in defeating such terror. It strikes at the heart of what we believe in. We know that if not stopped, the terrorists will do it again, this time possibly in Britain"[35] On October 16 Foreign Secretary Straw told the Commons that in providing military support for OEF

Britain was " . . . acting in self defence, our aims are to dismantle the terrorist network; to break the power of those who harbour the terrorists; and to end the threat to security at home."[36] The national interest logic for Britain's contribution was so compelling that the opposition Conservative and Liberal Democrats both expressed agreement with it.[37]

The threat from Al-Qaeda was at the heart of the British decision to contribute to ISAF as well. On October 22 the *Times* reported that Foreign Secretary Straw would commit British troops to a peace force in Afghanistan because "only when order is restored to Afghanistan will Britain be safe from terrorism at home."[38] British thinking on the peace force was based on the view that failed states become havens for terrorism—and Afghanistan's recent history confirmed that view. As Blair said when announcing that Britain would lead the peace force "[i]f the international community walks away from Afghanistan now it will make exactly the same mistake that was made ten or twelve years ago when it left Afghanistan to become what it became: a failed state."[39] Blair's logic was clear: to avoid another 9/11 Britain had to keep Afghanistan from becoming a future haven for Al-Qaeda, which it would do by spearheading the peace force. As Jack Straw told the International Institute for Strategic Studies on October 22, " . . . we have to be ready to bear the cost, because if we do not, the price we pay will be far greater. We will pay it in more terrorist atrocities, more lives lost and more economies disrupted."[40]

Interviews provide support for the claim that the Blair government's contribution to OEF was motivated by the perception that Al-Qaeda was a threat to the UK and its interests. A senior British intelligence official I spoke with—who was stationed in the United States at the time the decision was made—recalled that the British establishment had become increasingly concerned with Al-Qaeda's "abilities and ambition" but after the September 11, 2001, attacks, " . . . there was a very real threat to the UK and a very real perception of it."[41] Sir Lawrence Freedman noted that "Britain had felt terrorist attacks in the past. The view was 'they hate us as much as the Americans.'"[42] Theo Farrell who, as previously noted, believes threat was less important than alliance in this case, noted "British citizens were killed and yes Al-Qaeda was a threat. . . . "[43]

While little official evidence and published analysis supports the prestige explanation, it provides a plausible fit with this case. The widespread international support for a post–September 11 war to topple the Taliban regime meant that the war would be legitimate and thus Britain stood to gain in the eyes of its power competitors. The select nature of the coalition also meant that prestige was at stake. The UK was initially the United States' only ally other than indigenous Afghan groups. Thus, other states were likely

110 • America's Allies and War

to adjust their perceptions of Britain's power upward. The senior intelligence official I spoke with put it this way: "This factor certainly played a role. We are a second rate power with a third rate budget and first rate ambitions. We are so focused on convincing others of our prestige that we are always committing or promising to do things that are beyond our capabilities."[44] Theo Farrell agreed with the aforementioned way I posited prestige might have mattered in this case, saying, "You're absolutely right about Afghanistan: the wide recognition of the legitimacy of military action against the Taliban regime and the select nature of the coalition put British prestige on the table."[45] Without more evidence it is hard to say how significant this factor was, but it is plausible that it contributed to the outcome.

Electoral Politics

Electoral politics seem to have had no impact on this case. The public and the opposition favored military support, which was the only policy line the government appears to have ever considered. In an ICM poll of the British public published on September 18, 2001, two-thirds supported military action against terrorists.[46] In the same poll three-fourths of the British public said Blair had managed relations with the United States "about right" in the immediate wake of the attacks.[47] In a September 14, 2001, MORI poll, 74 percent of the public said they would support the involvement of British troops in a U.S.-led military action against those responsible for the 9/11 attacks.[48] From the moment of the September 11 attacks there was little doubt the Conservatives would provide total support for any contribution Britain made to a U.S.-led war against the perpetrators.[49] In the event, the Conservative Party and even the less hawkish Liberal Democrats favored British military support for the U.S.-led operations against the Taliban regime and Al-Qaeda.[50] Blair's Labour Party was also largely united in favor of military support. When a handful of Labour backbenchers finally were able to force a House of Commons vote on Britain's participation in OEF, the government won 373 to 13.[51] While the Conservatives, Liberal Democrats, and Labour backbenchers criticized aspects of the government's implementation of its participation in OEF, they did not take issue with the decision itself.[52]

An overwhelming majority of the public and the two opposition parties supported the Blair government's decision to contribute troops to OEF. In choosing to provide military support it is unlikely that Blair was fleeing the negative electoral consequences of refusing support because there is no evidence he or his government ever considered an alternative policy path. Moreover, it is unlikely that Blair chose support as a means to maximize electoral gains because the opposition parties' adoption of the government position meant that voters would not be able to reward the government for its policy choice. Further confirmation of this interpretation comes from an interview with Sir Robert Worcester, founder of the MORI poll. When I asked if the public had pushed the government to act, he replied, "No, the public backed up what the government wanted to do already."[53] The senior British intelligence official I spoke with put slightly more emphasis on public opinion but when I asked if this was the main factor in the decision he replied, "[n]o, of course not. The 12 September 2001 visit by Richard Dearlove and Eliza Manningham-Buller was clearly tied to the British intelligence assessment that Al-Qaeda was a threat to British interests."[54]

Identity and International Norms

When the 1997 election brought the Labour Party to power, Blair's new government made clear its ideas about Britain's identity in international relations. Britain was and would be a "force for good in the world."[55] Blair's first Foreign Secretary Robin Cook led the Foreign and Commonwealth Office in writing a new mission statement that enshrined the view of Britain as a moral country.[56] At first glance this view of British identity seems to fit well with the British decision to provide military support for OEF. For example, in his October 7 statement explaining Britain's contribution to OEF Blair said, "We have to act for humanitarian reasons to alleviate the appalling suffering of the Afghan people and deliver stability so that people from that region stay in that region."[57] In a late October speech designed to bolster support for the British effort in Afghanistan, Blair told the Welsh Assembly that "[w]hatever our faults, Britain is a very moral nation with a strong sense of right and wrong, and that moral fibre will defeat . . . the terrorists."[58] In January 2002, Jack Straw tied British identity to moral conduct in its foreign policy, saying, " . . . what we have now done is to establish a role for Britain in international affairs with which we are entirely comfortable. It is Britain not as a superpower but as a very powerful force for good."[59] The "force for good" story seemingly fits well with this case. The Taliban had a terrible human rights record and it is clear that the human rights situation of Afghans improved after the fall of the Taliban.[60]

Upon careful scrutiny, however, this explanation is flawed in several ways. First, as Paul Williams makes clear in a recent monograph, the British government began to turn away from the "force for good" mantra almost as soon as Cook voiced it.[61] In the dangerous post-9/11 world, the Blair government put even less time and energy into the moral factor than it had previously.[62] Indeed, the Blair government appeared generally willing to

112 • America's Allies and War

subvert the moral imperative to national interest, such as on the case of arms sales to Tanzania.[63] Second, while the British claimed to be acting to alleviate the suffering of Afghans, they were allied with the Northern Alliance, which during the mid 1990s "committed human rights abuses, atrocities, and acts that probably constituted war crimes . . . " and was responsible for "summary executions and atrocities" during the 2001 fall of Kunduz.[64] Given the Northern Alliance's record, there was little to guarantee that a post-Taliban government would lead to an improvement in human rights for the Afghan people. If the Blair government had been driven primarily by human rights, would it not have insisted on a strategy that did not rely so heavily on the Northern Alliance? Third, the identity and Afghan suffering argument cannot explain the timing of British action. The Taliban had a lengthy and widely known record of human rights abuses since coming to power in Afghanistan in 1996.[65] In her memoir Clare Short recalled that "[t]he humanitarian crisis in Afghanistan was very serious before September 11."[66] If Britain was truly motivated primarily by its desire to be a force for good and alleviate the suffering of Afghans, why did it wait to intervene or press for intervention until after the 9/11 attacks?

Interviews provide support for skepticism on the human suffering argument. When asked whether the Blair government intervened to mitigate the suffering of the Afghan people Theo Farrell responded, "No, I don't think that was a factor."[67] I asked the senior British intelligence official about the human suffering logic. He replied that while it was a useful addition to the government's rhetorical case, it was

> [m]uch less significant than the other factors we've discussed. It was all about the threat: the threat and the danger. The human rights side became part of the public rationale but it was not a driver of the decision. This logic did help broaden the domestic coalition in favor of Britain's participation. It is always helpful for governments who want to get the *Guardian* readers of the world on board to have a humanitarian logic. But it wasn't a driver.[68]

A norm of just punishment is the only norm that appears a plausible fit to explain Britain's decision to provide military support to U.S. military operations in Afghanistan. Blair's government referred to their commitment to capture and try or kill those responsible for the 9/11 attacks in a variety of statements in the weeks and months after the attacks. On September 14 Blair noted that "[we] have not just an interest but an obligation to bring those responsible to account."[69] On September 24, Blair said that the first of two clear objectives was " . . . to make sure those responsible for this atrocity are brought to account. . . . "[70] The justice norm is a less than

Afghanistan • 113

satisfying explanation of Britain's contribution to U.S. efforts in Afghanistan, however.

In Blair's most important statements on Britain's contribution he stressed the current and future threat to British citizens and downplayed the justice logic. In his October 7 statement he was explicit: "But even if no British citizen had died it would be right to act . . . " because "[w]e know the al-Qaeda network threaten Europe, including Britain, and, indeed, any nation throughout the world that does not share their fanatical views. So we have a direct interest in acting in our own self defense to protect British lives."[71] In fact, as weeks and months passed after 9/11 it is difficult to find Blair government statements referring to the justice logic for OEF. Moreover, while it was plausible to expect that U.S.-UK military operations in Afghanistan would degrade the ability of Al-Qaeda to launch future attacks, it was less likely that such action would result in those responsible for 9/11 being brought to justice. Those directly responsible for the attacks died during the attacks. Moreover, those most responsible for planning and supporting the attacks—Al Qaeda's leaders—were the least likely to be killed or captured by OEF, especially given that it commenced almost a month after the attacks.

Case Conclusion: Alliance

The senior British intelligence official I spoke with told me that alliance and threat were the two most important factors.[72] Some believe alliance was clearly more important than threat. Theo Farrell argued that if Britain had been motivated by threat, free riding would have been the optimal strategy as "[n]ot only would the threat have been reduced without British costs being incurred but, moreover, any remaining Al-Qaeda threat would have been less likely to be targeted at Britain due to its non-participation."[73] Only alliance value can explain why the Blair government chose to contribute, knowing that they could have taken a free ride.

The Blair government's decision to contribute to the U.S.-led war in Afghanistan provides support for proposition two. Policymaker and analyst statements—including interviews—document that the Blair government put high value on Britain's relationship with the United States and that this was a critical factor in the government's decision to provide support. Policymaker and analyst statements suggest that the Blair government believed that Britain's national interest (i.e., a reduced threat from terrorism) would benefit from the U.S.-led war. It would have been possible for the British to free ride off American action, however, and have the same outcome. While the British public and opposition Conservative Party

114 • America's Allies and War

favored support there is no evidence that this factor drove the decision. Evidence for the humanitarian logic and just punishment norm provides support for alternative proposition one. While a desire to improve the lives of the Afghan people is a plausible explanation it cannot explain why the Blair government did not lobby for the use of force earlier and it cannot explain the Blair government's inattention to Afghan suffering in other aspects of the case. Language consistent with a just punishment norm appeared shortly after the 9/11 attacks but then faded from public and private statements and OEF could not punish those directly responsible for the attacks as they died while perpetrating them.

France: Prestige

The French government, headed by center-right President Jacques Chirac and center-left Prime Minister Lionel Jospin, was eager to provide military support to OEF. As Chirac met with Bush on September 18 he made clear France's willingness to provide military support for American military operations in Afghanistan but he also suggested that in exchange France should be involved in formulating the goals and means of the intervention.[74] French officials also made clear that they would determine the nature of their contribution and how it could be used.[75] On October 9 *Le Monde* reported a statement by Chirac that the United States had in the previous few days asked France for its military participation in OEF and that France would respond positively to the American request.[76] The French provided a variety of aircraft: six Mirage fighter aircraft for close air support, two C-135-FR refueling aircraft, two Mirage IVs, and two C-160s for strategic reconnaissance and intelligence.[77] According to a RAND study, France was the only non-U.S. ally that provided jets that engaged in strike operations during the operation.[78] Finally, France contributed Special Forces to OEF.[79] France took the lead on pushing for a post-Taliban peace force, proposing that the European Union begin planning for such a force on October 2 (five days before the start of OEF).[80] On November 16 Chirac confirmed that a company of French troops had been sent to stabilize the city of Mazar-e-Sharif, which had fallen on November 9.[81] While the French originally thought they would commit three hundred troops to ISAF, they ended up initially committing 550.[82]

Alliance

In the period preceding the September 11, 2001, terrorist attacks the Chirac/Jospin government discounted France's alliance relationship with the

United States because they felt that Paris was unable to
Washington. Whereas senior Clinton administration (
to detect and resolve differences with the French, th'
with the new Bush administration.[83] As Henri Vern...
Cantaloube wrote, "[i]n Washington, no one lost sleep over Fren...
cerns."[84] French officials were taken aback by the new Bush administration's
policy on climate change and the International Criminal Court (ICC).[85]
Leaving aside the policies themselves Bush administration stances on climate change and the ICC indicated that it cared little about the probable
negative fallout with the United States' allies. French officials were also
generally concerned that the new administration would push the United
States toward unilateralism.[86]

The attacks themselves seem to have led the French to hope that the
United States would become more multilateral. A positive indication came
with regard to Jacques Chirac's visit to Washington, planned for
September 18. When the French Ambassador to Washington asked Bush's
National Security Adviser Condoleezza Rice if Chirac should cancel the trip
due to the 9/11 attacks she replied, "[C]ancel? No, no, on the contrary: it
should go ahead. It is in these dramatic moments that one has need of one's
friends."[87] In Paris, as elsewhere, there was a hope that the attacks would lead
the United States toward a more multilateral approach.[88] Of course, some
French analysts raised serious questions about how little influence the United
States was giving to its allies in the immediate wake of 9/11.[89] In addition,
the French were aware of the United States' relative power and believed
that—as Hubert Védrine put it—"[t]he United States are and will be a major
and central force for international stability."[90] Finally, it was reasonable for
French policymakers to do what they could—including a military contribution to OEF—to push the United States toward the multilateral path.[91]

There is some evidence to support the claim that concerns with the United
States' unwillingness to take allies' views into account led France to contribute
less than it was able to and otherwise would have.[92] On October 3, the
Financial Times quoted Prime Minister Jospin as saying, "[i]f France is asked
to be directly involved in military operations, this would imply our country
is fully associated with defining the political objectives and planning of these
actions."[93] Jospin's quote seems to provide broader insight about the role of
France's alliance relationship with the United States in French decision making. In the last months of 2001 the Chirac/Jospin government perceived little
ability to influence policy in Washington so it made sense for it to lean toward
a smaller contribution and guarantees that it would influence the process.

Interviews provide some evidence for the importance of alliance value in
this case. When I asked about concerns with the Bush administration's

- America's Allies and War

.lateralism, many noted that such concerns were not prevalent in the .mmediate wake of the 9/11 attacks.[94] As Pierre Hassner told me, " . . . solidarity was probably more important than concerns with unilateralism immediately after 9/11."[95] A number of those I interviewed stressed French solidarity with the United States as a contributing factor in the French decision. An adviser to the French Defense Minister told me that "French participation in Afghanistan was a way for Chirac to send a message to the United States that France was with them."[96] France's Ambassador to the United States at the time, François Bujon de l'Estang, told me that in addition to the French perception that Al-Qaeda was a threat, " . . . another reason was to demonstrate solidarity with the United States."[97] Finally, a relevant French Government Minister told me the government was motivated by the terrorist threat and humanitarian factors but then said, "France also had been a somewhat difficult ally and we wanted to return to the Gaullist ideal of being a state the United States knew it could count on in the really tough cases."[98] While there is evidence of concern with American unilateralism it also appears that alliance value was among the important factors in this case.

Threat and Prestige

The threat to France's national interest and prestige concerns effectively explain France's decision to provide military support for OEF. The Chirac/Jospin government believed France's national interest was implicated in U.S. military operations in Afghanistan because they believed Al-Qaeda and/or its affiliates were a threat to France. In the immediate wake of the 9/11 attacks the French government instituted a reinforced version of its Vigipirate plan for internal security. Prime Minister Jospin noted that France had been the target of terrorist attacks in the past and that "action against the risks of terrorism in our country is essential."[99] At the same time, Jospin said in a speech on September 24, "[c]onfronted with the terrorist threat, no country can comfort itself with the belief that it can protect itself in isolation. The struggle must, therefore, be taken beyond borders."[100] The well respected analyst François Heisborg contrasted the Kosovo War with the U.S.-led operations in Afghanistan. While, he said, NATO's motives in Kosovo were "serious and honorable," that war differed from the one in Afghanistan because "Milosevic was not going to attack Paris, London, or Berlin."[101]

In explaining OEF and France's decision to participate, the Chirac/Jospin government stressed that Al-Qaeda was a threat to all democracies, including France. Chirac addressed the French people as OEF began, stating: "[w]e need to know that these terrorist attacks affect us all. All the democracies are threatened. France immediately announced its solidarity. It indicated that it would lead with the United States this fight in which all men who love liberty must engage themselves with determination."[102] On October 25 the French President gave a speech in which he reminded the audience: "[w]e know that the heinous and insidious violence of terrorism threatens us equally, as it threatens all democracies."[103] Jospin made a similar case to the National Assembly on November 21, "We did not put ourselves in motion because of a local crisis but because we became aware that international terrorism had become a global threat."[104] He later reflected that if the United States had not led OEF, " . . . the risk of instability for the world would have been great."[105] On October 10, the French Foreign Minister Védrine explained that while France felt for the victims of the 9/11 attacks, " . . . we are engaged not only because of solidarity with the American people . . . but because it is in our interest to struggle against terrorism."[106] In parliamentary debates on Afghanistan, French politicians made clear that they thought France's national interest meant it should provide military support for U.S.-led efforts in Afghanistan.[107]

Leading figures in the Chirac/Jospin government offered a similar logic on the basis of national interests for their country's commitment to ISAF. In a November 21 speech to the National Assembly, Prime Minister Jospin said that " . . . it is essential for us, as for the entire international community, that Al Qaeda be crushed, that the Taliban regime be defeated, that the threat that the Afghan 'terrorist sanctuary' caused to weigh on the world disappears."[108] Jospin went on to make the case that the Taliban regime had been a sanctuary for Al-Qaeda because it was an illegitimate regime, isolated from the international community. Stabilization and reconstruction of Afghanistan were, thus, crucial in allowing Afghanistan to develop a legitimate government that would not be a sanctuary for terrorism in the future.[109]

Those I interviewed confirmed that the Chirac/Jospin government viewed Al-Qaeda as a threat and that this was among the most important factors in explaining the decision to provide a French military contribution to OEF. Ambassador Bujon told me that France "offered everything it had" to OEF because it " . . . knew that Al-Qaeda was capable of more attacks, including those against France. French intelligence was quite clear on this and French intelligence at the time on Al-Qaeda was better than the U.S.'"[110] A Defense Ministry official told me without a specific prompt on national interest, "we had to be there because of the threat posed by the Taliban and Al-Qaeda."[111] The official said the government was particularly sensitive to the threat given the Algerian terrorist attacks and attempted attacks on France during the 1990s.[112] The Government Minister I interviewed said that "[t]he real motive was to set an example for other

118 • America's Allies and War

countries considering hosting Al-Qaeda."[113] In this view the terrorist threat would be reduced, as groups would have fewer and fewer options for safe host sites.

The evidence suggests that prestige played an important role in the Chirac government's decision. The Chirac/Jospin government agreed on the importance of defending and, where possible, expanding France's prestige. As Jacques Chirac wrote, "France is a country that counts. Its voice is listened to and heard. It has an impact on the course of things."[114] As Jospin prepared for France's 2002 presidential elections, he said that under his government (in office since 1997) France mattered more in the international arena.[115]

Contributing to OEF was likely to impact a country's prestige. The international community almost universally supported U.S.-led military action against the Taliban regime.[116] Moreover, as the United States initially only chose to include Britain in OEF, it drew attention to the other large, militarily active European country—France—by its absence.[117] An adviser to Chirac recalled to Vernet and Cantaloube that Bush phoned Chirac thirty minutes before the war began but " . . . France was not, at that moment, a first-rank ally in Enduring Freedom."[118] For French power to be recognized as on par with Britain, it had to contribute to OEF. To see the importance of prestige in the French decision one needs only to look at what the French said after France chose to make its contribution. For example, President Chirac said, "I would like to remind you that the French involvement is, like that of Great Britain, the most important to have been put in place at the United States' request."[119] In short, if France contributed to OEF, its peers would be more likely to recognize it as a country willing and able to act along with other leading powers. As Jospin told the National Assembly on November 21, "[t]he Government will continue to affirm our solidarity in the struggle against terrorism. Alongside the President of the Republic it will make France's voice heard. . . . "[120] Political scientist Tom Lansford wrote that the French government's desire for *grandeur* was the single most important factor in the French decision to provide support.[121]

Interviews provide some support for this factor. One anonymous interviewee said of OEF that "[t]here were clearly prestige reasons for France to be involved."[122] A Defense Ministry official cited threat and solidarity as the main factors and then said, "Maybe another, more minor, reason is that other countries, like the UK were contributing and so France's rank was at stake."[123] Ambassador Bujon told me that he did not think France's prestige was important in this case, citing Britain's historical experience in Afghanistan as a reason why its prestige was implicated but France's was not.[124] Given the emotion surrounding the 9/11 attacks and U.S.-led action in Afghanistan those I interviewed may have been reluctant to admit prestige played a critical role in this case.

Electoral Politics

While the French public supported their government's decision to participate in OEF, there is little evidence electoral politics drove the outcome. As OEF opened in early October 2001, 64 percent of French respondents approved of the U.S.-led operations.[125] A SOFRES poll of mid-October 2001 showed 73 percent of respondents approved of French engagement at the side of the United States; as of the tenth of November, 71 percent approved.[126] The French public continued to approve of the U.S.-led military operations by a two-thirds margin as of April 2002.[127] At the time of France's decision to provide military support, France found itself in cohabitation government (as noted in the previous chapter). As indicated previously, Chirac and Jospin agreed that France should provide support for the United States, so neither of the two major political parties could possibly gain or lose in electoral terms relative to its rival on the decision to provide or refuse troops to Afghanistan.[128] While the French Communist Party opposed OEF, its position was hardly likely to have significant electoral ramifications.[129] In an interview Ambassador Bujon said public opinion did not push Chirac to contribute to the U.S.-led effort to overthrow the Taliban.[130] While the French Government Minister I interviewed did not say that public opinion drove government policy, he did caution that "I think it would have been very hard for the French government to have ignored the public desire to 'do something' given that the only thing to do was to use force."[131] In the end, there is little evidence that public opinion affected the French decision to provide military support.[132]

Identity and International Norms

French identity and related concepts figure in a variety of statements French officials made in the weeks after the September 11 terrorist attacks. The Chirac/Jospin government reacted to the attacks by offering French aid in solidarity with the United States. As Chirac said in a press conference after meeting with Bush on September 18, " . . . from the start I wanted to express to President Bush, who is my friend, and beyond him, to the American people, the total solidarity on the part of France and the French people, a solidarity of the heart."[133] Prime Minister Jospin and Foreign Minister Védrine made similar comments in the days after the attacks.[134] French government officials often also couched their reactions to the

120 • America's Allies and War

9/11 attacks in terms of values France shares with the United States as democracies.[135]

One problem with the solidarity and shared values explanation is that the statements to this effect were strongest in the period directly after the attacks—they faded as time passed and as France was forced to make and justify commitments of troops and planes. In key statements in October, November, and December, French officials focused more on the threat to France than on solidarity with the United States or common values. On October 9 Foreign Minister Védrine went so far as to make the point explicit, speaking of American military action in Afghanistan, "[t]he French government approves of it not only for reasons of solidarity but because the goals are its own, to know how to break Bin Laden's terrorist networks."[136] In a November 16 televised address announcing France's participation in what would become ISAF, Chirac explained that France was contributing "[f]or friendship, for solidarity. But also because we know that all democracies are in danger. . . . "[137] As documented previously, statements on threat and prestige did not vary substantially over time.

The norm of alleviating human suffering / improving human rights provides a plausible explanation of France's decision to provide military support. There is some evidence that leading figures in the Chirac/Jospin government were concerned with the suffering and human rights condition of the Afghan people. The Chirac/Jospin government made the case for OEF in humanitarian terms. For example, in response to a question from a French Senator asking about the devastation caused by OEF airstrikes Jospin replied, " . . . the alternative to not striking, in itself, would be simply the impunity of the Bin Laden system and the continuity of the Taliban's oppression of the Afghan people, and in particular, Madam, of the Afghan women."[138] As discussed previously, France took the lead in pressing for a postwar peace force. Comments by Hubert Védrine on November 14 indicate the French may have been motivated by Afghan suffering, saying as the Taliban fell and a UN relief effort loomed, "One could save from hunger, the cold of winter, and, therefore, death, many children, many people in the next three days. There is urgency."[139]

The central problem with the human suffering explanation is that it cannot explain why France was willing to deploy its military to alleviate the suffering of the Afghan people after the 9/11 attacks but did not consider acting or propose that others act prior. Moreover, as mentioned previously, Jospin—the leading voice for the humanitarian logic—made clear that he was concerned about the Afghan people because he believed that doing so would reduce the risk of future terrorist threats emanating from Afghanistan. As Jospin said to the National Assembly on November 21, "[t]he international community must force itself to not leave any people in a situation of lawlessness or without aid, as they could be vulnerable to become hostage to groups uniquely oriented toward destructive violence—internal and external."[140]

The Government Minister I interviewed made the case that in addition to signaling to potential hosts of terrorist groups, "[t]here was also a humanitarian dimension. French leaders were frustrated that they had not done anything against the Taliban regime, given how its Sharia regime rankled with the French notion of secularism."[141] When I asked Ambassador Bujon about the importance of the humanitarian factor he replied that it was "[n]ot very important. Not essential. It was a Socialist government and they always talk about human rights but it doesn't explain the policy."[142] Similarly, a Defense Ministry official I interviewed referred to the humanitarian logic as a post hoc justification rather than a cause of the Chirac/Jospin government's decision to participate.[143]

Case Conclusion

The Chirac/Jospin government's contribution to OEF provides further support for proposition two. Evidence from policymaker statements, including interviews, suggests that France's relationship with the United States played a role in the outcome, though there is evidence that the French were also concerned with American unilateralism. Myriad policymaker and analyst statements suggest that the Chirac/Jospin's decision was driven by a national interest in countering the terrorist threat. Of course, France's contribution could not have determined the outcome, so this factor cannot explain the case alone. Aspects of the case and numerous statements provide strong evidence that a desire to enhance France's prestige drove the decision. The French public supported their country's contribution to OEF but there was no opposition threat (given cohabitation), so the electoral concerns probably did not drive the Chirac/Jospin government's decision. There is some evidence to support the solidarity explanation and human suffering logic, so the case provides support for alternative proposition one. One may rebut the solidarity logic by noting that it is rooted in alliance value and that the logic of solidarity faded over time. The human suffering logic fails to explain the timing of France's contribution.

Italy: Alliance

In the immediate aftermath of the 9/11 terrorist attacks Silvio Berlusconi offered support for U.S.-led military efforts against Al-Qaeda and their state

122 • America's Allies and War

sponsors, making clear that Italy should have some input into the decision-making process.[144] On October 3, the United States issued a request for Italian planes and for some Italian assistance in fulfilling functions the U.S. military would be unable to provide while engaged in OEF.[145] A week later Berlusconi told a business group that "I will go to Washington to offer our intervention options; that is, what our armed forces are capable of putting on the battlefield." He further noted, "I am referring to air, naval, and perhaps even—but I hope and believe that they will not ask for this—ground troops."[146] On October 15, Italy sent its officers to CENTCOM headquarters in Tampa, Florida, presumably to continue to discuss Italy's contribution.[147] On November 3, Italy's Ministry of Defense confirmed that the United States had welcomed an Italian offer of men and means for the military effort against Al-Qaeda and the Taliban.[148] The Italian parliament voted in favor of the air and naval mission on November 7 and four Italian ships arrived in the Persian Gulf on December 4.[149]

In the November 7 Senate debate, Defense Minister Martino made clear that if Italy contributed ground troops to Afghanistan they would be " . . . in a successive phase, with tasks of supporting and providing armed escorts for humanitarian organizations."[150] While Italy's Foreign Ministry was willing to consider more robust missions, the Defense Ministry's position ultimately won out.[151] Martino explained his reluctance to recommend the deployment of Italian ground troops this way: "When there will be an accord between the factions, at that point the multinational force will be able to intervene, but until that occurs, it would not be peace-keeping but peace-enforcement, and I am not in favor of that, because one runs the risk of becoming the target between the adversaries."[152] On January 21, 2002, the *Corriere della Sera* noted that Italy's contribution to ISAF had arrived and its troops were working alongside their allies'.[153]

Alliance

Silvio Berlusconi's second government had only been in office a few months prior to the September 11, 2001, terrorist attacks. Yet, it was reasonable for the new Berlusconi government to value Italy's relationship with the United States, as the new government did not expect to have strong relations with leading European powers or the EU.[154] Moreover, the center-right Prime Minister had never made a secret of his pro-U.S. stance, saying during the 2001 election campaign, "I am on whatever side America is on, even before I know what it is."[155] Berlusconi responded to the 9/11 attacks with an immediate statement that put Italy's alliance with the United States up front. He said, "[o]ur country lined itself up immediately at the side of our

American allies and the president of the United States."[156] Berlusconi so valued Italy's relationship with the United States that he was reportedly "beside himself" when Bush did not thank Italy along with Britain, France, and Canada as he announced the opening of OEF.[157] Italy's Ambassador to the United States, Ferdinando Salleo, pressed for and attained a mid-October reception at the White House for Berlusconi.[158] During the visit Bush and Deputy Secretary of Defense Paul Wolfowitz thanked Italy for its willingness to provide support for OEF (as witnessed by the concurrent announcement that the Berlusconi government had sent Italian officers to CENTCOM).[159] Finally, just after the Prime Minister's trip to Washington, the Italian government announced that it would not, as previously agreed, purchase the European consortium–produced A400M military transport aircraft but would purchase the U.S.-made Joint Strike Fighter.[160]

Italy's alliance with the United States figured prominently in the Senate debates on an Italian contribution to OEF that took place on October 9 and November 7, 2001. In the October debate, Defense Minister Martino summed up the case for an Italian deployment this way: "[t]he adopted choices in this field cannot be one sided or seen as such, in that they are accomplished in the common interests of the country and in the path of traditions, interests, and alliances on which hinges the history of our republic."[161] In the November 7, 2001, debate, Berlusconi made the point more directly, stating, "[o]ur friendship toward the United States of America and our loyalty to our independent choice to stay in Europe and in the alliances we have signed are more than sufficient reasons to construct a vast national consensus around the work our armed forces will be called upon to accomplish."[162] Other parliamentarians also stressed Italy's relationship with the United States as a reason to support Italy's contribution to OEF, including former Prime Minister Guilio Andreotti, former Foreign Minister Lamberto Dini, and leading Berlusconi supporter Renato Schifani.[163]

Evidence from interviews provides additional support for the claim that Italy's high value for its alliance relationship with the United States led it to contribute to OEF and ISAF. In a conversation with an Italian Foreign Ministry official specializing in Afghanistan, I began with a general question as to why Italy had contributed and the official responded that "[t]he most important factor was Italian solidarity with its most important ally in NATO and an essential actor and friend in Italian foreign policy."[164] Another Foreign Ministry official with relevant expertise argued that "loyalty to the U.S. at its moment of greatest need" was the principle cause of Italy's decision.[165] In addition, a senior Italian diplomat working on the issue at the time told me that Italy's relationship with the United States—while not the most important factor—was "very important" as an explanation

124 • America's Allies and War

of Italian policy.[166] Finally, Lucio Caracciolo, editor of the popular foreign affairs journal *Limes*, told me, "[t]he only true reason for Italy to be there was to be with the U.S.—full stop; to protect Italy's relationship with America and its role as a member of NATO. There was no significant national interest in Afghanistan."[167]

Threat and Prestige

There is some evidence that the Berlusconi government was motivated by its perception that Al-Qaeda and a Taliban-controlled Afghanistan were a threat to Italy's national security. A number of the Berlusconi government's actions in the period immediately following the 9/11 attacks indicate that they believed Italy could be the target of an Al-Qaeda attack. On September 12, Berlusconi announced an array of security measures Italian authorities had taken, saying, " . . . we need to provide ourselves with many systems of protection of peace and security in our society; peace, liberty, and security are absolutely indivisible goods."[168] Three days after the attacks, Italy's Supreme Defense Council (*Consiglio Supremo di Difesa*) met to discuss threats to Italy and its National Committee for Security and Public Order met the day after, announcing increased security in airports, stations, ports, and military installations.[169] Though one might assume that these measures were designed primarily to address domestic fears in the days following the attacks, the government announced a series of new internal security measures roughly a month after the 9/11 attacks.[170] Evidence that Islamic radicals were operating in Italy spurred on these domestic security measures.[171] On October 11, the *Corriere della Sera* reported that the government had taken action against a terrorist cell that had been engaging in recruitment and planning for future attacks.[172] Two weeks later the paper published a report that the United States' CIA had warned that terrorists were plotting to attack an Italian tunnel.[173] Two days later Italy's domestic intelligence agency SISDe (*Servizio per le Informazioni e la Sicurezza Democratica*) announced that terrorist suspects had been arrested but also warned of future attacks in Italy.[174]

Analysts and political figures believed Italy was a potential target of Al Qaeda attacks and that this provided an excellent reason for its contribution to OEF. The day after the government announced its offer to OEF, the *Corriere della Sera*'s Franco Venturini wrote that it was no coincidence that the United States accepted a contribution from Rome shortly after Osama Bin Laden threatened Italy.[175] Meanwhile, columnist Sergio Romano referred to Italy as a potential "weak sheep" in Al Qaeda's sights.[176] Former center-left Foreign Minister Lamberto Dini said during the October 7

Senate debate that "[w]e cannot be neutral because we are all potential targets, even if attacks in Europe seem improbable to me."[177]

Leading figures in the Berlusconi government justified Italy's contribution as necessary to address a threat to its national interest. In the October 9 debate, Berlusconi said that Italy would do its part, "[w]e will do it to guarantee our security and our future."[178] Defense Minister Martino said that joining the antiterrorism coalition was in Italy's "precise national interest" and was consistent with "the role of our country in the international consensus and with our need for security."[179] Martino made even firmer statements in the November 7 Senate debate, saying of Italy's contribution: "[w]e understand the risks, implications, and costs. But we also understand that we undertake this operation to safeguard our national interests—vital, primary, and indefeasible."[180] Berlusconi again referred to the "danger" Italy faced in a November 18 statement to those departing for OEF.[181] This sample of statements shows that at the time the government argued that Italy had to contribute to OEF as a means to defend itself against the threat from Al-Qaeda.

Interviews revealed mixed support for the claim that a threat to Italy's national interest was an important factor in the government's decision to contribute to OEF. One Foreign Ministry official with relevant expertise said this factor was important when the initial decision was made.[182] Ambassador Silvio Fagiolo agreed when I asked him if national interest was more important than Italy's relationship with the United States.[183] A senior Italian diplomat told me Italy's national interest was at the heart of its Afghanistan policy because it was directly threatened and more broadly, "[t]he West could not allow there to be a country in the heart of Asia dominated by terrorism and drugs—a black hole, a threat to everyone."[184] Another Foreign Ministry official told me that national interest did not drive Italy's OEF policy because Italy was threatened by terrorists rooted in North Africa *not* South and Central Asia.[185] A well respected Italian journalist specializing in foreign affairs told me that the terrorist threat likely had little impact on government policy because "[t]here was—and is— a perception that Islamic radicals do not target Italy. The view might not be correct and is most certainly fragile but there you have it."[186] Lucio Caracciolo agreed that the usual view in Rome is that Islamic radicals do not target Italy but "[b]ecause of the environment of the period immediately after 9/11 it is possible that that general perception was suspended, especially with regard to concerns about an attack on the Vatican."[187]

Policymaker and analyst statements suggest that prestige was an important factor in this case. On the day after the 9/11 attacks Berlusconi said, "[w]e consider ourselves, with calm resolve, in the first rank."[188] A week after

126 • America's Allies and War

OEF began and Italy was not among the countries initially involved, columnist Franco Venturini wrote: "[n]ow, Italy should run after, not because it loves war but because it understands how much it may cost to not do so."[189] We can also see the importance of prestige by the way Italian government officials talked about and reacted to related developments. Italy's Ambassador to Washington, Giovanni Castellaneta, said after Italian officers joined CENTCOM in Tampa: "[s]o, now we can be considered equal to Germany."[190] At this point two events got the attention of those who emphasize Italy's prestige. On October 19 Tony Blair, Jacques Chirac, and Gerhard Schroeder held a meeting in Ghent to discuss Afghanistan. Many noted Italy's exclusion from the meeting, including former center-left Prime Minister Massimo D'Alema, who blamed the outcome on Berlusconi.[191] News that Blair, Chirac, and Schroeder planned a dinner in London to discuss Afghanistan on November 3 triggered renewed Italian prestige concerns. Berlusconi and other European leaders ultimately attained invitations.[192]

The announcement that Italy had negotiated a contribution with the United States led to a stream of comments about Italy's prestige. Venturini wrote that "[i]n the course of a few hours Italy . . . discovers itself catapulted into the top tier, finds again the rank that is its due. . . . "[193] Opposition figures even cited Italy's prestige as an important reason to support the Italian contribution to Afghanistan.[194] Berlusconi ally Renato Schifani offered the following logic during the debate on Italy's decision to contribute to OEF: "[w]hen we in the House of Freedoms have been called upon to safeguard Italy's international prestige, we have always done it, we have never backed down. When Italy's good name is in question one cannot and one must not withdraw one milimeter."[195] Admiral Guido Venturoni, Chair of NATO's military commission, cited prestige as an important reason for Italy's contribution.[196]

Interviews provide abundant support for the view that prestige played a central role in Italy's decision to provide a contribution to OEF. All of those I spoke with about Afghanistan said that prestige played an important role in the Berlusconi government's decision. Many agreed that it was important that Britain and France had contributed. One Foreign Ministry official noted that because of the U.S.-UK "special relationship," a British contribution did not create major issues for Italian prestige but because France and Germany were contributing Italy had to be involved.[197] When I asked a senior Italian diplomat about the importance of prestige in this case he explained that he did not mention it initially because "it is always a factor for Italy."[198] The diplomat, like *Limes* editor Caracciolo, cited Italy's persistent opposition to permanent UNSC seats for Germany and Japan as evidence that Italian governments are very prestige conscious.[199] Ambassador

Silvio Fagiolo told me that in the post–Cold War era, "Italy wanted to prove to be an equal of other leading European countries and military action was a means to that end."[200] In a similar vein an Italian journalist I interviewed said of the Berlusconi government's decision, "[b]ecause Italy does little in international relations the only way it counts is to contribute its troops to peace operations. In this way Italy can be considered among the four great countries in Europe."[201]

Electoral Politics

Very little evidence exists that electoral politics drove the Berlusconi government's decision to provide a contribution to OEF. Polls showed that the Italian public supported their government's contribution but by a very slim margin. Renato Mannheimer of the *Corriere della Sera* reported on November 9 that while a month earlier 70 percent of Italians favored their country's involvement in Afghanistan, only 51 percent favored an Italian contribution at the time of the parliamentary vote.[202] The Catholic Church offered rare approval for the war, saying it was a U.S.-led war of self-defense.[203] Less than two weeks into OEF, however, the Vatican began to call for a bombing pause.[204] One week into the war the most committed Italian pacifists engaged in a 150-kilometer peace march from Perugia to Assisi.[205] The Berlusconi government responded by organizing a pro-U.S. march.[206] Observers such as Angelo Panebianco believed that as the Italian contribution began, public support was anything but firm.[207] Given the thin margin and the uncertain trajectory of Italian public opinion, it would not have made good sense to bet one's electoral future on a contribution to OEF.

Leading center-left opposition figures announced immediately after the 9/11 attacks that they would support the use of force, given the circumstances.[208] Leaders of the center-left and most of the rank and file supported the government's pro-U.S. line in the October 9 Senate debate.[209] Civilian casualties from the bombing campaign led to some center-left criticism of the conduct of the war.[210] In the November 7 debate, the center-left voted in favor of an alternative resolution that supported an Italian contribution but offered a few caveats.[211] Stefano Folli of the *Corriere della Sera* wrote that " . . . the government's political support is clear like never before."[212] Still, the fact that the center left had not itself been clamoring for an Italian contribution meant that the government would not have risked electoral ramifications had it refused to provide military support.

Electoral politics may, however, provide an explanation of the previously outlined limitations on Italy's contribution. The Berlusconi government's

128 • America's Allies and War

public announcement that it hoped that the United States would not announce ground troops does not make sense from alliance value or prestige perspectives but it makes perfect sense as a means to calm anticipated concerns about casualties from the Italian public. This interpretation is consistent with Alastair Campbell's notation in his diary from immediately after the 9/11 attacks that Berlusconi said privately that he supported military action "provided not too many people die"[213]

None of those I interviewed said that public opinion or electoral politics led the Berlusconi government to decide in favor of an Italian contribution to OEF. A senior Foreign Ministry official noted that 51 percent in favor of an Italian contribution is quite high relative to analogous cases.[214] When I asked about Berlusconi's stated hope that the United States would not ask for ground troops, most referred to the domestic political scene. A senior Italian diplomat reminded me that governments in Rome always have "a terror of coffins coming home."[215] The foreign affairs journalist I interviewed told me that the government was caught between wanting to be a good ally for the United States and the desire to limit what he perceived to be a potential domestic political liability.[216] Finally, Lucio Caracciolo believes that while Berlusconi may have underestimated the Italian public's willingness to support a ground war, " . . . he made a prudent assessment. He didn't want to risk his political future on a potentially bloody war in Afghanistan."[217]

Identity and Norms

There is a plausible story about Italy's identity and its decision to contribute to the U.S.-led war against the Taliban and postwar stabilization efforts. Some in Italy seem to have seen the 9/11 attacks as an opening salvo in a religious clash between Islam and Western Christianity that put Italy's identity as a Catholic nation in jeopardy and, thus, required a response. Journalist Oriana Fallaci—who was living in New York City at the time— wrote an intense polemic to this effect, which the *Corriere della Sera* began to publish in serial form on September 29.[218] Fallaci framed Osama Bin Laden as representative of Islam and asserted that the West was clearly superior to it. A few days earlier Silvio Berlusconi told journalists that "[w]e should be aware of the superiority of our civilization, made up of principles and values that have contributed much to the quality of life for the community." He went on to say that "[i]n our countries there is respect for human rights—of religion and politics—that, certainly, there is not in Islamic countries."[219] In the October 9 debate on Italian support for the U.S.-led war in Afghanistan, Berlusconi cited defense of Western values as one reason to support the government's line.[220] While it is true that the views Fallaci and Berlusconi expressed were controversial in Italy, it is possible that Berlusconi's government was motivated by them in deciding to contribute to OEF.

Logical and empirical problems arise with the identity explanation, however. First, without the security threat element, the threat to identity would not have been salient. Osama Bin Laden's statements pre-date the 9/11 attacks and should have provoked a defense of Italian identity earlier if threat to identity were the primary reason for action. It seems more likely that the 9/11 attacks made the Al-Qaeda threat to all aspects of Western life—including values—clear, and thus responding to the threat became important. There is some evidence that Berlusconi government officials deemed the security threat to trump the threat to Western values. In the November 7 debate, Defense Minister Martino said that the war in Afghanistan was "a struggle of civilization against barbarity" necessary in order to safeguard shared values but " . . . above all to defend the more specific interests and expectations of our national community."[221] Second, if the Berlusconi government truly saw Al-Qaeda and radical Islam as a fundamental threat to Italy's identity, why would it have been so reluctant to commit ground troops?

Perhaps the Berlusconi government was motivated instead by outrage at the Taliban regime's abysmal human rights record. The Taliban regime was indisputably one of the world's worst violators of widely accepted human rights. Moreover, an international norm that states should use force and intervene against governments that are particularly brutal to their citizens was in place as of 2001. The Berlusconi government made some statements that implied that it saw Afghanistan in this context. On November 19, Berlusconi wrote to the head of Italy's parliamentary commission on childhood that Afghanistan faced "[a] humanitarian tragedy provoked by an oppressive and merciless regime that, hosting Islamic terrorist bases, has transformed that country into a theater of a regrettably inevitable war and has inflicted new suffering on men, women, and, above all, children."[222]

This explanation has several shortcomings, however. One problem has to do with timing. As noted in the previous cases, the Taliban had ruled Afghanistan since 1996 and there was little doubt about its treatment of its citizens from the start. One might argue that the Berlusconi government seized upon the post-9/11 environment to participate in action to resolve a problem that it had long been concerned with. Unfortunately, there is little evidence that the Berlusconi government officials were sufficiently concerned with the Taliban regime's human rights records before 9/11 that they sought military action to overthrow it. Finally, there is the problem

130 • America's Allies and War

that in providing military support for the overthrow of the Taliban the Berlusconi government does not appear to have been concerned with the human rights record of the Northern Alliance, who were the leading local allies of the United States. In the October 9 debate, Senator Luigi Malabarba drew attention to the concerns of Afghan women about the prospects for human rights under the Northern Alliance.[223] The *Corriere della Sera* reported on Northern Alliance abuses on November 30—there is no evidence that those reports led the Italian government to reconsider its support for OEF.[224]

Interviews provided little support for the importance of Italian identity or the responsibility to protect.[225] An Italian Foreign Ministry official told me that the suffering of the Afghan people " . . . had only a limited place in the Italian decision making process. The public and policymakers had not paid attention to Afghanistan since the Soviet withdrawal and had little idea of the human rights of Afghans."[226] A senior Italian diplomat told me that the humanitarian aspect was critical in delivering the support of the "women's lobby" in the parliament but otherwise its primary effect was to impact how Italian troops were used in Afghanistan.[227] In the other interviews I did not explicitly ask about human rights and none of those I spoke with volunteered it—or Italy's identity—as a significant factor.

Case Conclusion

The Berlusconi government's contribution to OEF provides support for proposition two. Numerous policymaker and analyst statements provide strong evidence that Berlusconi valued Italy's relationship with the United States and that this factor best explains the Italian decision. Many policymakers and analysts in public and private (e.g., interviews) confirmed that the Berlusconi government contributed to OEF to address the threat from Al-Qaeda. As Italy could have taken a free ride off U.S. efforts, this logic cannot be the dominant one, however. Policymakers and analysts agreed that Italy's prestige played an important role in this case. The Italian public and opposition favored support for OEF, but there is no evidence this factor affected the outcome (though fragile public support may have led the Berlusconi government to refuse to contribute ground troops). There is some evidence that the Berlusconi government saw the 9/11 attacks as an attack on Italy's identity and that it was responding to a humanitarian intervention norm, so the case provides support for alternative proposition one. The identity explanation cannot make sense of the outcome without the security threat element, however. The humanitarian intervention argument cannot explain the timing of the Berlusconi government's concern with human rights in Afghanistan or its lack of concern with its allies' violation of human rights.

Conclusion

Britain and France believed Al-Qaeda was a threat to their national interest and explained their contributions by referring to the threat. Italy's interest was a little less clear but the Berlusconi government appears to have been convinced that Al-Qaeda was a threat to it as well. If national interest had been the only factor in this case, however, contribution would not have made sense as it was widely believed after September 11, 2001, that the United States was willing and able to take successful military action against the Taliban and Al-Qaeda without allied support. Because the United States had just suffered the 9/11 attacks, alliance value was very clearly on the line and it was a factor in each country's decision—the evidence suggests it was the dominant factor in the British and Italian cases. Prestige was also a factor in all three cases because of the widespread support for the campaign and due to its exclusive nature. The evidence suggests that the Chirac/Jospin government made a military contribution primarily to defend France's prestige. Domestic support for the war helped each of the three governments but the lukewarm public support in Italy (and the Berlusconi government's concern that it might deteriorate significantly with casualties) may explain that country's reluctance to contribute ground troops to OEF. Finally, little evidence supported the causal impact of identity and norms in this case.

CHAPTER 6

Iraq

When the United Nations Security Council (UNSC) unanimously adopted resolution 1441 on November 8, 2002, it seemed as if the United States and its allies agreed that Iraq's WMD were a problem and UN inspections were the way to solve it.[1] The rift became apparent as UN inspectors began to report back. The Bush administration argued that Iraq's failure to comply fully with United Nations Monitoring, Verification and Inspection Commission (UNMOVIC) indicated that it was intent on concealing its WMD. Others, such as Jacques Chirac's government in France, emphasized UN inspectors' requests for more time to continue their investigations. On March 20, 2003, the United States initiated war against Iraq. George W. Bush's administration argued—among the many rationales it offered—that Saddam Hussein's Iraq was a regional and global threat because of its chemical and biological weapons (CBW) stockpiles, nuclear ambitions, and ties to terrorist groups. Tony Blair's government in Britain was George Bush's closest ally during the crisis, providing total political support and 46,000 troops for the war. In Italy Silvio Berlusconi's government publicly supported the Bush administration's firm line with Iraq but provided no military support for the war. Chirac's government in Paris actively opposed the U.S.-led war and refused a military contribution. How can we explain such divergent behavior by America's leading European allies?

The United Kingdom: Alliance

The United Kingdom was the only American ally to provide a significant contribution of ground troops during the combat phase of Operation Iraqi Freedom (OIF). It is hard to pinpoint exactly when the Blair government made the final decision to provide military support: the decision appears to have been made in stages.[2] Blair spokesperson and confidante Alastair

134 • America's Allies and War

Campbell recorded that the British government began planning for a role in a possible U.S.-led war against Iraq in July 2002. The planning was necessary because the government believed that the Bush administration had decided that force would be necessary.[3] At a July 2002 meeting on Iraq, Britain's Chief of Defence Staff, Admiral Sir Michael Boyce, discussed three options for British participation: bases only, bases with maritime and air assets, and a ground contingent of roughly 40,000 troops.[4] An assistant to Blair's Foreign Policy Adviser Sir David Manning recorded at the time that the core conclusion of the meeting was "[w]e should work on the assumption that the UK would take part in any military action."[5] According to Bob Woodward, the Bush administration believed it had guaranteed British military support in a September 2002 meeting between Bush and Blair.[6] On October 17 Campbell recorded that the Blair government was holding out before making a final decision.[7] It appears that a final decision point came at the end of February when it became clear that a UNSC resolution explicitly authorizing the use of force (which the Blair government had pressed the Bush administration to pursue) would not pass. At that point, Blair's leading biographer, Anthony Seldon, recounts that Bush made clear to Blair that he could withdraw his country's offer of support—instead Blair chose to take his government to war alongside the United States.[8] The Blair government ultimately engaged roughly 46,000 of its military personnel in the formal combat phase of OIF (March 20, 2003–May 1, 2003).[9]

Alliance

Britain valued its alliance relationship with the United States in the period prior to the 2003 Iraq War and the evidence indicates that alliance value was a critical factor in the Blair government's decision to provide military support. Analysts agree that in the period prior to the Iraq War British Prime Minister Tony Blair was convinced that providing support for the United States would translate into greater influence with the Bush administration. Campbell wrote in July 2002 that Blair " . . . felt maximum closeness publicly was the way to maximize influence privately."[10] Blair and his advisers were also convinced that the closest possible relationship with the United States was in Britain's national interest. As Philip Stephens put it, "The prime minister was unapologetic about his relationship with Bush, judging it in his country's vital strategic interests to stay close to Washington regardless of who occupied the White House."[11] Robin Cook believed that American power best explains why Blair valued Britain's relationship with the United States so much.[12] A close adviser to Blair reflected after the Iraq War that "[t]he U.S. had the power, and that is where Blair turned his

Iraq • 135

attention."[13] In a September 2002 interview, Blair created a furor when he said that he agreed with Robert McNamara that the "special relationship" meant that the UK should be willing "to commit themselves to pay the blood price."[14]

Several issue areas provided evidence to British officials that their country was capable of influencing American policy.[15] As noted, the British were the only foreign officials to have a role in the planning and implementation of Operation Enduring Freedom in Afghanistan. Moreover, while British pressure for a multinational peace force for post-Taliban Afghanistan met initial resistance, the Bush administration ultimately agreed to the creation of a UK-led force. Afghanistan demonstrated that Britain had influence over the United States that other countries could not match.[16] In the period leading up to the Iraq War, it appeared that Britain would also be able to get the Bush administration more engaged in the Middle East peace process. After much British lobbying, Bush embraced the "two-state solution" for the Israeli-Palestinian conflict in April 2002.[17] In September 2002, Bush promised Blair that he would make a major effort for Middle East peace, which later emerged in his "Roadmap for Peace."[18] Bush announced his willingness to publish the roadmap on March 14, just days before the initiation of the Iraq War.[19] Finally, the Blair government also influenced the Bush administration's Iraq policy. Blair combined with American Secretary of State Colin Powell to overcome initial resistance to pursue what came to be UNSC resolution 1441.[20] Peter Riddell writes that "[t]he best evidence, from both sides of the Atlantic, is that the Prime Minister's desire, and political need, for a UN resolution helped reinforce the President's tilt in that direction. . . . "[21] The Blair government also successfully pressed the Bush administration to join it in pushing for explicit UNSC authorization for the U.S.-led use of force against Iraq.[22] On March 5, 2003, Blair told Cook: "[l]eft to himself, Bush would have gone to war in January. No, not January, but back in September."[23]

What of those who argue that Blair ultimately failed to receive the influence he thought he would get in exchange for British support in Iraq? As the UK's Ambassador to the United States Christopher Meyer later wrote, "There comes a point where, if you hug too close, it becomes an end in itself."[24] *The Times'* Peter Riddell has written that Blair's gamble that he would get influence over Washington ultimately failed.[25] While this criticism has merit, the critical point for this chapter is that prior to the war Blair's government *thought* it could influence the United States and that it was reasonable for it to think so. Many at the time believed Blair had substantial influence over Bush—including those who opposed the war and criticized the government's Iraq policy more broadly.[26] Clare Short, the

136 • America's Allies and War

Secretary for International Development, believes that Blair got Bush to announce the Road Map and in her memoirs she criticizes the Prime Minister mainly for not pressing Bush more firmly on the Middle East and other issues.[27]

There is much evidence that Britain's alliance relationship with the United States was a central factor in Britain's decision to provide military support for OIF. In a survey of Blair's foreign policy, Paul Williams cites the UK-U.S. relationship as the first of three factors he uses to explain the British decision to participate in the U.S.-led war in Iraq: "Blair's government went to war, in part, because it believed the benefits of demonstrating its solidarity with the United States would outweigh the potential costs."[28] Government insiders had a similar view. Prior to a summit with Bush on Iraq, David Manning told Blair: "[C]onversations with [my] U.S. counterpart Condoleezza Rice convinced me that Bush wants to hear your views on Iraq before taking decisions. He also wants your support."[29] Because of Bush's desire to hear Blair's views and gain his support, Manning concluded in his memo to Blair: "[t]his gives you real influence. . . . "[30] Campbell recalled a meeting between Blair and Robin Cook in which the Prime Minister said, "I'm not going to let the U.S. go unilateral. It would be wrong and this way I get to influence them."[31] Robin Cook, who was the Leader of the House of Commons (and a former Foreign Secretary), believed Blair's perception of the value of Britain's alliance with the United States was the most important factor in explaining British policy.[32] Cook recalls Blair's statement during a March 2002 Cabinet debate on Iraq that "I tell you that we must steer close to America. If we don't we will lose our influence to shape what they do."[33] Permanent Undersecretary at the Foreign and Commonwealth Office, Michael Jay, told Blair biographer Anthony Seldon of Britain's relationship with the United States, "That's what led him ultimately to support the war."[34] Ambassador Meyer explained Blair's Iraq policy this way: " . . . [W]hatever Bush chose to do, Blair wanted to be with him."[35] In his March 18, 2003, address to the House of Commons Blair recognized those who feared American unilateralism, saying, "[b]ut the way to deal with it is not rivalry, but partnership."[36] In his January 2010 testimony to the Iraq Inquiry (popularly known as the Chilcot Commission), Blair tried to downplay the desire for influence over the United States as a factor in his government's decision, probably in an attempt to silence domestic critics who labeled him Bush's "poodle."[37] Blair's previously cited private statements from the period during which the decision was made and Iraq Inquiry testimony by other high-ranking policymakers such as Jack Straw and Geoffrey Hoon suggest that attaining influence over the United States played a critical role in the decision.[38]

Iraq • 137

Interviews provided significant support for the central role of the U.S.-UK alliance relationship in the Blair government's decision to provide troops for the Iraq War. While those I interviewed disagreed on whether Blair might have attained more from Bush, they agreed that in the period prior to the Iraq War Blair believed he could influence Bush and most thought that it was reasonable for him to do so.[39] Anglo-American relations expert Alan Dobson suggested the Blair government—like any British government—valued the U.S.-UK relationship because "you can never be sure when a future Falklands will come" (wherein fundamental British national interests would require American support).[40] Eight of nine of those I asked about the role of the alliance on the outcome agreed it was a very important factor.[41] Three of those told me the alliance with the United States was the most important factor in the Blair government's decision. Clare Short told me that "[f]or Blair not falling out with the U.S. was at the top of the list of reasons for British participation."[42] When I asked Peter Riddell of *The Times* whether the WMD threat or U.S. alliance was more important, he replied, "[f]or Tony Blair, it goes back to his view that Britain has to stick with the U.S."[43] Bernard Jenkin, Shadow Defence Secretary at the time, said, "Tony Blair told the House of Commons that the main thing was that the substance of our relationship with the United States was at stake."[44]

Threat and Prestige

A satisfying explanation of the British decision to provide support for the U.S.-led war against Iraq should illustrate why the British supported an invasion of Iraq in spring 2003 whereas they had not done so previously. Evidence linking a threat to Britain's national interest with the Blair government's decision facilitates this end. The 9/11 terrorist attacks set the story in motion. To be clear: the Blair government did not believe Iraq had been responsible for the 9/11 attacks. Rather, the 9/11 attacks led the Blair government to a profound concern with the possibility of future attacks, especially if terrorist groups such as Al-Qaeda were to acquire WMD. After 9/11, the Blair government sought to address potential threats before they became real.[45] Anthony Seldon cites a Number 10 aide as saying that 9/11 was crucial for Blair "because the balance of risk that he was willing to accept changed dramatically after that day."[46] As Defence Secretary Geoffrey Hoon said during the September 23, 2002, cabinet meeting, "[t]he key issue in answering the question 'Why now?' is September 11th."[47]

The Blair government believed Saddam Hussein's regime possessed large stockpiles of chemical weapons, chemical and biological agent, and the capacity to make more.[48] As Blair stressed in making the case for Britain's

138 • America's Allies and War

participation in the war, when United Nations Special Commission (UNSCOM) inspectors departed Iraq in 1998 they left behind 10,000 liters of anthrax, up to 6,500 chemical munitions, 80 tons of mustard gas, unspecified amounts of sarin and botulinum toxin, and a VX nerve agent program.[49] The Iraqis claimed, but offered little proof, that they had destroyed the weapons and agent stockpiles.[50] As of 2003 most analysts believed that Iraq possessed CBW.[51]

If the Blair government truly believed Hussein's Iraq possessed CBW, why did it encounter such difficulty in presenting the intelligence on WMD? The trouble began when the government published the September 2002 dossier, which included the claim that the Iraqi military could deploy chemical or biological weapons within forty-five minutes of an order to do so and the claim that the Iraqis sought to purchase uranium "yellowcake" from Niger.[52] Both claims were later proven false. The situation worsened with the government's publication in February 2003 of what became known as the "dodgy dossier" because four of its nineteen pages were exposed as having been copied almost word for word from the Internet.[53] While the subsequent Hutton inquiry and Butler Review did not fault the Blair government for unduly pressuring intelligence officials, the two dossiers raise questions about the role of the WMD threat in the government's decision.[54] If the Blair government sought only to "fix" intelligence around a prior decision to go to war, did it truly believe Iraq's WMD were a threat to British interests?[55]

The Blair government's perception of Iraq's WMD threat was consistent with its presentation of the two dossiers. The Blair government's threat perception was rooted in the UNSCOM findings from the 1990s of Iraq's chemical weapons, biological and chemical agent stocks, and the potential to create more. Moreover, there was no evidence that the Iraqis had destroyed the weapons and agent UNSCOM had documented. According to John Kampfner's *Blair's Wars*, in the period prior to the war Blair received frequent assessments on Iraq from the Joint Intelligence Committee (JIC) and its Chairman John Scarlett that "Saddam had not accounted for his weapons and therefore must be hiding them."[56] A September 9, 2002, JIC report judged that "Iraq currently has available, either from pre–Gulf War stocks or more recent production, a number of biological warfare (BW) and chemical warfare (CW) agents and weapons. . . . "[57] The Blair government—and even experts opposed to the war—had difficulty imagining why Hussein's regime would secretly destroy the weapons, agents, and programs and refuse to provide proof that it had done so.[58] As Robin Cook said of the September 2002 dossier, "[p]ersonally, I never doubted that Number 10 believed in the threads of intelligence which were woven in to the dossier."[59] Clare Short has said the intelligence at the time supported the view that Iraq had chemical and biological programs, probably had weapons stocks, and sought nuclear weapons—Blair's mistake was to exaggerate the imminence of the threat.[60] Christopher Hill wrote of the assessment that Iraq had WMD "[t]he whole elite was guilty of tracked thinking and 'groupthink' in this respect, and the dissenters, like Brian Jones or David Kelly in the Ministry of Defence, did not get further than thinking the conclusion drawn up was too firm, and had been 'sexed up'."[61] As the Blair government believed Iraq possessed a chemical and biological arsenal, the two dossiers were designed to persuade skeptics in the domestic and international audience of the threat. Peter Riddell suggests that the Hutton and Butler inquiries show that "Mr. Blair exaggerated the immediate threat from Iraq, but he genuinely believed—as did British and other intelligence agencies—that Saddam Hussein possessed weapons of mass destruction and the intention to develop more."[62]

The Blair government believed that Hussein was willing and able to hide the missing chemical and biological arsenal from UNMOVIC as he had hitherto done. In the wake of 9/11, Blair and his advisers were afraid that anything but a complete picture of Iraq's WMD might hide a reality even worse than they feared. As one Blair aide told John Kampfner, "[m]y worry was not that the stuff was made up, but that we were seeing only a part of the picture and failing again."[63] Blair said that Iraq's December 2002 declaration on its WMD (in which it denied possessing any) was "only waffle that indicated that he was not serious about co-operating."[64] The House of Commons Intelligence and Security Committee had access to all the same intelligence assessments as the government and concluded in a September 2003 report that " . . . there was convincing evidence that Iraq had active chemical, biological and nuclear programmes and the capability to produce chemical and biological weapons."[65]

Believing that Iraq possessed these weapons, stocks, and programs did not necessarily mean that Iraq was a threat to British interests, however. Cook writes that a week before the release of the September dossier Blair received a memo from Jonathan Powell that the dossier " . . . does nothing to demonstrate a threat, let alone an imminent threat."[66] A March 2002 "options paper" from the Overseas and Defence Secretariat Cabinet Office noted that Saddam Hussein " . . . has used WMD in the past and could do so again if his regime were threatened. . . . "[67] The September 9, 2002, JIC assessment concluded that Saddam Hussein was likely to use WMD against coalition forces "[s]hould he feel his fate is sealed. . . . "[68] In a March 2002 memorandum, Jack Straw argued that Iraq posed a "unique and present danger" because it "invaded a neighbor" and "has used WMD and would use them again."[69] While there appears to have been some concern

140 • America's Allies and War

that Hussein's regime might use WMD against British interests, analysts believed such an outcome was unlikely unless the regime was threatened.

Some in the Blair government feared that Hussein's Iraq might share its CBW or know-how with terrorist groups. This fear began with Hussein's animosity toward the British and American governments and the view that he would strike out at them by any means available to him. In the Blair government's view, Hussein was a brutal killer with a history of aggression, including his invasion of Kuwait in 1990. Moreover, Hussein had a history of supporting terrorist groups, most notably the paramilitary wing of the Palestinian group Hamas. As Blair said in his March 18, 2003, address to the House of Commons, "[d]o not be in any doubt at all—Iraq has been supporting terrorist groups."[70] Groups like Hamas did not have a history of threatening British interests but Al Qaeda did. Many—including Britain's Defence Intelligence Service—have pointed out that Al Qaeda viewed Hussein as an infidel and thus the two entities were not likely allies.[71] The JIC reported that senior Iraqi officials had met senior Al-Qaeda operatives, that the latter sought WMD expertise from the former, and that some accounts suggested Iraq had trained Al-Qaeda terrorists. The October 2002 report concluded that there was "no intelligence of current cooperation" between Iraq and Al-Qaeda, however.[72] In the Blair government's view, Hussein's Iraq might pass WMD to Al Qaeda or other Islamic radical terrorist groups because they shared common enemies: the United States and Britain.[73]

In a March 18, 2003, speech to the House of Commons, Blair outlined " . . . why I believe that the threat we face today is so serious and why we must tackle it." The Prime Minister made clear his view that the world faced two major threats: tyrannical regimes with WMD and extreme Islamist terrorist groups. He further noted that even though the picture was not completely clear, the possibility that the two threats could merge justified British action.

> At the moment, I accept fully that the association between the two is loose—but it is hardening. The possibility of the two coming together—of terrorist groups in possession of weapons of mass destruction or even of a so-called dirty radiological bomb—is now, in my judgment, a real and present danger to Britain and its national security.[74]

Ian Duncan Smith speaking on behalf of the Conservative opposition similarly argued: " . . . the main reason why we will be voting for the motion is that it is in the British national interest."[75]

Blair has said that the question of whether Britain could have prevented the United States from invading Iraq is moot as—in his view—the war was in Britain's national interest. As the Prime Minister told Alastair Campbell on March 6, 2003, " . . . Saddam is a real problem, for us as much as anyone . . . "[76] In contrast, John Kampfner reports that as of summer 2002 Blair would have preferred to focus on combating terrorist networks but he and his advisers "concluded that the game had moved on to Iraq."[77] Recent testimony to the 2010 Iraq Inquiry makes clear that while almost all relevant actors in the Blair government believed Hussein's Iraq possessed WMD, none believed Iraq posed an imminent threat to Britain or its interests.[78] Jack Straw clarified to the Inquiry that " . . . when we were talking about a threat, we were talking about a threat in the future."[79]

Interviews provided mixed support for the importance of national interest in this case. Most interviewees agreed that Blair government officials believed—reasonably—that Saddam Hussein's Iraq possessed WMD programs and perhaps stocks.[80] A number of them, including a Minister working on Iraq at the time, said the Blair government was not concerned that Hussein would use WMD against Britain or its interests in the absence of a war.[81] The picture was slightly more mixed on the potential for Hussein to share WMD with terrorist groups. The anonymous Blair minister said that while Hussein " . . . didn't have extensive ties with Al-Qaeda, he could have passed [WMD] off to another, similar group."[82] Bernard Jenkin and an anonymous analyst agreed.[83] Others I spoke with did not believe the government was concerned about an Iraq–terrorist group WMD connection.[84] Philip Stephens, for example, recalled no sense of concern at the time with the potential for Iraq to share WMD with terrorist groups.[85] Journalist Peter Riddell told me that Blair officials tried to use the Iraq/terrorism/WMD link to sell or justify the war.[86] An anonymous security analyst at a prestigious London think tank said Blair officials stressed the Iraq/WMD link more than other factors because they believed it would sell best in Britain.[87]

Electoral Politics

One might think that if public opinion did not matter in this case, then it never will. A Populus poll taken for *The Times* 7–9 February 2003 found three-fifths of the British public said their country should only wage war against Iraq if the UN authorized it.[88] Knowing British public opinion, Foreign Secretary Jack Straw warned that if the Blair government waged war without a second resolution, the "only regime change that will be taking place is in this room."[89] Was Blair just being courageous by defying public opinion in defense of what he thought best for British national interest? Blair's government knew it would be shielded from the public's

142 • America's Allies and War

electoral wrath because the opposition Conservatives made clear early on that they would support war against Iraq.[90] While the Liberal Democrats opposed the war, the Blair government knew that they were not a serious rival.[91] The main point for the Blair government was that any voter making an Iraq protest vote would be lost to Labour but would not be a simultaneous gain for the Conservatives, thus minimizing the electoral fallout.

Some believed the Blair government might suffer significant Cabinet defections or a backbench rebellion so large that it would trigger a no confidence vote. In the end, only two high profile Cabinet members expressed their opposition to the war—Robin Cook and Clare Short—and only Cook resigned prior to the war. While 139 of 413 Labour MPs voted against the government, the government did not have to rely on the Conservative Party's support to survive.[92] More Labour backbenchers voted for the war because they knew that Blair had led them to two consecutive victories at the polls and that the Iraq War would not fundamentally affect Labour's future electoral prospects.

Interviews provided support for this perspective on electoral politics. Sir Robert Worcester, founder of the MORI poll, said the distribution of the electorate and the electoral system insulated the Blair government from public outrage on the Iraq War.[93] A few interviewees declined to speculate on whether the Blair government would have been forced to refuse support for the United States had the opposition Conservatives chosen to oppose the war.[94] Clare Short suggested that had a Conservative government faced the same public majority against war and if the Labour opposition had sided with the public, it would have been very difficult for the government to participate.[95] Others agreed with Short's hypothetical.[96] Bernard Jenkin agreed that Conservative support for Blair provided important "cover" for him.[97]

Identity and Norms

As noted, the Blair government believed that Britain was and should be a "force for good in the world."[98] In the House of Lords debate on Iraq in September 2002, Roy Jenkins characterized Blair as " . . . seeing the matters in stark terms of good and evil."[99] This view of British identity provides an initially plausible explanation of the British decision. For example, in his March 18, 2003, address to the Commons, Blair first provided a summary of the Hussein regime's human rights abuses and then said that if the war's opponents were to prevail, " . . . for the Iraqi people, whose only true hope lies in the removal of Saddam, the darkness will simply close back over. They will be left under his rule, without any possibility of liberation—not from us, not from anyone."[100] This explanation is inconsistent with prior British policy on Iraq, however, and cannot explain the timing of the British decision to support an invasion of Iraq. While Blair had commented on the nastiness of Hussein's regime in the past, he did not advocate a ground war that would result in regime change until after 9/11.[101] In fact, many argued that the pre-9/11 Anglo-American sanctions policy toward Iraq was blind to the suffering of the Iraqi people. Robin Cook recorded in his diary that when Jack Straw made the case during Prime Minister's questions that war was preferable to sanctions because the Iraqi people suffer from sanctions, he was heckled because " . . . he had never before shown interest in the suffering of the Iraqi people from sanctions."[102]

Even a cursory look at Blair and Straw's statements on Iraq makes clear that their reference to the Iraqi people's suffering emerged only in February 2003 as it got closer to the war (by almost all accounts after the Blair government had already decided to participate), most likely as an effort to persuade Labour backbenchers and core Labour voters.[103] Blair even said during the March Commons debate that he presented the moral argument not as a cause for action but so that " . . . if we do act, we should do so with a clear conscience and a strong heart."[104] In his January 2010 testimony to the Iraq Inquiry, Blair noted that " . . . there are many regimes that I would like to see the back of, but you can't just go through, I am afraid, and remove all the dictatorships. People often used to say to me about Mugabe in Zimbabwe and the Burma regime and so on, but you have to have a basis that is about a security threat."[105]

In saying that the moral argument was not the reason for Britain to act against Iraq Blair cited as the primary reason " . . . the terms set out in resolution 1441—that is our legal base."[106] In the same speech Blair said Britain had to wage war against Iraq because it "must uphold the authority of the United Nations."[107] Jack Straw closed the March 18 debate by saying that if Britain waged war against Iraq "[t]he world will become a safer place, and, above all, the essential authority of the United Nations will have been upheld."[108] The Butler Report found that in addition to the WMD threat and U.S. concerns, the Blair government favored force because of " . . . Iraq's perceived continuing challenge to the authority of the United Nations."[109] A number of those who testified before the Iraq Inquiry said the Blair government acted to defend the UN.[110] Did the Blair government decide to send its troops to fight alongside the Americans in Iraq in 2003 as a means to defend the United Nations?

The U.S.-led war against Iraq exceeded the terms of the UNSC resolution 1441, violated international law on the use of force, and defied the authority of the United Nations. Resolution 1441 warned Iraq of serious

144 • America's Allies and War

consequences if it did not comply with the details therein but it did not explicitly authorize UN member states to take military action against Iraq to force it to comply. Post–World War II international law on the use of force is rooted in the UN Charter and state norms regarding it. The UN Charter allows states to use force in self-defense when an armed attack has occurred.[111] Of course, an armed attack had not occurred prior to the U.S.-led initiation of hostilities. The UN Charter permits the use of force in only one other case: when the UNSC explicitly authorizes its members to take "all necessary means" to enforce a resolution. International legal scholars took serious issue with Attorney General Goldsmith's attempt to offer a legal defense of the war.[112] Goldsmith, who had initially said resolution 1441 did not provide sufficient legal cover, argued on March 7, 2003, that no resolution subsequent to 1441 was necessary because 1441 did not explicitly state such a requirement.[113] Peter Riddell puts the response well: "[t]he real reason why Resolution 1441 did not contain any reference to the need for a further decision sanctioning force was, of course, that this was politically unacceptable to the United States."[114]

International legal scholars agreed that the 2003 Iraq War violated international law.[115] In the period preceding the war, Michael Wood and Elizabeth Wilmshurst, the Foreign Office's top legal advisers, made clear to the Foreign Secretary that in the absence of explicit UNSC authorization Britain would be joining an illegal "war of aggression."[116] Moreover, unlike the WMD threat, upholding the integrity of the UN appeared rarely in private exchanges of the period and when it appeared, defense of the UN was secondary to concern with threat.[117] Blair recently acknowledged to the Iraq Inquiry that while the Cabinet had discussed Iraq twenty times, the Attorney General had only been present twice.[118] In his March 7, 2003, legal opinion on the war Goldsmith said only that "a reasonable case" could be made in defense of the war: that "[a]rguments can be made on both sides."[119] At best, international law permitted action—no one made the case that international law compelled Britain to participate. Finally, if Britain had truly been motivated by a desire to uphold the authority of the UN, it would have waited for UNMOVIC inspectors to finish their work. If at that point it viewed Iraq as still having failed to comply with resolution 1441, it would have negotiated a new UNSC resolution explicitly authorizing the use of force. Goldsmith's legal advice to Blair specified that the "safest legal course" would have been to attain a UNSC resolution subsequent to 1441.[120]

Interviews provided little support for the view that the Blair government was driven primarily by a desire to improve the lives of the Iraqi people. Shadow Defence Secretary Jenkin believed the Blair government's public

Iraq • 145

case for war was much about concern for the Iraqi people but said that would never have been enough on its own to justify involving the UK in the invasion of Iraq, because the plight of the Iraqi people did not have a direct impact on UK national interest, though it did strengthen the justification for such action in the national interest.[121] Others suggested this factor was important to only some members of the Blair government, such as Clare Short.[122] When asked about the importance of the humanitarian logic the security analyst I spoke with said, "[i]n isolation, not important. It is clear that if the British government was sincere at particular moments, it wasn't sincere about this concern all the time. Consider the 1991 Shi'a uprising, for example."[123] Peter Riddell pointed out that had humanitarian concerns been more important the Blair government would have insisted more on an effective postwar stabilization and reconstruction process.[124]

Interviews provided mixed support for the view that the Blair government sought to defend international law and the UNSC's authority. The anonymous Blair government minister said the government acted to defend the UNSC but then also admitted that the government did not seriously consider proposals to grant UN inspectors more time because of the military imperative of fighting the war before the heat of the Iraqi summer.[125] If the government wanted primarily to defend the UNSC, it would have pushed for more time for inspections and insisted that it would only join a UNSC-sanctioned war against Iraq (even if it had to wait until fall of 2003 to do so).[126] I asked Philip Stephens if going to war without a second resolution was not destroying the UN in order to save it and he replied that Blair " . . . shared the American view that the UNSC is only worth having if it works. Despite being a lawyer he wasn't particularly concerned with or focused on the international legal arguments. . . . "[127] Rosemary Hollis said that for the Blair government international law was "an afterthought" whereas Clare Short said the claim that the Blair government sought to defend the UNSC was "a lie."[128]

Case Conclusion

Peter Riddell summed up his view of the case this way: "Blair's conviction about the evils of Saddam and his weapons was matched by his overriding determination to see that America was not left alone to face terrorism."[129] While both factors were important, alliance value was probably more important than threat. Blair and his advisers knew that the UK's military contribution to OIF was unlikely to determine the outcome of the war.[130] As Blair's Foreign Policy Adviser David Manning told the Iraq Inquiry, "[t]he Americans could have done this operation without us. We always

146 • America's Allies and War

knew that."[131] Had the Blair government been motivated solely or mostly by threat it could have taken a free ride and allowed the United States to fight and win against Iraq alone. A counterfactual may illuminate the importance of alliance in the Blair government's decision. Would the Blair government's behavior through the crisis have been the same had the United States not pressed for military action so firmly from start to finish? While Blair had been concerned with Iraq's WMD since he had been in office, there is substantial evidence that Iraq became a central issue for the British government in 2002 because of the United States' lower risk tolerance in the wake of the 9/11 attacks.

Moreover, it seems likely that, as Anthony Seldon says, had the Blair government not been so committed to its alliance relationship with the United States, the UK might have embraced one of many proposals of March 2003 to allow UN weapons inspectors more time.[132] In late February and early March 2003 British officials sought a compromise position " . . . involving specific benchmarks for Iraqi compliance. The problem was timing. The United States firmly resisted any deadline lasting into the late spring or early autumn."[133] The overwhelming majority of the British government officials and advisers asked about the issue by the 2009–10 Iraq Inquiry confirmed that the U.S. government put very firm limits on the inspections regime, primarily due to what they claimed was a military imperative of waging war no later than mid to late March 2003.[134] For example, Baroness Usha Prashar asked Sir Jeremy Greenstock, the UK's Ambassador to the UN, whether as of March 2003, " . . . the military tail was wagging the diplomatic dog?" and Greenstock replied, "Yes, of course. In the United States it was, and, therefore, it affected the United Kingdom, because there was already an understanding between the United Kingdom and the United States that, if force in the end had to be used, then the United Kingdom would also use force in partnership with the United States."[135]

A number of the players directly involved with the story told the Iraq Inquiry that more time for inspectors to pursue specific benchmarks would have increased the probability of disarming Iraq or confirming that it had disarmed itself, thus avoiding war.[136] In the event that Iraq did not allow the benchmarks to be met, more time would have increased the likelihood of gaining explicit UNSC authorization (which would have made the war more legitimate, legal, and palatable in the British domestic political arena).[137] Given that, as outlined previously, the Blair government did not believe Iraq was an imminent threat to Britain or its interests, what other than the high value that it placed on its alliance with the United States can explain its unwillingness to allow inspectors more time?[138] Had the Blair government demanded more time in March 2003 it is likely the United States would have gone to war without Britain but doing so would have been extremely disruptive to the U.S. war plan and, thus, would have likely hurt the UK-U.S. alliance.[139] Alastair Campbell records that when Jack Straw suggested that Britain could choose to refuse support to the United States Blair replied that doing so " . . . would be the biggest shift in foreign policy for 50 years and I'm not sure it's very wise."[140]

The Blair government's decision to provide military support for the Iraq War provides support for proposition two. Numerous policymaker and analyst statements (including eight of nine relevant interview responses) suggest that the Blair government's value for the UK's relationship with the United States was among the most important factors in this case. There is some evidence that Blair and his advisers chose to contribute because of their concerns with Iraq's WMD. There is little evidence, however, that the Blair government believed Iraq would use WMD unless it was attacked and there is only mixed evidence that the government was concerned Hussein's regime might share WMD with terrorist groups. Moreover, while alliance value can explain why Britain was unwilling to give UN inspectors more time, WMD threat cannot explain that critical aspect of the story. The British public was firmly opposed to the Iraq War in the absence of explicit UNSC authorization but there is some evidence that Blair believed he could avoid the electoral ramifications of defying the public because of support from the opposition Conservative Party. This case did not provide support for alternative proposition three. Rebuttal points cast doubt on the "force for good" identity explanation—including its inability to explain the timing of British support for war. Moreover, there is no evidence that identity triumphed over international norms because of its intensity.

France: Threat

France did not provide military support for the 2003 Iraq War though it is unclear when the Chirac government made its decision. As of September 2002, Chirac refused to take the military option off the table.[141] French General Jean-Patrick Gaviard visited Washington in early January 2003 to discuss the possibility of a French military contribution of up to 15,000 troops.[142] French opposition to the war began hardening on January 20 after a UN meeting on terrorism when French Foreign Minister Dominique De Villepin said, "[w]e believe that nothing today justifies military action." When asked if France would veto a new resolution, he replied, "Believe me, in a matter of principles, we will go to the very end."[143] Philip Gordon and Jeremy Shapiro argue that De Villepin's statement marks the French

148 • America's Allies and War

decision not to provide military support.[144] Chirac was not as hard-line as his Foreign Minister, perhaps to preserve flexibility.

France's political opposition to the war escalated after De Villepin's January 20 UN statement. France opposed extending NATO's protection to Turkey in the event that Iraq attacked it because of Ankara's support for the U.S.-led war.[145] On March 9, De Villepin traveled to Angola, Guinea, and Cameroon to lobby those rotating members of the UNSC to vote against a second resolution on Iraq.[146] On March 10, Chirac said that as of "this evening" France would veto any new ultimatum to Iraq "whatever the circumstances."[147] As noted, Chirac made clear that—absent dramatic discoveries or Iraqi violations—his government would veto any resolution that allowed the United States and UK to determine when military action was appropriate.[148]

While France opposed the Canadian and Chilean proposals of March 11 and March 14 for a three-week deadline for the inspection regime, on March 16 Chirac spoke of a possible thirty- or sixty-day deadline.[149] Four days later the United States initiated war against Iraq and the French military played no role.

Alliance

The French value for their alliance with the United States continued to wane after the French decision to contribute to OEF. First, the U.S. decision not to use NATO for its war against the Taliban in Afghanistan and only to share planning responsibilities with the British led the French to expect that their influence with the Americans would be minimal.[150] After the 9/11 attacks, French decision makers became increasingly convinced that when neoconservatives in the Bush administration said that multilateralism and alliances unduly constrained the United States they were expressing the administration's consensus view.[151] Moreover, the Chirac government viewed the Bush administration's assertive defense of American power and interests as directly challenging France. George-Henri Soutou says the French believed the United States was " . . . the main obstacle to the achievement of French goals" such as an independent European defense, closer relations with Russia, and strong ties between France and North Africa.[152] Thus, while French public statements often celebrated the country's alliance with the United States, the reality was different. Journalists Henri Vernet and Thomas Cantaloube characterize France-U.S. relations during the Bush-Chirac era as " . . . a false semblance of friendship and soaring proclamations about common "values" that mask with great difficulty two divergent views of the world."[153]

As the United States leaned toward the use of force against Iraq it also made clear it would not consider allies' views—with the possible exception of Britain. Bush administration officials derided French skepticism about the threat from Iraq's WMD and the ties between Hussein's regime and terrorist groups. Gilles Delafon and Thomas Sancton wrote in *Le Monde* in February 2003 that the Bush administration's lack of consultation was at the heart of the split between Paris and Washington over Iraq. They contrasted the Bush administration with its predecessor, saying, "[b]ut above all—and that is the essential difference—Bill Clinton and Jacques Chirac did not cease to remain in contact. The American president regularly consulted his counterpart."[154] Bush administration officials had little interest in speaking with their French counterparts, let alone giving them any influence on American policy. After U.S. Secretary of Defense Donald Rumsfeld warned the French and Germans that in opposing the United States they were isolating themselves, French Defense Minister Michèle Alliot-Marie replied, "[t]o be an ally is not to say 'my idea is completely correct and those who disagree with me must be dismissed or excluded.' To be an ally is a status that implies dialogue and the respect of one's partners."[155] De Villepin and Chirac were aware that their decision to refuse military support and politically oppose the U.S.-led war against Iraq could lead to a worsening of their alliance relationship with the United States.[156] Given the already bad state of France-U.S. alliance relations, though, they felt that they had little to lose.

Interviews support the view that the Chirac government's low value for France's relationship with the United States contributed to the outcome. Some suggested that the lack of influence was an important element of the story. Etienne de Durand of the *Institut français des relations internationales* (IFRI) told me that "[t]he Bush administration's preventive war doctrine, especially in that the United States said it would be willing to go to war without the consent of NATO or the UN, meant the exact opposite of what France wanted: a seat at the table."[157] Bruno Tertrais of the *Fondation pour la recherche stratégique* (FRS) remarked that France's independent nuclear force may allow it to be less dependent on the United States than other of Washington's allies.[158] A senior French Foreign Ministry official stressed, "France's commitment to independence" as a significant factor in the Chirac government's decision.[159] Moreover, the Chirac government knew that France's relationship with the United States might suffer as a result of the French decision not to contribute. A very high-ranking official at the Policy Planning (*Centre d'Analyse et de Prévision*) section of the Foreign Affairs Ministry in the period preceding the war recalled that " . . . there was a recognition that our opposition to the war would be costly to our relationship

150 • America's Allies and War

with the United States."[160] In the end, of course, France's relationship with the United States did not lead the Chirac government to contribute or, it appears, to seriously consider doing so. As Nicole Gnesotto told me, "When something like Iraq occurs, many other countries look to how the United States will react first, France doesn't do that."[161] As a senior French Foreign Ministry official put it, "[i]n the end it came down to a choice between the alliance and national interest and we chose the latter."[162]

Threat and Prestige

Strong evidence indicates that the Chirac government did not perceive Iraq to be a significant threat to French interests and did not believe France would lose prestige by refusing to contribute. It is important to remember that while Jacques Chirac was skeptical of claims that Iraq possessed CBW, many French policymakers—including many in French intelligence— believed Iraq had CBW stocks.[163] In the end, French intelligence could not conclude definitively that Iraq did or did not have WMD.[164] The French view that Iraq probably continued to possess WMD explains their support for UNSC resolution 1441.[165] In January 2003, Chirac said Iraq's disarmament was "a problem for peace and for collective security."[166] For the Chirac government, Hussein's WMD were a problem but it did not expect he would use his arsenal outside Iraq, so the threat did not justify the use of force. French decision makers were also very skeptical of Iraq's ties to Al-Qaeda or other terrorist groups that might target the West and, as such, thought it highly unlikely that he would share his WMD with them.[167]

The Chirac government's behavior during the crisis is consistent with its perception that Iraqi WMD was not a significant and direct threat to France. French decision makers believed that UN inspectors were the key to determining if Iraq had WMD.[168] Chirac also knew, however, that it was rational for Iraq to refuse to destroy or prove it had destroyed its WMD if it believed that the United States had already decided to wage war against it (so as to maintain a deterrent).[169] This sensitivity to Iraq's perspective provides one reason why France opposed an automatic trigger for UNSC resolution 1441 and made clear that it interpreted the threat of "serious consequences" in the resolution as in no way authorizing member states to act against Iraq without further, explicit authorization from the Security Council.[170] On 13 and 14 January, Chirac's envoy Maurice Gourdault-Montagne visited Washington, D.C. When Gourdault-Montagne returned to Paris, he reported that the Bush administration had decided that the United States would wage war against Iraq unless Saddam Hussein was forced from power or overthrown.[171] After the January visit, the Chirac government believed that Washington was committed to war and a new UNSC resolution would only serve to legitimize the American decision.[172] From the French perspective, only UN inspectors could determine that Iraq was in "material breach" of resolution 1441 and only then should the UNSC explicitly authorize UN member states to enforce the resolution by force.[173]

The French view that Iraq's WMD were not a significant and direct threat to French interests seems to have played a significant role in the government's decision to refuse military support. When asked by *The New York Times* in September 2002 "[d]o you consider Saddam Hussein a very dangerous man today? For the region? For the world?" Chirac replied, "I find that he is especially dangerous to his own people, who are living under extraordinarily difficult circumstances. . . . "[174] Saddam Hussein might threaten Iraqis but he did not threaten Frenchmen. Gordon and Shapiro refer to divergent perceptions of Iraqi threat as "the first and most basic transatlantic difference."[175] UNMOVIC head Blix recalled, "[i]n the view of President Jacques Chirac, Iraq did not represent an immediate threat that justified an immediate war."[176]

Far from seeing a war against Iraq as likely to resolve a threat to French interests, the Chirac government viewed the prospect of a U.S.-led war against Iraq as itself a threat to France's interests. French officials feared that a U.S.-led war against Iraq might lead to global instability as other countries could feel justified in initiating preventive wars without having to first seek the approval of a respected international organization.[177] Members of the Chirac government also believed a U.S.-led war against Iraq would cause regional instability and turn into a potent recruitment tool for Islamic radicals.[178] The French were further concerned that Iraq would turn into a quagmire. In November 2002, De Villepin's Strategic Affairs Adviser Bruno Le Maire wrote in his diary that Chirac opposed French participation in U.S. planning for war because "[t]he slope is too slippery. Once we are there, we will not be able to leave."[179] Chirac apparently lectured Bush on the negative ramifications of an Iraq war, including regional instability, recruitment for terrorists, and regional instability during a November 2002 private bilateral meeting in Prague.[180]

Gordon and Shapiro wrote that the French " . . . genuinely thought the war was a bad idea and worried that a Western occupation of Iraq could turn into a quagmire that would serve as a recruiting tool for al Qaeda."[181] As De Villepin said on January 20, "[g]iven that we can disarm Iraq with pacific means, we do not need to . . . put in danger regional stability or even enlarge the rift between peoples and cultures, and increase terrorism."[182] Outside observers such as Alastair Campbell and Hans Blix documented the Chirac government's concern with the Iraq war's negative ramifications.[183]

152 • America's Allies and War

Blix reflected after meeting with Chirac on January 17, 2003, that France's Iraq policy " . . . seemed to be dominated by the conviction that Iraq did not pose a threat that justified armed intervention."[184] Chirac offered this statement as the bottom line for France's opposition to the Iraq War as the war was about to begin: "Today, Iraq does not represent an immediate threat that in itself justifies an immediate war."[185]

The Chirac government demonstrated a profound interest in maintaining or improving France's prestige in the international system in the period prior to the Iraq War. Dominique De Villepin has said that his action as Foreign Minister was " . . . marked by the wish for French independence, the will to assume our rank and our mission to show our convictions and to refuse compromises."[186] Specifically, some argue that the leading role France has played in European integration and enlargement drove France's desire for more prestige.[187] One can also see the constant French calls for a multipolar world as an attempt to decrease American prestige while increasing France's.[188] Chirac said the following to French ambassadors: " . . . [C]an France pretend to remain master of its destiny? Can it continue to make its voice heard in communicating its response on the great questions that pose themselves to mankind? I have the conviction that it can and it must."[189] In sum, the Chirac government was focused on preserving or enhancing French prestige.

Few expected the U.S.-led war against Iraq to garner much international support. Consequently, if France refused military support, it would not lose prestige relative to its peers and might even gain some by leading the political opposition to the war. As Chirac told *The New York Times* in September 2002, "It's not Schroder and I on one side, and Bush and Blair on the other; it's Bush and Blair on one side and all the others on the other side."[190] Established and rising powers such as Germany, Russia, China, and India made clear their opposition to a potential U.S.-led war.[191] Opposition to the war was so widespread globally that it led former U.S. Ambassador to Israel Martin Indyk to say, "The reality is that the French were in respectable company."[192] The Chirac government demonstrated that it viewed the Iraq crisis as a contest over prestige as it made vigorous efforts to isolate governments that politically supported the United States, like Britain, Spain, and Italy.[193] The French also took great pains to bolster countries—especially those on the UNSC—opposed to the war.[194] Chirac's concern for French prestige may also explain his statement that EU candidate countries that signed the Vilnius Declaration supporting the United States' Iraq policy were "not well raised" and "missed a good opportunity to stay quiet."[195] Finally, Chirac referred to France's majority position in the international community to explain why it was not providing military support

Iraq • 153

to OIF. In his brief address on March 18, 2003, Chirac made clear that "The French position is shared by the great majority of the international community."[196]

Interviewees provided very strong support for role of threat, while there was less support for the importance of prestige in this case. The policymakers and analysts agreed that the consensus view in Paris at the time was that Saddam Hussein's Iraq possessed CBW and programs.[197] Those I interviewed also told me that the Chirac government did not perceive Iraq's weapons as a threat because they did not expect Hussein to use them against France or its interests (even if he were technically able to do so) or share them with terrorists.[198] A senior French Foreign Ministry official clarified the government's perspective at the time "Saddam Hussein's own goal was his survival after sanctions. He was not going to frighten any of his neighbors or anyone else if left alone."[199]

Interviewees further stressed that the Chirac government was not concerned Hussein would share his WMD with terrorists. The senior Policy Planning official I interviewed recalled a paucity of evidence of ties between Iraq and terrorist groups and that "[e]ven if he wanted to strike at the United States he wouldn't have given or sold WMD to terrorist groups because he wouldn't have been able to exercise control over the groups after giving them the weapons."[200] When I asked Frédéric Bozo about the concern that Hussein's regime might share WMD with terrorists he replied " . . . that link was never bought here. The intelligence was weak and it did not square with everything we knew about Saddam Hussein."[201] The FRS's Bruno Tertrais summed up the thinking in the Chirac government: "[m]ost importantly, there was no evidence of Saddam Hussein's willingness to use or transfer his weapons to others and the evidence that existed was too flimsy to base a war on."[202] Finally, some interviewees stressed the government view that war would actually harm French interests by destabilizing the Middle East. As a senior French Foreign Ministry official recalled, " . . . we believed that there was a serious danger of regional instability resulting from a U.S.-led war against Iraq."[203] Similarly, the high-ranking Policy Planning official said Chirac feared the Iraq War would lead to a "clash of civilizations" whereas Nicole Gnesotto recalled concerns that "the region would explode."[204]

Many interviewees agreed that France's political opposition to the war led to an increase in its prestige. Of those, however, almost all argued that prestige was of minor or no causal importance in the decision to refuse military support. Nicole Gnesotto said gains in prestige were a positive side effect of French policy but did not cause it.[205] Etienne de Durand suggested that "France's lack of military participation cannot be explained by *grandeur*

154 • America's Allies and War

but this might explain its diplomatic stance."[206] Frédéric Bozo pointed out that de Villepin worked so hard to bolster opposition to the war in the UNSC because " . . . of France's position as a permanent member with a veto right."[207] Bozo also noted that France's desire to preserve its international status as a major power is the key to understanding why it must preserve its permanent seat on the Security Council.

Electoral Politics

While electoral politics provide a plausible explanation of this case, it does not appear that they significantly influenced the outcome. On the one hand, a number of details of the case make electoral politics a plausible explanation of France's decision to refuse support. First, the Chirac government does appear to have entertained the prospect of providing military support to a U.S.-led war against Iraq. As noted, General Gaviard discussed the prospect of a French contribution with his American counterparts in early January 2003. Second, French public opinion firmly opposed a U.S.-led war against Iraq. As of September 2002, 65 percent of French respondents opposed a war against Iraq and by February 2003, 77 percent did so.[208] Finally, the leading opposition to Jacques Chirac's center-right government, the Socialist Party, made clear its opposition to a U.S.-led Iraq war as soon as the prospect of such a war emerged.[209]

Was Chirac, then, just pandering to the French public in refusing French military support for a U.S.-led Iraq war? In this view, Chirac seriously considered providing military support but was kept from doing so by his fear of domestic electoral losses to the Socialist opposition. While plausible, the details of the case suggest that threat—not electoral politics—drove the French decision. First, General Gaviard's January visit seems to have been driven by the possible contingency—slim as of early January—that Iraq might decide to severely impede UN inspectors or that the inspectors would uncover WMD and Iraq would refuse to destroy them. As inspections continued and Blix and his colleague Mohamed El Baradei reported on their progress (beginning January 9 and continuing through March 2003), the Chirac government became increasingly convinced that Iraq was not a threat to French interests and, thus, did not justify war.[210] A Chirac government insider said of the Gaviard mission: "[s]imply, we could not exclude the hypothesis wherein Saddam Hussein would commit a blunder."[211] Bruno Le Maire wrote that " . . . we never arrived at the moment of the crisis where French military participation was seriously envisaged."[212] As an anonymous Chirac government figure told *Le Monde*'s Claire Trean at the end of January, "The question of a military intervention would pose itself if we were certain that Iraq possessed weapons of mass destruction and it refused to destroy them; it cannot pose itself only on the absence of certainty that Iraq does not have them."[213]

Chirac's government never agreed with the U.S. position that war was necessary because Iraq was an imminent threat, neither is there any evidence that it considered providing military support after the Gaviard visit. Moreover, the Chirac government did not order any preparations for war.[214] Obviously, it would have been politically difficult for the Chirac government to provide military support for the U.S.-led war against Iraq, but there is no evidence that it ever seriously considered doing so. Leading analysts, such as the Brookings Institution's Philip Gordon and Jeremy Shapiro, agree that the domestic political arena does not provide a convincing explanation of the French decision.[215] While French popular opposition to war may have contributed to the way De Villepin and Chirac communicated French policy, there is little evidence that public opinion drove the core policy decision.[216]

Interviews strongly supported this view of electoral politics. When I asked Frédéric Bozo whether the overwhelming majority of the French opposed forced Chirac to refuse military support for the United States, he replied, "No, that's not right. I think earlier polls showed less opposition. Chirac could have made the case for war, like Mitterrand in the 1991 Gulf War."[217] Bruno Tertrais felt that public opinion did not necessarily prevent Chirac's government from making a relatively small, symbolic commitment.[218] Other interviewees stressed that the Chirac government never seriously considered providing a military contribution (and, thus, public opinion did not force him to decline the United States' request). The senior Policy Planning official expanded on the point:

> From the start and throughout the French government never considered going to war in the circumstances in which it was initiated. If, however, we are discussing the very unlikely event that Saddam Hussein would have said a blunt "no" to 1441 or if he had engaged in blatant defiance of and opposition to the UN inspectors, France would have participated in military operations.[219]

Identity and Norms

The constructivist explanation provides a plausible explanation of the Chirac government's decision to refuse support. In this case French identity was tied to the defense of two major international norms. On February 21, 2003, Chirac provided the following view of French identity: "France acts to

156 • America's Allies and War

defend principles—not specific situations—the principles of law, of morality, principles that unify the international community more and more."[220] In his March 18 address Chirac said, "France acted in the name of the primacy of law and in view of its conception of relations among peoples and nations."[221] Given these statements and those previously cited, one could explain France's decision to refuse military support as rooted in a view that France should defend international law and the authority of the UNSC.

Chirac government officials certainly believed a U.S.-led war against Iraq would violate international law if initiated in the absence of a resolution subsequent to UNSC 1441.[222] Chirac and his advisers also said repeatedly that the United States should not initiate war without explicit authorization from the UNSC.[223] Yet, several reasons make this explanation less than compelling. First, even the French recognized that international law was not the most important reason for their decision to refuse military support.[224] Second, the explanation gets the causality backwards as France played a significant role in the lack of UNSC authorization for the war: as a permanent member of the UNSC it threatened its veto and it attempted to persuade other members to withhold support from a second resolution.[225] Third, France has a record of ignoring international law and the UNSC when it feels doing so is necessary. Kosovo provides an excellent recent case.[226] Fourth, while France may have been concerned for the authority of the UNSC in this case, this concern seems to be rooted in a French desire to defend the prestige of the country's permanent seat and veto, rather than a desire to uphold the norm of Security Council authority per se.[227]

Interviews provided minimal support for the claim that international law or the defense of the UNSC drove French policy in this case. The FRS's Camille Grand said that had France favored war it could have "finessed" the international legal picture, adding, "[i]n diplomatic terms the lack of international legal approval worked well as cover for our real opposition."[228] A number of interviewees suggested that international law on the use of force and the defense of the UNSC played a role in the Chirac government's decision. They admitted, however, that had France seen Iraq as a threat to national interest, international law and the UNSC would not have determined the outcome.[229] The Policy Planning official succinctly articulated this point: "[i]f France had truly believed that Iraq was a threat but couldn't get explicit UNSC authorization, it would have gone to war. There is no doubt."[230] When I asked whether France was not itself responsible for the UNSC outcome and, thus, the lack of international legal support for the war, I got a mixed response. Interviewees noted that countries like China and Russia would have opposed the war even if France had abstained. They also recognized, however, that France's high profile opposition to the war [made] it possible for small countries already predisposed to oppose the war to [feel] safer in so doing.[231] Some I spoke with said that in opposing the war Fran[ce] was trying to defend its permanent seat on the UNSC. The Policy Planning official said, "Chirac believed that to justify its permanent seat France should speak its mind to show that it is a state that deserves veto rights. . . . "[232]

Case Conclusion

The Chirac government's refusal to participate in the Iraq War provides additional support for proposition one. Policymaker and analyst statements, some from interviews, suggest that the Chirac government had a relatively low value for its alliance relationship with the United States and some interviewees believed this played a role in the outcome. Numerous policymaker and analyst statements confirmed that because the Chirac government did not believe Iraq would use WMD or share them with terrorists, they did not see war against Iraq as addressing a threat to France's interests. Instead, they saw a U.S.-led war as potentially destabilizing and, hence, a potential harm to France's national interest. Because there was little nascent international support for the war, it was reasonable for Chirac to believe that a refusal to provide support would not hurt France's prestige. It does not appear that the Chirac government refused support to avoid the electoral ramifications of voter and opposition Socialist Party hostility to a military contribution. The defense of UNSC authority explanation is a plausible fit and, as such, provides support for proposition two. There are a number of rebuttal points to the argument, however. For example, in defending the UNSC France was defending a central component of its prestige. Moreover, interviewees did not suggest that a desire to defend UNSC authority was a critical factor in this case.

Italy: Electoral Politics

On November 22, 2002, the *Corriere della Sera* reported that the American Ambassador to Italy, Mel Sembler, had delivered a letter from the U.S. government to the Italian government seeking its military contribution to a potential U.S.-led war against Iraq.[233] While the Berlusconi government subsequently claimed that it had not been asked to contribute troops, nothing in the reports of the U.S. request supports this claim.[234] Moreover, Berlusconi government officials made statements indicating they seriously considered providing a military contribution. In Washington on January 21, 2003, Foreign Minister Franco Frattini said, "[a] decision taken by the

Allies and War

..., sufficient for Italy to participate in an operation ...[235] Berlusconi had already made clear that his ...rted the aggressive American stance toward ...o. State Department spokesperson noted that ...pports the necessity for resolute action to confront the ...s weapons of mass destruction."[236] Ultimately, the Berlusconi ...it announced that Italy would not provide a formal military ...ibution to the Iraq War.[237]

The Berlusconi government took a number of steps short of a formal military contribution to the Iraq War that indicate a desire to contribute. Italy contributed to the war effort in October 2002 by sending roughly one thousand additional troops to Afghanistan "in substitution" for American forces redeployed to the Persian Gulf.[238] Shortly before the war began, the Italian government announced that it would grant the United States access to its bases and air space.[239] After the March 19 Council of Supreme Defense (CSD) meeting with President Ciampi, Berlusconi clarified that Italy's bases could not be used for direct attacks on Iraq. It later emerged, however, that Italy's bases were used for direct attack on Iraq. For example, in late March 2003, a thousand U.S. paratroopers flew directly from Vicenza to engage Iraqi forces in the North of the country.[240] Finally, as formal hostilities were winding down in late April 2003, it emerged that a contingent of SISMI (Italy's military intelligence service) agents were in Iraq during the months preceding the war working with their American and British counterparts to weaken the Iraqi regime and enhance the allied intelligence picture, thus facilitating the U.S.-led war.[241]

Alliance

The Berlusconi government highly valued Italy's relationship with the United States.[242] Foreign Minister Franco Frattini has argued that Italy's relationship with the United States enhances its international profile.[243] Moreover, Italian government officials stress that Italy benefits from the influence it gets over the United States through institutions like NATO. As Berlusconi told European colleagues in a September 2002 conference, if allies did not support the United States, which he referred to as "the military power incomparably stronger than any other nation," it would be more likely to "choose the path of isolationism, distancing itself from multilateral institutions."[244] In February 2003, the Prime Minister said Europe would be causing a "self-inflicted wound" in not supporting the United States.[245]

Berlusconi had sufficient access to Bush in the period preceding the Iraq War to view it as an asset worth maintaining with a military contribution to the Iraq War. Berlusconi was the first Italian Prime Minister to be invited to Camp David, where the *Corriere della Sera* reported he would tell Bush that Italy "will certainly do its part" in responding to the Iraqi threat.[246] From Camp David Berlusconi told the press: "I represent a country that is a loyal, faithful ally of the United States."[247] He added that he appreciated Bush's decision to pursue a new UNSC resolution—Berlusconi had lobbied Bush to go the UN route.[248] As of February 12, 2003, the *Corriere della Sera* reported there had been four cases of direct Bush-Berlusconi contacts in three weeks' time.[249] Journalist Paola Di Caro wrote that "Italy remains a loyal ally of the United States, consulted and considered in crucial moments like this one. . . . "[250] On the occasion of a late January Berlusconi visit to the White House, Franco Frattini remarked that "Italy is the only country which is not a member of the Security Council consulted by Bush."[251] Bush invited Berlusconi to the White House in January 2003 alongside Tony Blair, a pairing former Italian Foreign Minister Gianni De Michelis referred to as "an important diplomatic success" for the Prime Minister.[252] The alliance was not just of value because of the influence and prestige it yielded in the period preceding the Iraq War: it promised to continue to yield a variety of benefits in the future as well. Some believe Italy's support for the United States' Iraq policy played a critical role in the Pentagon's 2005 decision to award a lucrative contract for presidential helicopters to a subsidiary of the Italian firm Finmeccanica.[253] More broadly, U.S. Secretary of State Colin Powell reportedly assured Franco Frattini that if Italy continued its supportive line with regard to Iraq it would " . . . count more than it [currently] does not having a seat on the UN Security Council."[254]

Analyst assessments and policymaker statements from the period suggest that alliance value was among the most important factors leading the Berlusconi government to favor the U.S. position on Iraq. The *Corriere della Sera* chose to headline a March 19 article on Italy's tortured Iraq policy: "Support for America the Only Firm Point."[255] On March 12, Ministry of Foreign Affairs Undersecretary Alfredo Mantica said of the looming Iraq crisis: "It seems obvious to me that loyalty to NATO and the transatlantic relationship will be determinant in deciding our behavior."[256] Defense Minister Antonio Martino responded to criticisms from the left of the goverment's Iraq policy by noting: "On the left many seem to forget that the alliance with the United States is a fundamental pillar of our foreign policy."[257] Similarly, Deputy Prime Minister Gianfranco Fini warned, "we cannot separate ourselves from the alliance with the Americans," we have to "maintain a close relationship with them."[258] The Berlusconi government's value for Italy's relationship with the United States should have led it to provide at least a token military contribution. Other factors must explain the lack of contribution.

160 • America's Allies and War

Interviewees said alliance value played an important role in the Berlusconi government's Iraq policy. Those I interviewed agreed that Berlusconi's government valued Italy's relationship with the United States highly. Some stressed the Berlusconi government's view that Italy had gained from the relationship with the United States; for example, in the Bush administration's opposition to a UNSC seat for Germany.[259] Others stressed that American power was the critical factor in the government's value for the U.S.-Italy relationship.[260] By far the most common explanation for Italy's political support for the United States during the Iraq crisis was the U.S.-Italy relationship. For example, Ambassador Silvio Fagiolo cited Berlusconi's decision to sign the *Wall Street Journal* editorial supporting the U.S. position as a critical indicator of Italy's support for the United States.[261] Lucio Caracciolo noted that "Italy's alliance with the U.S. is a cornerstone of Italian foreign policy, so for Italy's relationship with the U.S. Berlusconi would suffer the [domestic political] costs of political support."[262]

Interviewees were divided on why the U.S.-Italy relationship did not translate into a symbolic military contribution during the war. Some claimed that the United States never requested Italian military participation or did so insincerely.[263] Ambassador Sembler's previously documented request for Italian military participation rebuts this claim. Ambassador Fagiolo, who said only that he was unaware of a formal request, noted that the United States probably restrained itself out of a desire to avoid embarassing its allies but he admitted that Washington would have benefitted politically from more countries providing military support.[264] Senator Fiorello Provera, President of the Senate Foreign Affairs Committee at the time, noted that while the United States did not ask Italy for more than Berlusconi was able to provide, he is "convinced that the Italian government wanted to do more but the situation at the time did not permit it."[265] Senator Provera cited—as I document later—Italian public opinion as the central factor limiting the Berlusconi government. Several interviewees agreed that because of the U.S.-Italy relationship Berlusconi would have preferred to provide a symbolic military contribution to OIF. A parliamentary foreign affairs staff member recalled that because of the domestic resistance to war "[f]or Berlusconi the trick was to be loyal to the American ally, while limiting its contribution to the post-war phase."[266]

Threat and Prestige

There is some evidence that the Berlusconi government perceived Iraq to be a threat to Italy's national interest. Public statements emphasized that Iraq had CBW and had ties to terrorist groups with whom it might share

CBW. Foreign Minister Frattini later wrote that the governing center-right coalition shared the Bush administration's view that containment was insufficient in the face of the terrorist threat: that it was necessary to "go to the root of problems, face up to them, and resolve them."[267] Members of the Berlusconi government said publicly that they believed that terrorism threatened Italy. Antonio Martino said if there were no preventive war against Iraq and "[i]f one day another attack were to occur, like September 11th, perhaps even in Europe, we would be responsible for not having prevented it."[268] In the months preceding the war, Italy's military intelligence service warned of an Al-Qaeda threat to Italy.[269] As Berlusconi put it: "[t]errorism is a problem for everyone and the big problems that it causes are not only [for] the Americans. It is not only a problem of the right or left but of the whole country."[270] At times, government officials seemed concerned that Saddam Hussein might use WMD against Italy's interests. As Berlusconi said in January 2003, "Saddam is dangerous . . . we are afraid there could be a new attack, as terrible as 9/11. An attack accomplished with the biological and chemical weapons Iraq possesses."[271] Umberto Bossi, a leading figure in Berlusconi's governing coalition, said promoting peace included actions that " . . . would prevent Saddam from using arms against the West."[272]

Frattini and Berlusconi argued that the U.S. drive against Iraq made sense given Iraq's WMD and the possibility that Hussein's regime might share them with terrorists. Frattini warned Italy's Senate that " . . . the Iraqi regime posssesses weapons of mass destruction that could be supplied to terrorist movements. . . . "[273] Berlusconi argued with regard to Al Qaeda: "[t]hey could not be so organized without the support and aid of a state and one is right to deduce that this state could be Iraq." He added that "[t]he Iraqi dictator needs to provide an account of where the weapons of mass destruction he said he had have ended up."[274] After Colin Powell's presentation on Iraqi WMD to the UNSC, Berlusconi urged resolve as "Iraq has not actively cooperated with inspectors, that he has not provided credible proof that the elimination of [his] weapons of mass destruction took place . . . " and "has continued to keep up ties with international terrorism."[275] While it is possible that Frattini and Berlusconi were parroting the White House's rhetoric, it is striking that a respected figure such as the *Corriere della Sera*'s Franco Venturini wrote: ". . . . if in the old bipolar order Iraq could be considered not dangerous for the West, after September 11th everything is changed and Iraq, with its chemical and bacteriological weapons, could be a base to support terrorism."[276]

Berlusconi recognized that the United States was perhaps more concerned with the threat emanating from Iraq than other countries. Berlusconi

162 • America's Allies and War

said the 9/11 attacks made the United States like a family that cancer has devastated that gives a substantial share of its resources to cancer research.[277] The Prime Minister also contended that because Saddam's Iraq posed such a threat it was not possible to respond to "the new American strategic preoccupations" with "a shrug of the shoulders."[278] In early February, Berlusconi said that Saddam Hussein "never had the will to disarm" and Bush's fear of "a new spectacular attack" like September 11 was founded on a legitimate view of Iraq as a threat.[279] Berlusconi later claimed that he had privately warned Bush about the negative ramifications of war in the period preceding it. On February 9, Pier Ferdinando Casini reported that "from conversations—including private ones—with Silvio Berlusconi it is clear that he does not fail to underline to the Americans the great risks of a unilateral initiative."[280]

Some evidence suggests that the Berlusconi government believed that the threat from Iraq justified the use of force against it. As early as September 2002, Berlusconi wrote in an article published in *Il Foglio*, " . . . either things change or it will be necessary to act concretely, with all diplomatic and political means possible, and without excluding the military option to preserve global security from a real threat."[281] In Italy's Senate the Prime Minister argued regarding Iraq that "terrorist networks nourished by state complicity" and weapons of mass destruction required intervention "because this constitutes—beyond a moral obligation—a true national interest. . . . "[282] Only a month before the war began, Berlusconi told the Senate that "serious consequences" were the only way to attain " . . . the difficult goal of disarming Iraq and destroying the chemical weapons that Baghdad undoubtedly possesses but has hidden until now. . . . "[283] Others close to the government expressed similar views. Renato Schifani, a close ally of the Prime Minister, voiced his concern with " . . . the 6,500 chemical bombs and 8,000 liters of anthrax still present in Iraq. . . . "[284] As of March 2003, Berlusconi made clear he agreed with Bush and Blair that UN inspections were not working to end Iraq's WMD threat. After a summit with German Chancellor Gerhard Schroeder, Berlusconi said UN inspections demonstrated that Iraq "did not have the will to cooperate" and that "[d]isarmament without war depends entirely on the Iraqi dictator."[285]

One could see the Berlusconi government's political support for U.S. policy toward Iraq as a bid for prestige. As noted, Berlusconi was the first Italian Prime Minister to be invited to Camp David and he had a striking level of access to Bush at a moment of great international tension. As Berlusconi said in the Senate on September 25, 2002, "[t]he government's actions have guaranteed for Italy a clear and irrefutable increase in prestige at the international level, definitively assigning it the role it deserves as founding member and third largest contributor to the European Union, fifth largest industrial power, sixth largest contributor to the United Nations, and third nation in the world for men committed to UN peace operations."[286] The problem with this line of argument is that many of the countries Italy measures itself against in prestige terms (e.g., France, Germany) only hardened their opposition to the war as time went on and, hence, were unlikely to grant Italy prestige even if it had provided a military contribution.

Very little evidence from interviews supports the claim that threat played a major role in the Berlusconi government's decision. Most of those I spoke with said Berlusconi government officials did not perceive Iraq as a threat to Italy or its interests. For example, when I asked a parliamentary foreign affairs staff member about the Iraqi threat logic he responded: "No, it was almost completely about solidarity with the United States. Italy wasn't convinced there was a threat. In fact, the tendency was the exact opposite."[287] A center-right Senator I interviewed—who was the head of a relevant parliamentary committee at the time—said, "In the Persian Gulf war we had a sense that Iraq was a real threat. In the 2003 Iraq War there was not the same view that Iraq was a threat."[288] Others I spoke with stressed that while the Italian government officials believed Iraq had WMD, they did not see it as a threat to Italy.[289] Ambassador Fagiolo told me that he believes the Berlusconi government did not even try to assess the threat itself, instead relying on a logic analogous to that of the Cold War PCI relative to the USSR that "it is better to be wrong with the United States than right against it."[290] None of those I spoke with said that a perception that Iraq was a threat drove the Berlusconi government's policy.

Electoral Politics

Evidence supports the claim that public opposition to the war countered the Berlusconi government's preference to provide military support for the United States. In mid-September 2002, the *Corriere dela Sera* reported that 50 percent of Italians were opposed to war, even with a UN mandate.[291] While Berlusconi recognized popular resistance early on, he appears to have initially believed that he could persuade Italians to change their minds. On January 30, Berlusconi told reporters that he was "giving Bush a hand" in drawing attention to the Iraqi threat "[b]ecause we in government have been mistaken, we have not spoken enough about Saddam's chemical weapons stocks. That is why in Europe sixty-five percent of citizens are opposed to war. But they will change their minds."[292] The Italian public did not change its mind about a U.S.-led war against Iraq and whether Italy should

164 • America's Allies and War

support it. A month prior to the war the *Corriere*'s polling expert Renato Mannheimer reported that 85 percent of Italians opposed a U.S.-led war without UN authorization (interpreted to mean a second UNSC resolution) whereas 71 percent were opposed even with UN authorization.[293] The Vatican's vocal public opposition to the war most certainly contributed to the number of those opposed.[294] President Ciampi's opposition was also probably significant in the swell of opposition.[295]

Berlusconi's major problem was that the center-left opposition had taken a firm stance opposed to war. As early as September 10, 2002, the *Corriere della Sera* reported that the center-left opposition was united in opposition to war against Iraq in the absence of explicit UN authorization.[296] The center-left remained united in opposition to war without UN authorization, though centrist elements split on the questions of war authorized by the UN and United States' use of Italy's bases.[297] As it became clear that the United States and UK would not attain a second UN resolution, Berlusconi knew that voters opposed to the war could express their view by voting for the center-left in future legislative elections (to be held no later than summer 2006).

Journalists and analysts have explained the Berlusconi government's policy by emphasizing public opinion and electoral politics. Two weeks before war began, Paola Di Caro reported that Berlusconi had cited polling figures when meeting with Bush to make the case that " . . . a second UN resolution is crucial because we need to do all we can to avoid unilateral actions that public opinion would not understand."[298] On March 15, Stefano Folli wrote that Berlusconi did not attend the prewar summit in the Azores because " . . . he is throwing lots of water into the wine of his interventionism. With an eye to the polls, to pacifist opinion (even his own [coalition]), to the Church."[299] Professor Massimo Teodori wrote that " . . . fear of unpopularity and the Catholic world's pressure . . . " best explains the "oscillation" in the government's support for the United States.[300]

Interviews provided mixed support for the view that the Berlusconi government's decision was determined by electoral politics. Some denied that electoral politics had an impact on the decision. The center-right Senator, for example, said that while there was public opposition to the war, this did not restrain the government because " . . . it never had any intention of providing military support."[301] Others suggested electoral politics had a significant impact on the outcome. Ambassador Fagiolo noted that in the period prior to the war Berlusconi suffered from low approval ratings and reelection thinking influenced his decision.[302] The parliamentary foreign affairs staffer explained that Berlusconi " . . . found a middle ground between providing as much political support as he could but didn't go against public opinion by offering military support."[303] Responding to an overall question on why the Berlusconi government provided political but not military support Senator Provera said: "[b]ecause the presence of strong conditioning on public opinion by the Italian left represented a deterrent to military support. In 2003 loss of life would have been intolerable and manipulated for political propaganda."[304] Finally, because one could see the electoral explanation as a criticism that Berlusconi lacked "courage" or was too much driven by polls his political allies might have been reluctant to agree to it. In fact, two of the three interviewees who disagreed with the electoral explanation of this case shared a political affiliation with Berlusconi.

Peace Identity and International Law

Perhaps the Berlusconi government chose not to contribute to the U.S.-led war because of its identity and international legal norms. Franco Frattini told the *Corriere della Sera* that he would explain to Colin Powell " . . . we are bearers of a culture of tolerance and repudiation of war."[305] Similarly, on February 14 Berlusconi said, "Italy has a long tradition of peace and a natural inclination to pursue peace until the last, very last minute, as I said in parliament and I also confirm [this point] after the inspectors report."[306] Article 11 of Italy's constitution with its repudiation of war as a means to solve international disputes reflects Italy's identity and many referred to it as a reason why Italy could not provide military support for the United States.[307]

Some evidence casts doubt on the role Italy's identity and international legal norms played in the Berlucsoni government's decision, however. Italy's identity did not keep it from waging war in Kosovo (without UN authorization) and Afghanistan.[308] While some understand Article 11 to mean that Italy can use force when authorized by the UN or NATO, neither Italy's identity nor Article 11 allows it to wage war under any circumstances. During a Senate debate on March 12, Giulio Andreotti noted that the intent in drafting Article 11 had been the repudiation of all war.[309] That Italy waged war in Kosovo and Afghanistan indicates that government could have found a way to reconcile the war with Italy's identity and its constitution. For example, Umberto Bossi contended with reference to Iraq's WMD threat that "[p]eace is not the absence of war. Peace is the absence of conditions that lead to war. Therefore, it is sancrosanct to act to eliminate those conditions. We have to be realistic."[310] Berlusconi told the Senate on February 6, "Italy, even in its recent tour of talks with other European leaders, clarified that it does not want war, but neither does it intend to put

166 • America's Allies and War

its head in the sand" regarding Iraqi threat.[311] Moreover, it is unlikely that Italy's identity was the principal factor here because in the final debate in the Italian parliament prior to the war a resolution that "excludes participation or collaboration of any kind by Italy against Iraq" was defeated in favor of a resolution endorsing Berlusconi's statement on Iraq, which said the war was legitimate and found sufficient authorization in previous UN resolutions.[312] Finally, if Italy's peace identity prevented it from participating in the Iraq War, why did it not keep Italian military intelligence agents from working with their American counterparts to pave the way for victory in the war (as documented earlier in this chapter)?

Perhaps the Berlusconi government was motivated primarily by international law and the UNSC. One might suggest that the lack of explicit UNSC authorization made it impossible for Italy to contribute to the Iraq War. Problematically for this interpretation, Berlusconi and other members of the government stated repeatedly that they believed the war complied with international law and was authorized by the UNSC. Following Colin Powell's presentation at the UNSC, Berlusconi said Powell had demonstrated that Iraq was in violation of resolution 1441.[313] On March 6, Berlusconi stated that a resolution subsequent to 1441 "is not necessary but is desirable."[314] On March 16, Maurizio Gasparri said, "the UN needs to pose to itself the problem of the weight of previous resolutions, that according to many observers already authorize a war against Saddam."[315] In his statement closing the March 19 Senate debate, Frattini stressed that the war's legitimacy "resides in the combined terms of sixteen UN approved resolutions. . . . "[316] Berlusconi opened the March 19 Senate debate by declaring that the U.S.-led use of force against Iraq was legitimate because of " . . . previous resolutions adopted by the Security Council, 678 in 1990, 687 in 1991, and 1441 in 2002, from the combined terms of which emerges with clarity that the cease fire stipulated at the conclusion of the 1991 conflict fails in case of violation of the obligation to forcibly disarm and the elimination of weapons of mass destruction."[317] In sum, Berlusconi officials' statements indicate that they believed the 2003 Iraq War complied with international law and was authorized by the UNSC. As such, international law and norms on the use of force cannot explain the outcome of this case.

Interviews provided little support for the view that Italian identity and/or international law were critical factors in this case. One interviewee suggested that President Ciampi's interpretation of Article 11 and the March 19 CSD meeting were the determining factors in this case.[318] Ambassador Fagiolo stressed that the legal basis for war was lacking but added: "Probably when the polls clearly showed opposition, Berlusconi determined that Italy could not provide even a symbolic contribution. As Speaker of the U.S. Congress Tip O'Neill said, 'All politics is local.'"[319] Several interviewees disagreed with the claim that the CSD meeting had an impact on government policy. The parliamentary foreign affairs staffer I spoke with said that the CSD meeting " . . . was useful in allowing Berlusconi to avoid taking a controversial public position."[320] Similarly, Lucio Caracciolo said, "Article 11 was useful for Berlusconi given that he had decided not to provide military support."[321] Responding to a question about the importance of President Ciampi, Article 11, and UNSC authorization, Senator Provera responded that such factors were "[n]ot very significant: less important than the massive propaganda developed at the time."[322] The center-right Senator I interviewed told me that Berlusconi had privately agreed with him that the war should have UN support.[323] Did the Berlusconi government withold military support because of the lack of a subsequent UNSC resolution? As noted, the government said repeatedly that the war *was* fully authorized by the UNSC despite domestic political incentives to conclude otherwise. In an interesting footnote, in April 2003 the Berlusconi government announced it would send a "peace" force to Iraq even if there were no new UNSC resolution—in defiance of President Ciampi's call for it to wait for UN authorization.[324]

Case Conclusion

The Berlusconi government's refusal to make a military contribution to the 2003 Iraq War supports proposition four. Policymakers and analysts agree that the Berlusconi government highly valued Italy's alliance relationship with the United States. Numerous interview responses and published policymaker and analyst statements suggest that high alliance value led the Berlusconi government to provide political support for the United States and to desire to make a military contribution. There is less evidence that the Berlusconi government provided political support because it saw Iraq as a threat to Italy. The Italian public opposed the Iraq War and so did the center-left opposition. Analysts and several interviewees believe Berlusconi refused to provide support because of electoral concerns. This case also provides support for alternative proposition two. Italy's peace identity and international legal norms should have led the Berlusconi government to refuse support. Italy's identity has not kept it from waging war in other cases, however, or from helping the United States to succeed in Iraq. The international legal argument is problematic as the Berlusconi government publicly insisted that the U.S.-led war was legal. Interviews provided little support for the alternative explanation.

168 • America's Allies and War

Conclusion

Alliance was an important factor in this case. The Blair government's high value for Britain's relationship with the United States appears to have been the most important factor in its decision to provide a military contribution to a war in March 2003. The relatively lower value the Chirac government had for France's relationship with the United States partly explains why it never really considered providing military support in the absence of a second UNSC resolution. The Berlusconi government's value for Italy's alliance with the United States tells us why it wanted to provide a military contribution and why it provided such firm political support for the Bush administration's Iraq policy. The Blair government believed Iraq threatened Britain and its interests but it did not believe the threat was imminent, so this cannot explain why Blair and his advisers were unwilling to give UN inspectors more time. The view from Paris was different. The Chirac government believed a U.S.-led war against Iraq was more threatening to French interests than Iraq's CBW. While Berlusconi government officials publicly agreed with the U.S. assessment of the Iraqi threat, evidence from interviews indicates that most in Rome were not convinced. Public opposition to war was high in all three countries. Blair's government could ignore public opposition to the war because it had the support of the opposition Conservative Party, however. Chirac benefitted from public opposition to the war but it does not appear that the public drove his decision. Only in Rome did popular opposition to war have a decisive impact. Berlusconi knew that if he defied the overwhelming majority of Italy's public, disgruntled voters could shift their support to the center-left opposition. Given that prospect, Berlusconi rationally chose to refuse the American request for military support.

CHAPTER 7

Improving Transatlantic Alliance Burden-Sharing

In 1954 Dwight D. Eisenhower responded to the suggestion that the United States should contribute troops to Vietnam even if France refused by noting that "[w]ithout allies and associates the leader is just an adventurer like Genghis Khan."[1] Since World War II, America has often, but not always, gone to war with allies at its side. This book has sought to explain why some of the United States' leading postwar allies—Britain, France, and Italy—sometimes provide and sometimes refuse military support for U.S.-led military operations. Chapter 1 established that all three states have a consistent, albeit not perfect, record of contribution. Chapter 2 provided two explanations of allies' decisions—rooted in neoclassical realism and constructivism—and ten propositions specifying the conditions under which allies were more or less likely to contribute. Chapters 3 through 6 applied the explanations and propositions to seven U.S.-led military operations from Vietnam through the 2003 Iraq War. This chapter evaluates the extent to which the cases supported the propositions and the individual variables. It then discusses some of the general conclusions one can draw from the cases. The chapter closes by drawing on the book's conclusions to offer advice to American policymakers seeking to improve transatlantic burden-sharing in the future.

Evaluating the Propositions and Factors

The case studies in Chapters 3 through 6 provide the basis for several conclusions about the neoclassical realist explanation, the alternative constructivist explanation, and the relative utility of the different variables (causal factors). Table 7.1 summarizes the findings from each of the twenty-one cases as to support for the propositions and alternative propositions. The

Table 7.1 Evaluating the propositions

	Vietnam			Lebanon			P Gulf			Somalia			Kosovo			Afghanistan			Iraq '03		
	Britain	*France*	*Italy*	*Britain*	*France*	*Italy*	*Britain*	*France*	*Italy*	*Britain*	*France*	*Italy*	*Britain*	*France*	*Italy*	*Britain*	*France*	*Italy*	*Britain*	*France*	*Italy*
P1		SU								SU										SU	
P2					SU	SU	SU	SU	SU		SU	SU	SU	SU	SU	SU	SU	SU	SU		
P3																					
P4																					SU
P5																					
P6	SU																				
P7			NS	SU																	
AP1						SU	SU	SU		NS	SU	SU				SU	SU	SU			
AP2	SU	MS	MS												NS					SU	SU
AP3				NS	MS				MS				MS	MS					MS		

SU (Support—even if rebuttal points)

NS (No support)

MS (Minimal support-no evidence of causal force)

overall pattern is striking: the cases provide much more support for the neoclassical realist explanation's propositions than they do for the constructivist explanation's propositions. Alliance value, threat and prestige, and electoral politics do a better job explaining British, French, and Italian decisions than identity and international norms.

Twenty of twenty-one cases provided support (i.e., the posited independent and dependent variable combinations matched and there was some evidence for causal force) for neoclassical realist propositions. Only one case—Italy and Vietnam—did not support the relevant neoclassical realist proposition (i.e., the independent variable values suggested an alternative outcome). Eleven of twenty-one cases provided support for the constructivist propositions. Seven more cases provided minimal support for the constructivist propositions (i.e., the independent and dependent variable combinations matched but there was no evidence of posited causal force). Three cases did not support the relevant constructivist propositions: the Thatcher government's contribution to the Multinational Force (MNF) in Lebanon, the Major government's refusal to provide military support for U.S.-led security and relief efforts in Somalia, and the D'Alema government's contribution to the 1999 Kosovo War. Overall, the neoclassical realist propositions explained almost all of the cases whereas the constructivist propositions only explained about half the allies' decisions.

Some of the neoclassical realist propositions received more of a test than others. The most important propositions for the neoclassical realist explanation received the most support. Proposition two said that high alliance value, high threat and/or implicated prestige, and an electorally irrelevant or a supportive public combine to make support highly likely. Proposition two applied to fourteen of twenty-one cases and found support in all fourteen. The range of cases is sufficiently diverse to include the Mitterrand government's decision to provide troops for the U.S.-led action in Lebanon, the Italian contribution of aircraft to the Kosovo air war, and the Blair government's decision to offer 46,000 soldiers for the 2003 Iraq War. Proposition one made mirror opposite claims to proposition two, positing that low alliance value, low threat and prestige, and an irrelevant or relevant, opposed public combine to make support highly unlikely. Three cases provided support for proposition one: de Gaulle's refusal to provide military support for the American War in Vietnam, the Major government's refusal to provide a military contribution for UNITAF in Somalia, and the Chirac government's refusal to provide military support for the 2003 Iraq War.

Proposition four made the novel claim that the public can force a government leaning toward support—because of alliance, threat, or prestige—to refuse it when the opposition party/coalition joins with the public (and the public is in other ways electorally relevant). Only one case fit proposition

172 • America's Allies and War

four—the Berlusconi government's refusal to provide military support for the 2003 Iraq War—thus confirming the claim from Chapter 2 that it is rare for the public and opposition to join together to push their government to refuse support when alliance value and threat/prestige favor it.[2] Proposition six suggested that an electorally relevant public can help tip the scales between high alliance value and low threat (and prestige not implicated). The Wilson government's refusal to provide British troops to the U.S.-led Vietnam War provided support for proposition six. Proposition seven posits that high alliance value, low threat (and prestige not implicated in the case), and electorally irrelevant public opinion make support somewhat likely. The Thatcher government's contribution to the MNF provided support for this proposition whereas the Moro government's refusal to provide support for the U.S.-led war in Vietnam did not provide support for proposition seven.

None of the twenty-one cases fit the independent variable combinations for propositions three and five. While theoretically possible, there may be reasons why real-world cases rarely, if ever, fit the posited configurations. Proposition three suggested that an electorally relevant public favoring a contribution could counteract low alliance value and low threat/prestige. This kind of case might be extremely rare because—as noted—the opposition and the public rarely join against the international-level variables. Proposition five suggested that an electorally relevant public favoring support can be decisive when alliance value is high but threat is low and prestige is not implicated (or vice versa). As with proposition three, the absence of cases indicates that the British, French, and Italian publics and oppositions do not clamor for the provision of support when the imperative is not clear. This makes sense given that military action is always risky in international and domestic political terms. The reluctance of the public and opposition to offer support when the signals are not clear is also consistent with the allies' relative power positions: while the United States is so powerful that it can afford to act when its alliances, national interests, and prestige are not on the line, Britain, France, or Italy do not have that luxury.

Eight of twenty-one cases supported alternative proposition one, which argued that an identity consistent with the case of intervention and an international norm favoring intervention make contribution likely. Alternative proposition two argued that an identity contrary to the case of intervention and an international norm opposed to it make intervention unlikely. Alternative proposition two fit three of six cases where it applied: the Wilson government's refusal to provide support for the Vietnam War and the Chirac and Berlusconi government's decisions to refuse support in the 2003 Iraq War. In two of the six cases the constructivist propositions got the independent variable and outcome combinations correct but there was no evidence that the relevant variables caused the outcomes. In a final case (the D'Alema government and the Kosovo War) identity and norms predicted no military support but the government provided it. Finally, none of the cases supported alternative proposition three. In five of the six cases there was evidence to support identity or norms but the other variable predicted the opposite outcome and there was no evidence that the intensity of the former variable overrode the latter. In the case of the Thatcher government's contribution to the U.S.-led efforts in Lebanon, no evidence supported the identity explanation and the international norm wrongly predicted a refusal to contribute.

What does process-tracing analysis tell us about the relative causal weight of the different independent variables (see Table 7.2)? Consider a related question as well: while proposition two explains fourteen of twenty-one cases, is there variance within the cases as to which variables matter more than others? In six of twenty-one cases there was strong evidence that alliance value was among the most important factors in explaining the outcome (in one of the seven cases there was strong evidence but also a convincing rebuttal of the factor).[3] In fourteen cases there was strong evidence that a threat to national interest or implicated prestige was among the most important factors in the decision to provide or refuse support (there were three additional cases with strong evidence for threat or prestige and convincing rebuttals). In nineteen of twenty-one cases threat or prestige predicted the right outcome and there was at least some evidence that it played a role in the outcome. There is strong evidence that alliance value and/or threat was among the most important factors in seventeen cases. The cases suggest that an ally is most likely to provide military support when it values its alliance with the United States and the action is targeted at a threat to its interests (or its prestige is implicated).

There was some evidence that electoral politics mattered in two cases. While, as noted, it is rare for public and opposition to align against alliance and national interest, when this happens it can be decisive. Thus, the book suggests that in rare cases where the public and opposition jointly urge no support, the government may ignore high alliance value and threat and refuse a military contribution. In two cases there was strong evidence that identity was among the most important causal factors and in four additional cases there was strong evidence that international norms were among the most important factors. Though strong evidence supported these constructivist factors in six of twenty-one cases, rebuttal points cast doubt on their effectiveness in explaining the outcome in each of those six cases.

What Have We Learned?

The case study analysis allows a number of conclusions. Chapter 1 noted that it is puzzling that the United States' smaller allies contribute to

Table 7.2 Evaluating the causal factors

	Vietnam			Lebanon			P Gulf			Somalia			Kosovo			Afghanistan			Iraq '03		
	Britain	France	Italy	Britain	France	Italy	Britain	France	Italy	Britain	France	Italy	Britain	France	Italy	Britain	France	Italy	Britain	France	Italy
Alliance	OD	PD	OD	ED	PD	SE	ED	ED	SE	PD	ED	PD	ED	ED	SE	SE	ED	SE	SE	ED	OD
Threat/ Prestige	ED	SE	SE	OD	SE	SE	SE	SE	SE	ED	SE	SE	SE	SE	SE	SE†	SE	SE†	SE†	SE	OD
Electoral	PD	PD	PD	PD	PD	PD	PD	PD	PD	PD	ED	ED	PD	PD	PD	PD	PD	PD	ED	PD	ED
NCR	ED*	SE	SE*	ED	SE	SE	SE	SE	SE	ED	SE	SE	SE	SE	SE	SE	SE	SE	SE	SE	ED
Identity	ED†	PD	PD	PD	ED	SE†	N/A	N/A	OD	N/A	N/A	N/A	ED†	SE†	OD	ED†	ED†	ED†	ED†	ED†	ED†
Norms	ED†	N/A	N/A	OD	OD	ED†	SE†	ED†	SE†	OD	SE†	SE†	OD	OD	OD	ED†	ED†	ED†	OD	ED†	PD
CIST	ED†	PD	PD	PD	ED*	SE†	SE†	ED†	SE†*	OD	SE†	SE†	ED†*	SE†*	OD	ED†	ED†	ED†	ED†*	ED†	ED†

KEY

OD (opposite direction)

PD (predicted direction) little/no evidence

ED (evidence) some evidence that impacted outcome

SE strong evidence that critical

N/A did not develop this factor in this case

Note: Chapter Two outlines the bases for classifying factors.

†Indicates that important rebuttal points made to cast doubt on the evidence.

NCR neoclassical realist

CIST constructivist

Note: Overall causal weight score is based on the highest scoring individual variable for that explanation.

*Some evidence or strong evidence for one or more factors. Should not be taken to ignore the fact that another factor made opposite direction predictions in the case.

U.S.-led operations rather than leave it to bear the burden alone. Free-riding is the optimal strategy when allies have a national interest in having a problem solved (e.g., keeping Hussein's Iraq from controlling too much of the world's oil) and they know that the United States will act and that the success of the U.S.-led operation is not contingent on their cooperation. Why would they contribute rather than let the United States solve the problem for them? Alliance value and prestige provide a solution to this puzzle. States frequently contribute because they want to maintain their state's valued alliance relationship with the United States or so that they can maintain or enhance their international prestige. Free riding does not convince the United States of an ally's value nor does it convince other states that the free rider is willing or able to deploy its military when push comes to shove. The only way for allies to maintain alliance value and prestige is to contribute, so it is rational for them to contribute more often than free-riding logic would lead us to expect.

What do the cases tell us about whether alliance value or threat and prestige are more important in allies' military support decisions? Much of the burden-sharing literature suggests the alliance relationship is the more significant factor. For example, the "single most important finding" of Bennett, Lepgold, and Unger's edited volume is that the American manipulation of alliance dependence (or anticipated dependence) to get allies to contribute was critical in many countries' contribution decisions for the Persian Gulf War.[4] This book's cases suggest that alliance value is important—there is strong evidence that it was among the most important factors in a third of the cases. The cases demonstrate, however, that alliance value is significantly *less* important than threat and prestige: strong evidence supported threat and prestige in twice as many cases as alliance value. Thus, the burden-sharing literature has failed to sufficiently emphasize threat and prestige relative to alliance value. That alliance value is less important than threat and prestige is particularly striking given that American primacy characterized five of the book's seven cases. Despite America's unrivaled power and a request for support (or allied understanding that the United States desired it), allies made up their minds most often on the basis of whether the target threatened their interests or their prestige was implicated. In the end, the historical record supports Lord Palmerston's view: "We have no eternal allies, and we have no perpetual enemies. Our interests are eternal and perpetual, and those interests it is our duty to follow."[5]

One should not take from the book that alliance and threat/prestige are contradictory forces, however. The cases show that alliance and threat/prestige tend to covary (i.e., alliance value is high when the target is a threat or prestige is implicated and vice versa). Why is this so? While a thorough

176 • America's Allies and War

answer would require further study, the cases offer the basis for speculation. First, it stands to reason that allies that value their relationship with the United States also share many interests in common with it. Targets that threaten the United States sufficiently to spur the United States to use force also often threaten allies' interests. Second, alliance value may be interrelated with threat assessment. Allies with influence over the United States—a key component of alliance value—may contribute to its view that force is necessary relative to a particular target (e.g., the UK and the Kosovo War). States that value their alliance with the United States may also be more likely to accept American threat assessments (e.g., Italy and the 2003 Iraq War case).

The cases also demonstrate that previous studies of alliance burden-sharing have erred in overlooking the importance of prestige (i.e., the social recognition of a state's power). The cases covered in this book show that governments are more likely to make a military contribution when their prestige is implicated in the target of the use of force by prior interactions, geography, or by the fact that the state's peers are going to contribute. Strong evidence supported the claim that prestige was among the most important factors in government decisions in eleven of twenty-one cases. In nine of those cases prestige contributed to the causal force of threat, while in two of the eleven cases (the Mitterrand and Amato governments' decisions to contribute to UNITAF) prestige was the single most important factor in explaining the outcome.[6] In short, prestige often plays a significant role in allies' decisions to provide military support and previous studies have failed to recognize this fact.

The cases also yield some novel conclusions about the relationship between domestic politics and alliance burden-sharing. Public opposition to their country's military participation can constrain governments but only in rare cases where both it and an electorally relevant opposition party or coalition join forces to oppose a government that would otherwise prefer to make a contribution. The public and electorally relevant opposition did not join together in any of the fifteen cases where allies contributed to U.S.-led military action. In some of the fifteen support cases the public supported the government. In cases where the public opposed their country's military contribution, the opposition either supported the government or was too small to threaten the government's survival. The scarcity of cases where the public and an electorally relevant opposition joined to oppose a government leaning toward providing support is consistent with the logic outlined in Chapter 2.

The cases also generate conclusions about identity, norms, and their relationship to burden-sharing. Identity and norms do not provide an effective explanation of alliance burden-sharing. The cases show, however, that identity and norms recur in policymaker and analyst statements with some regularity. In the twenty-one cases covered in this book norms and identity served mainly as government justifications for decisions already made. Governments use identity and normative rhetoric to disarm those in their domestic polity (constituents, members of their parliamentary party, members of the opposition) they anticipate will oppose the use of force. The cases also show that the specific nature of a military operation provides governments with varying ability to use identity and normative rhetoric. The Kosovo War, for example, was rife with opportunities to make the case that humanitarianism drove government decisions whereas governments had considerably less success attempting to make a similar case for the 2003 Iraq War. Finally, there is evidence in a few cases that identity worked through public opinion to constrain the kind of military support a government could provide (e.g., Italy and Afghanistan).

Improving Transatlantic Burden-Sharing

While America's allies have contributed regularly to U.S.-led uses of force over the past three decades, there is room for improvement. The conclusions from the case analysis provide firm ground for several specific recommendations for how American policymakers can improve transatlantic burden-sharing, alliance relations, and decisions about the use of force.

Alliance value was among the most important factors in explaining roughly a third of the cases. Alliance value is also the easiest factor for policymakers in Washington to manipulate. First, American policymakers should be aware that alliance value varies: regardless of what pundits might say about what should be true, it is not a given that the United States' allies always have a high value for the alliance nor is it a given that particular allies always have a high (the UK) or low (France) value for the relationship.[7] Second, American administrations should give allies more influence. The cases show that the more influence allies have with the United States, the more they value the alliance. Granting allies influence means first granting their highest-ranking officials access to their American counterparts as often as possible. Granting influence also means changing policy in ways that take into account an ally's preferences or concerns. The United States should grant allies more influence on issues of importance to the allies and it should consult with allies in the lead-up to a potential use of force. Recall, for example, that George H. W. Bush made an important change to a January 1991 letter to Saddam Hussein as a result of feedback from François Mitterrand.[8]

178 • America's Allies and War

Of course, no American administration should make concessions to allies on issues of vital importance when they do not expect to get a significant contribution from an ally. However, American policymakers should not make the mistake of making a simple cost-benefit calculus and ignoring the ally if they do not need it at that moment. A look at alliance value across the cases shows that if an ally is denied influence in one instance, that experience has an impact on its alliance value assessment for the next instance of the use of force. The Chirac government experience of being excluded from U.S. decision making on Afghanistan contributed to a low alliance value assessment in the lead-up to the Iraq War.

The book's conclusions regarding threat and prestige also yield policy advice. Analysis of the extent to which the target threatens an ally's national interest and implicates its prestige is the single best way to know whether it is disposed to contribute. Such analysis can tell U.S. policymakers how likely an ally is to contribute and, thus, about the utility of offering influence or other incentives to persuade the state to contribute. In some cases an ally may have strong incentives to contribute regardless of alliance value (e.g., France and Somalia) whereas in other cases it may be a waste of U.S. time and effort to try to persuade an ally that has no interest or prestige incentive to contribute. The book also suggests that U.S. policymakers should try to construct the largest possible coalitions because when large coalitions appear likely, any fence-sitting states will be motivated to contribute rather than lose prestige relative to their peers.[9] Finally, U.S. policymakers may try to persuade allies (e.g., by exposing them to secret intelligence) that the use of force addresses a true threat to the ally's national interest. Leaders in Washington should be careful, however, to avoid publicly denigrating allies for their assessments and/or questioning their motives, neither of which will change the ally's decision and both of which are likely to worsen alliance value.

The preceding case analysis also provides some insight into how American policymakers should act with regard to allies' domestic political arena. In the period preceding the use of force, leaders in Washington should take note of the ally's domestic political scene, focusing on the opposition's stance on their government's provision of military support. If the public opposes a military contribution but the opposition supports it, the allied government can offer support and minimize the electoral fallout. This insight can help U.S. policymakers understand which allies feign domestic constraint and which are truly limited in their ability to provide support. While the United States can try to influence the decisions of the allied public and opposition, doing so may backfire. When the allied public and opposition make firm decisions to oppose support it is best for

Improving Transatlantic Alliance Burden-Sharing • 179

American leaders to stop pressuring the allied government to contribute as doing so is a recipe for electoral disaster.

In applying the lessons presented here, policymakers in Washington may confront a case wherein they have little prospect of getting more than a handful of allies to provide support. In such cases, the book's neoclassical realist explanation can facilitate a more thorough evaluation of whether force is the best option. Obviously, the calculus should begin with the American President and his advisers' assessment of the costs, benefits, and efficacy of the use of force relative to alternative means of attaining the same policy objective.[10] The cost-benefit analysis should not stop there, however. This book's framework makes possible a preliminary assessment of whether allies are likely to contribute, which alters the equation. If few or no allies provide military support, the United States has to bear the costs of action alone. If few or no allies join the U.S.-led effort, the operation will most likely suffer in terms of domestic and international legitimacy, as outlined in Chapter 1. Lower domestic and international legitimacy means that the operation will be less likely to be effective. Even if the operation is effective, its low international legitimacy will reflect poorly on the United States' image in the world and that should be seen as a negative externality (unintended consequence) of the action that should be included in the calculus of whether to use force. In short, when America cannot get its allies to go to war, it should consider whether war is such a good idea after all.

Notes

Chapter 1

1. For an overview, see Daniel F. Baltrusaitis, *Coalition Politics and the Iraq War: Determinants of Choice* (Boulder, CO: First Forum Press, 2010), 3–5.
2. Philip H. Gordon and Jeremy Shapiro, *Allies at War: America, Europe, and the Crisis over Iraq* (New York: McGraw Hill, 2004), 123, 150, 152.
3. Mancur Olson, Jr., and Richard Zeckhauser, "An Economic Theory of Alliances," *Review of Economics and Statistics* 48, no. 3 (August 1966): 266–79.
4. Todd Sandler and Keith Hartley, *The Political Economy of NATO: Past, Present, and into the 21st Century* (Cambridge: Cambridge University Press, 1999), 22–57.
5. For scholarship applying collective action problems to military operations, see Joseph Lepgold, "NATO's Post-Cold War Collective Action Problem," *International Security* 23, no. 1 (Summer 1998): 78–106.
6. Wallace J. Thies, *Why NATO Endures* (Cambridge: Cambridge University Press, 2009), 96–97.
7. Richard E. Rupp, *NATO after 9/11: An Alliance in Continuing Decline* (New York: Palgrave Macmillan, 2006), 100–101.
8. Robert Kagan, *Of Paradise and Power: America and Europe in the New World Order* (New York: Vintage Books, 2004), 98.
9. Rajan Menon, *End of Alliances* (Oxford: Oxford University Press, 2007).
10. Christopher A. Preble, *The Power Problem: How American Military Dominance Makes Us Less Safe, Less Prosperous, and Less Free* (Ithaca, NY: Cornell University Press, 2009).
11. Stephen J. Cimbala and Peter K. Forster, *Multinational Military Intervention: NATO Policy, Strategy and Burden Sharing* (Farnham: Ashgate, 2010).
12. "Security and Stability in Afghanistan," Hearing of the House Armed Services Committee, Washington, D.C., December 11, 2007.
13. Ibid. Admiral Mullen stressed that some allies were contributing well and he was cognizant of the political limits on allies' ability to contribute.
14. Andrew Purvis, "Coalition of the Unwilling," *Time*, March 26, 2008.

182 • Notes

15. Vincent Morelli and Paul Belkin, "NATO in Afghanistan: A Test of the Transatlantic Alliance," Congressional Research Service, Washington, D.C., December 3, 2009.

16. Frederik Logevall, "America Isolated: The Western Powers and the Escalation of the War," in *America, the Vietnam War, and the World: Comparative and International Perspectives,* ed. Andreas W. Daum, Lloyd C. Gardner, and Wilfried Mausbach (Cambridge: Cambridge University Press, 2003), 175–96.

17. David B. Ottaway, "French Troops Land in Beirut," *The Washington Post,* September 25, 1982; Richard W. Nelson, "Multinational Peacekeeping in the Middle East and the United Nations Model," in *The Multinational Force in Beirut 1982–1984,* ed. Anthony McDermott and Kjell Skjelsbaek (Miami: Florida International University Press, 1991), 13.

18. Joseph Lepgold, "Britain in Desert Storm: The Most Enthusiastic Partner," in *Friends in Need: Burden Sharing in the Persian Gulf War,* ed. Andrew Bennett, Joseph Lepgold, and Danny Unger (New York: St. Martin's Press, 1997), 70–71; Isabelle Grunberg, "Still a Reluctant Ally: France's Participation in the Gulf War Coalition," in *Friends in Need,* ed. Bennett, Lepgold, and Unger, 115; Lawrence Freedman and Efraim Karsh, *The Gulf Conflict, 1990–1991: Diplomacy and War in the New World Order* (Princeton, NJ: Princeton University Press, 1995), 356.

19. George Graham, "Bush Orders 28,000 Troops into Somalia to Aid Relief," *Financial Times,* December 5, 1992; Claudio Lindner, "'Pronti a partire', conferma Ando," *Corriere della Sera,* November 30, 1992.

20. John L. Hirsch and Robert B. Oakley, *Somalia and Operation Restore Hope: Reflections on Peacemaking and Peacekeeping* (Washington, D.C.: United States Institute of Peace Press, 1995), 45.

21. Ivo H. Daalder and Michael E. O'Hanlon, *Winning Ugly: NATO's War to Save Kosovo* (Washington, D.C.: Brookings Institution, 2000), 147–49.

22. Nora Bensahel, *The Counterterror Coalitions: Cooperation with Europe, NATO, and the European Union* (Santa Monica: RAND, 2003), 11, 57–58.

23. Wayne A. Silkett, "Alliance and Coalition Warfare," *Parameters* (Summer 1993): 74–85.

24. Glen Kessler, "United States Puts a Spin on Coalition Numbers," *The Washington Post,* March 21, 2003.

25. For the 2003 Iraq War, see "America's Image Further Erodes, Europeans Want Weaker Ties," Pew Global Attitudes Project, Washington, D.C., March 18, 2003, http://people-press.org/reports/pdf/175.pdf. For the Persian Gulf War, see Craig R. Whitney, "War in the Gulf: Europe; Polls Show Support for War, Even in Germany," *The New York Times,* January 29, 1991; Michael Inyon, "Broad Backing for 'Just War' Against Aggressor," *The Times* (London), February 5, 1991.

26. Kagan, *Of Paradise,* 150.

27. Jeremy Greenstock, "Oral Evidence Transcript," *The Iraq Inquiry,* London, November 27, 2009, 38, http://www.iraqinquiry.org.uk/transcripts.aspx.

Notes • 183

28. Jean-Marie Colombani and Walter Wells, *Dangerous De-Liaisons: What's Really Behind the War Between France and the U.S.* (Hoboken: Melville House, 2004), 124.

29. Patricia A. Weitsman, "Wartime Alliances Versus Coalition Warfare," *Strategic Studies Quarterly* (Summer 2010): 113–36.

30. William Drozdiak, "War Effort Restrained by Politics, Clark Says," *The Washington Post*, July 20, 1999. Anonymous interview, 3/30/09.

31. "International Security Assistance Force (ISAF): Key Facts and Figures," http://www.isaf.nato.int/images/stories/File/Placemats/Apr-16-2010-placemat.pdf.

32. For an example, see Jamie Findlater, "Italian Carabinieri to Begin Training Iraqi National Police Forces," *American Forces Press Service*, September 21, 2007, http://www.defense.gov/news/newsarticle.aspx?id=47526.

33. Steven Kull, "What Kind of Foreign Policy Does the American Public Want," Program on International Policy Attitudes, University of Maryland, October 20, 2006, http://www.worldpublicopinion.org/pipa/pdf/oct06/SecurityFP_Oct06_rpt.pdf.

34. James Addison Baker, *The Politics of Diplomacy: Revolution, War, and Peace, 1989–1992* (New York: Putnam, 1995), 278.

35. The book excludes the 1950–1953 Korean War because the U.S.-led effort was undertaken under United Nations auspices and Italy was not yet a member of the United Nations, so it was not possible for Italy to contribute.

36. The book excludes NATO's 1995 air strikes against Bosnia because of its limited duration (about three weeks) and small size (NATO aircraft flew roughly a tenth of the sorties in Bosnia that they flew in Kosovo).

37. Hugh Smith, "What Cost Will Democracies Bear? A Review of Popular Theories of Casualty Aversion," *Armed Forces and Society* 31, no. 4 (Summer 2005), 507.

38. A number of first-rate studies of U.S.-German relations exist in English. See, for example, Wolfram Hanrieder, *Germany, America, Europe: Forty Years of German Foreign Policy* (New Haven, CT: Yale University Press, 1991). No equivalent studies exist of U.S.-Italy relations since World War II.

39. A good example of a rigorous comparative study with Germany as one country among other Western democracies is Brian C. Rathbun, *Partisan Interventions: European Party Politics and Peace Enforcement in the Balkans* (Ithaca, NY: Cornell University Press, 2004).

40. Jason W. Davidson, "Italy-U.S. Relations since the End of the Cold War: Prestige, Peace, and the Transatlantic Balance," *Bulletin of Italian Politics* 1, no. 2 (2009): 289–308.

Chapter 2

1. Robert Kagan, *Of Paradise and Power: America and Europe in the New World Order* (New York: Vintage Books, 2004), 98. For a more complex perspective, see Vittorio Emanuele Parsi, *The Inevitable Alliance: Europe and the United States Beyond Iraq* (New York: Palgrave Macmillan, 2006).

184 • Notes

2. See, for example, Robert J. Lieber, *The American Era: Power and Strategy for the 21st Century* (Cambridge: Cambridge University Press, 2005).
3. Jean-Marie Colombani and Walter Wells, *Dangerous De-Liaisons: What's Really Behind the War Between France and the U.S.* (Hoboken: Melville House, 2004), 25.
4. See, for example, Colin L. Powell, "Interview on Fox News Sunday with Tony Snow," March 16, 2003, Washington, D.C., http://www.state.gov/secretary/former/powell/remarks/2003/18751.htm.
5. For a recent public articulation of this view, see "President Bush Participates in Joint Press Availability with Prime Minister Gordon Brown of the United Kingdom," April 17, 2008, Washington, D.C., http://www.whitehouse.gov/news/releases/2008/04/20080417-4.html. For an overview, see John Dumbrell, *A Special Relationship: Anglo-American Relations from the Cold War to Iraq,* 2nd ed. (Houndmills: Palgrave Macmillan, 2006).
6. See, for example, Elizabeth Pond, "The Dynamics of the Feud over Iraq," in *The Atlantic Alliance under Stress: U.S.-European Relations after Iraq,* ed. David M. Andrews (Cambridge: Cambridge University Press, 2005), 30–55.
7. See, for example, "Presidential Debate in Coral Gables, Florida," *Weekly Compilation of Presidential Documents* 40, no. 40 (Washington, D.C.: Government Printing Office, 2004), 2177.
8. Philip H. Gordon and Jeremy Shapiro, *Allies at War: America, Europe, and the Crisis over Iraq* (New York: McGraw Hill, 2004).
9. Andrew Bennett, Joseph Lepgold, and Danny Unger, "Burden-Sharing in the Persian Gulf War," *International Organization* 48, 1 (Winter 1994): 39–75.
10. Andrew Bennett, Joseph Lepgold, and Danny Unger, *Friends in Need: Burden Sharing in the Persian Gulf War* (New York: St. Martin's Press, 1997).
11. Ibid., 347–49.
12. David P. Auerswald, "Explaining Wars of Choice: An Integrated Decision Model of NATO Policy in Kosovo," *International Studies Quarterly* 48, no. 3 (September 2004): 631–62.
13. Ibid., 643–46.
14. Jürgen Schuster and Herbert Maier, "The Rift: Explaining Europe's Divergent Iraq Policies in the Run-Up of the American-Led War on Iraq," *Foreign Policy Analysis* 2, no. 3 (July 2006): 223–44.
15. Daniel F. Baltrusaitis, *Coalition Politics and the Iraq War: Determinants of Choice* (Boulder, CO: First Forum Press, 2010).
16. While I do not explicitly review literature that addresses related questions—such as that on contributions to peace operations and analysis of intervention decisions—I do incorporate it as I outline my argument. For peace operations, see Hirofumi Shimizu and Todd Sandler, "Peacekeeping and Burden-Sharing, 1994–2000," *Journal of Peace Research* 39, no. 6 (November 2002): 651–68. For intervention, see Brian C. Rathbun, *Partisan Interventions: European Party Politics and Peace Enforcement in the Balkans* (Ithaca, NY: Cornell University Press, 2004).

17. Gideon Rose, "Neoclassical Realism and Theories of Foreign Policy," *World Politics* 51 (October 1998): 144–72; Randall Schweller, "The Progressiveness of Neoclassical Realism," in *Progress in International Relations Theory: Appraising the Field,* ed. Colin Elman and Miriam Fendius Elman (Cambridge, MA: MIT Press, 2003); Brian Rathbun, "A Rose by Any Other Name: Neoclassical Realism as the Logical and Necessary Extension of Structural Realism," *Security Studies* 17, no. 2 (April–June 2008): 294–321.

18. In addition to the sources cited previously, see Charles A. Kupchan, "NATO and the Persian Gulf: Examining Intra-Alliance Behavior," *International Organization* 42, no. 2 (Spring 1988): 317–46.

19. The logic is similar to what Glenn Snyder refers to as entrapment. Glenn H. Snyder, "The Security Dilemma in Alliance Politics," *World Politics* 36 (July 1984), 467.

20. One might argue that states with low alliance value provide support to create value. This alternative is problematic. It requires the state to have faith that its support will increase its value to the ally and concomitantly change the latter in ways that increase the alliance's value for the former. While possible, this logic requires the smaller state to make real sacrifices today for future gains dependent on a complex series of contingent events. The case studies are the best judge of this alternative's merit.

21. For alliance dependence, see Bennett, Lepgold, and Unger, *Friends in Need.* Note: they draw their usage from Snyder, "The Security Dilemma in Alliance Politics," 471–73. For relative power, see Schuster and Maier, "The Rift."

22. One factor I do not consider here is whether the state has an alternative larger ally. See Snyder, "Security Dilemma in Alliance Politics," 472. Britain, France, and Italy did not have an alternative larger ally across the time period under study.

23. On the related concept of "tethering," see Patricia Weitsman, *Dangerous Alliances: Proponents of Peace, Weapons of War* (Stanford: Stanford University Press, 2004), 21–24.

24. Kenneth N. Waltz, *Theory of International Politics* (New York: McGraw Hill, 1979), 118.

25. Stephen M. Walt, *The Origins of Alliances* (Ithaca, NY: Cornell University Press, 1987).

26. The logic is similar to bandwagoning (i.e., allying with the stronger coalition). Waltz, *Theory of International Politics,* 126.

27. It may be difficult to influence a unipolar ally. Stephen M. Walt, "Alliances in a Unipolar World," *World Politics* 61, no. 1 (January 2009): 86–120.

28. For analysis, see Richard N. Haass, rev. ed., *Intervention: The Use of American Military Force in the Post–Cold War World* (Washington, D.C.: Brookings Institution Press, 1999), 71. Perhaps the clearest recent policy pronouncement was the Clinton administration's PDD-25. See http://www.fas.org/irp/offdocs/pdd25.htm.

186 • Notes

29. My definition of national interest builds on Daryl Press's notion of "important interests." Daryl G. Press, *Calculating Credibility: How Leaders Assess Military Threats* (Ithaca, NY: Cornell University Press, 2005), 26–27.

30. If the target were such an existential threat, the state would be forced to respond—it would not have the luxury of choosing whether to provide or refuse military support. Moreover, none of the governments viewed any of the seven targets of U.S.-led intervention as existential threats.

31. It also makes sense to expect the United States to structure missions with the cost limitations (relative to national interest) of the contributing parties in mind.

32. "Transcript of President's Address on Somalia," *The New York Times*, December 5, 1992.

33. Robert Gilpin, *War and Change in World Politics* (Cambridge: Cambridge University Press, 1981), 30–33. For a historical review of the importance of prestige in states' motivations, see Evan Luard, *Types of International Society* (New York: The Free Press, 1976), 147–69. For research on rank and peace operations, see Laura Neack, "UN Peace-Keeping: In the Interest of Community or Self?" *Journal of Peace Research* 32, no. 2 (May 1995): 181–96.

34. Anthony Downs, *An Economic Theory of Democracy* (New York: Harper Collins, 1957), 28.

35. Jon Western, *Selling Intervention and War: The Presidency, the Media, and the American Public* (Baltimore: Johns Hopkins University Press, 2005).

36. The basis for this idea is Downs, *Economic Theory*, 54.

37. It would be—ceteris paribus—rational for the opposition to do so. Kurt Taylor Gaubatz, *Elections and War: The Electoral Incentive in the Democratic Politics of War and Peace* (Stanford: Stanford University Press, 1999), 78.

38. On the notorious lack of public attention to foreign affairs, see Richard Sobel, *The Impact of Public Opinion on U.S. Foreign Policy since Vietnam* (Oxford: Oxford University Press, 2001), 12.

39. For related claims, see ibid., 15; Joe D. Hagan, *Political Opposition and Foreign Policy in Comparative Perspective* (Boulder, CO: Lynne Rienner, 1993), 91.

40. On the timing of elections and the use of force, see Miroslav Nincic, "Elections and U.S. Foreign Policy," in *The Domestic Sources of American Foreign Policy: Insights and Evidence,* ed. Eugene R. Wittkopf and James M. McCormick, 4th ed. (Lanham: Rowman and Littlefield, 2004), 117–27. See also, Gaubatz, *Elections and War.*

41. One might ask why the government is not more concerned with pleasing its base. The government's base is less significant for the outcome because they are less likely to vote for the opposition (though they may abstain, this is less dangerous for the government than swing voters because when the government loses a base voter the opposition does not gain one).

42. Some research suggests that elite consensus makes public support for the use of force more likely. Eric V. Larson, *Casualties and Consensus: The Historical Role of Casualties in Domestic Support for U.S. Military Operations* (Santa Monica: RAND, 1996).

Notes • 187

43. The aforementioned government logic is different—an opposed, electorally relevant public is a fait accompli the government must concede to or suffer the consequences.

44. On the importance of party history and platform, see Rathbun, *Partisan Interventions*.

45. For a critique of neoclassical realist scholarship on similar grounds, see Jeffrey W. Legro and Andrew Moravcsik, "Is Anybody Still a Realist?" *International Security* 24, no. 2 (Fall 1999): 5–55.

46. On the relative importance of realist to non-realist factors, see Rathbun, "A Rose," 303.

47. On a realist logic for the relationship of the variables, see ibid., 300.

48. Rose, "Neoclassical Realism," 146. See also, Schweller, "Progressiveness," 325–32.

49. Taliaferro, Lobell, and Ripsman write (p. 25) that "systemic forces ultimately drive external behavior" but that societal forces may stand between systemic imperatives and outcomes. In *Neoclassical Realism, the State, and Foreign Policy,* ed. Steven E. Lobell, Norrin M. Ripsman, and Jeffrey W. Taliaferro (Cambridge: Cambridge University Press, 2009).

50. Randall L. Schweller, *Unanswered Threats: Political Constraints on the Balance of Power* (Princeton, NJ: Princeton University Press, 2006), 63–66.

51. For a recent scholarship on prestige from realist and non-realist perspectives, see William C. Wohlforth, "Unipolarity, Status Competition, and Great Power War," *World Politics* 61, no. 1 (January 2009): 28–57; Deborah Welch Larson and Alexei Schevchenko, "Status Seekers: Chinese and Russian Responses to U.S. Primacy," *International Security* 34, no. 4 (Spring 2010): 63–95.

52. One might ask why I do not instead evaluate an alternative explanation stressing the party/coalition in power like Rathbun's *Partisan Interventions*. The party explanation does not provide a plausible explanation of the cases. In most cases the government and opposition agreed on whether their country should provide support.

53. For an overview, see Alexander Wendt, "Constructing International Politics," *International Security* 20, no. 1 (Summer 1995): 71–81.

54. See, for example, Michael N. Barnett, "Identity and Alliances in the Middle East," and Thomas Risse-Kappen, "Collective Identity in a Democratic Community," in *The Culture of National Security: Norms and Identity in World Politics,* ed. Peter Katzenstein (New York: Columbia University Press, 1996); Chrisopher Hemmer and Peter J. Katzenstein, "Why is There No NATO in Asia? Collective Identity, Regionalism, and the Origins of Multilateralism," *International Organization* 56, 3 (Summer 2002): 575–607; and Jae-Jung Suh, *Power, Interest, and Identity in Military Alliances* (New York: Palgrave Macmillan, 2007).

55. Martha Finnemore, *National Interests in International Society* (Ithaca, NY: Cornell University Press, 1996), 85–88.

188 • Notes

56. For a description of these methods, see Stephen Van Evera, *Guide to Methods for Students of Political Science* (Ithaca, NY: Cornell University Press, 1997), 58–67.

Chapter 3

1. Sylvia Ellis, *Britain, America, and the Vietnam War* (Westport, CT: Praeger, 2004), 4–5.
2. Ibid., 7.
3. Ibid., 3.
4. Ibid., 4–5. See also, Logevall, "America Isolated: The Western Powers and the Escalation of the War," in *America, the Vietnam War, and the World: Comparative and International Perspectives,* ed. Andreas W. Daum, Lloyd C. Gardner, and Wilfried Mausbach (Cambridge: Cambridge University Press, 2003), 183.
5. For U.S. requests and British responses, see Ellis, *Britain, America, and the Vietnam War,* 115, 116, 123, 164, 168.
6. Ibid., 173. In addition to political support the British had a small training mission in South Vietnam. Ellis, *Britain, America, and the Vietnam War,* 2–3.
7. Alan P. Dobson, *Anglo-American Relations in the Twentieth Century* (London: Routledge, 1995), 137.
8. David Sanders, *Losing an Empire, Finding a Role: British Foreign Policy since 1945* (Houndmills: Palgrave, 1990), 171.
9. Dobson, *Anglo-American Relations,* 128. Sanders, *Losing an Empire,* 173.
10. Thomas Alan Schwartz, *Lyndon Johnson and Europe: In the Shadow of Vietnam* (Cambridge: Harvard University Press, 2003), 81–83.
11. See Dobson, *Anglo-American Relations,* 68; Schwartz, *Lyndon Johnson and Europe,* 68; Ellis, *Britain, America, and the Vietnam War,* 19. See also, Jonathan Colman, *A 'Special Relationship'? Harold Wilson, Lyndon B. Johnson and Anglo-American Relations 'at the summit,' 1964–68* (Manchester: Manchester University Press, 2004), 49–50.
12. Harold Wilson, *The Labour Government, 1964–1970: A Personal Record* (London: Weidenfeld and Nicolson, 1971), 50.
13. Logevall, "America Isolated," 184.
14. Wilson, *Labour Government,* 80. See also Ellis, *Britain, America, and the Vietnam War,* 50.
15. Johnson administration officials knew that the left wing of Wilson's Labour party was vehemently opposed to the war. Schwartz, *Lyndon Johnson and Europe,* 86.
16. Ellis, *Britain, America, and the Vietnam War,* 28. See also ibid., xv.
17. Sanders, *Losing an Empire,* 175. See also, Dean Rusk and Daniel S. Papp, *As I Saw It* (New York: W.W. Norton, 1990), 455.
18. Ellis, *Britain, America, and the Vietnam War,* 95. See also p. 174.
19. Logevall, "America Isolated," 183.

Notes • 189

20. Schwartz, *Lyndon Johnson and Europe,* 12; Ellis, *Britain, America, and the Vietnam War,* 1.
21. Wilson, *The Labour Government,* 42.
22. Ellis, *Britain, America, and the Vietnam War,* 100. Ellis notes that an April 1965 poll measured the first majority opposed to the U.S.-led war.
23. Ellis, *Britain, America, and the Vietnam War,* 60. See also p. 28.
24. Ellis, *Britain, America, and the Vietnam War,* 128. See also pp. 97 and 172. Colman, *A 'Special Relationship'?* 58–59.
25. Schwartz, *Lyndon Johnson and Europe,* 86.
26. Vietnam was not a major issue in the elections. Ellis, *Britain, America, and the Vietnam War,* 153.
27. Ibid., 29.
28. Colman, *A 'Special Relationship'?* 42.
29. Ibid.
30. Ellis, *Britain, America, and the Vietnam War,* 29.
31. Ibid., 270.
32. Ibid.
33. Charles de Gaulle, *Memoirs of Hope: Renewal and Endeavor* (New York: Simon and Schuster, 1971), 256.
34. Rusk and Papp, *As I Saw It,* 454.
35. Charles G. Cogan, *Oldest Allies, Guarded Friends: The United States and France since 1940* (Westport, CT: Praeger, 1994), 132–33.
36. Jean Doise and Maurice Vaïsse, *Politique étrangère de la France: Diplomatie et outil militaire, 1871–1991* (Paris: Éditions du Seuil, 1992), 538.
37. Frédéric Bozo, *La politique étrangère de la France depuis 1945* (Paris: La Découverte, 1997), 28–29.
38. Bozo, *La politique étrangère de la France depuis 1945,* 42.
39. Schwartz, *Lyndon Johnson and Europe,* 13. See also, Doise and Vaïsse, *Politique étrangère de la France,* 179.
40. Schwartz, *Lyndon Johnson and Europe,* 14.
41. Frank Costigliola, "The Vietnam War and the Challenges to American Power in Europe," in *International Perspectives on Vietnam,* ed. Lloyd C. Gardner and Ted Gittinger (College Station: Texas A&M University Press, 1999), 144.
42. France continued to derive value from the North Atlantic Treaty. Stanley Hoffman, *Decline or Renewal: France since the 1930s* (New York: Viking Press, 1974), 319.
43. Logevall, "America Isolated," 180. See also, Yuko Torikata, "Reexamining de Gaulle's Peace Initiative on the Vietnam War," *Diplomatic History* 31, no. 5 (November 2007), 919.
44. Marianna Sullivan, *France's Vietnam Policy: A Study in French-American Relations* (Westport, CT: Greenwood, 1978), 12, 26.
45. De Gaulle, *Memoirs of Hope,* 200.
46. Logevall, "America Isolated," 180.

190 • Notes

47. De Gaulle, *Memoirs of Hope,* 256. See also, Torikata, "Reexamining de Gaulle's Peace Initiative," 915–16.
48. Torikata, "Reexamining de Gaulle's Peace Initiative," 923. See also p. 918, 934.
49. Costigliola, "The Vietnam War," 150. See also, Sullivan, *France's Vietnam Policy,* 25–26.
50. De Gaulle, *Memoirs of Hope,* 171; Hoffman, *Decline or Renewal,* 283; Bozo, *La politique étrangère de la France depuis 1945,* 3.
51. Cogan, *Oldest Allies, Guarded Friends,* 3; Doise and Vaïsse, *Politique étrangère de la France,* 553; Torikata, "Reexamining de Gaulle's Peace Initiative," 914.
52. Torikata, "Reexamining de Gaulle's Peace Initiative," 913, 922.
53. Sullivan, *France's Vietnam Policy,* 27. See also p. xii.
54. Ibid., 78.
55. Ibid., 75.
56. Ibid., 78.
57. Philip H. Gordon, *A Certain Idea of France: French Security Policy and the Gaullist Legacy* (Princeton, NJ: Princeton University Press, 1993), 15.
58. Alistair Horne, *A Savage War of Peace: Algeria 1954–1962* (London: Pan Books, 1977).
59. Logevall, "America Isolated," 187–88.
60. Luigi Vittorio Ferraris, *Manuale della politica estera italiana, 1947–1993* (Roma: Laterza, 1996), 138. Leo J. Wollemborg, *Stars, Stripes and Italian Tricolor: The United States and Italy, 1946–1989* (New York: Praeger, 1990), 113, 117.
61. Leopoldo Nuti, "The Center-Left Government in Italy and the Escalation of the Vietnam War," in *America, the Vietnam War, and the World,* ed. Daum, Gardner, and Mausbach, 170–76.
62. Wollemborg, *Stars, Stripes and Italian Tricolor,* 21–22.
63. Ibid., 46.
64. Giuseppe Mammarella and Paolo Cacace, *La politica estera dell'Italia. Dallo Stato unitario ai giorni nostri* (Roma: Laterza, 2006), 218. See also Sergio Romano, *Guida alla politica estera italiana. Da Badoglio a Berlusconi* (Milano: BUR, 2004), 127.
65. Mammarella and Cacace, *La politica estera dell'Italia,* 219.
66. Wollemborg, *Stars, Stripes and Italian Tricolor,* 39. See also Ferraris, *Manuale della politica estera italiana,* 135.
67. Wollemborg, *Stars, Stripes and Italian Tricolor,* 80–81.
68. Mammarella and Cacace, *La politica estera dell'Italia,* 215; Wollemborg, *Stars, Stripes and Italian Tricolor,* 98.
69. Ferraris, *Manuale della politica estera italiana,* 192. Mario Sica, *Marigold non fiorì. Il contributo italiano alla pace in Vietnam* (Firenze: Ponte alle Grazie, 1991), 31, 32.
70. Wollemborg, *Stars, Stripes and Italian Tricolor,* 113.
71. Ferraris, *Manuale della politica estera italiana,* 191.
72. Wollemborg, *Stars, Stripes and Italian Tricolor,* 118–19. See Logevall, "America Isolated," 192.

Notes • 191

73. Nuti, "The Center-Left Government in Italy," 266–68; Ferraris, *Manuale della politica estera italiana,* 138–39.
74. Sica, *Marigold non fiorì. Il contributo italiano alla pace in Vietnam*, 48–49.
75. Ferraris, *Manuale della politica estera italiana,* 191.
76. Ibid., 191.
77. Mammarella and Cacace, *La politica estera dell'Italia,* 106. See Nuti, "The Center-Left Government in Italy," 265. Sica, *Marigold non fiorì. Il contributo italiano alla pace in Vietnam,* 30.
78. Paul Ginsborg, *A History of Contemporary Italy: Society and Politics, 1943–1988* (London: Penguin, 1990), 442.
79. Ferraris, *Manuale della politica estera italiana,* 174.
80. Nuti, "The Center-Left Government in Italy," 266; Wollemborg, *Stars, Stripes and Italian Tricolor,* 113, 117.
81. For a good overview, see Richard W. Nelson, "Multinational Peacekeeping in the Middle East and the United Nations Model," in *The Multinational Force in Beirut 1982–1984,* ed. Anthony McDermott and Kjell Skjelsbaek (Miami: Florida International University Press, 1991).
82. J. A. Kenney and Peter Woolley, "Some Lessons from British Participation," in *The Multinational Force in Beirut*, ed. McDermott and Skjelsbaek, 159.
83. Paul Sharp, *Thatcher's Diplomacy: The Revival of British Foreign Policy* (New York: St. Martin's Press, 1999), 105.
84. Ibid., 107.
85. See Margaret Thatcher, *The Downing Street Years* (London: Harper Collins, 1993), 253–56. See also, George P. Shultz, *Turmoil and Triumph: My Years as Secretary of State* (New York: Charles Scribner's Sons, 1993), 135–45.
86. Sharp, *Thatcher's Diplomacy,* 101.
87. "Britain Asked to Send Troops to Lebanon," *The Times* (London), November 8, 1982.
88. Henry Stanhope, "Small British Team May Go to Beirut," *The Times* (London), November 16, 1982.
89. John Dumbrell, *A Special Relationship: Anglo-American Relations from the Cold War to Iraq,* 2nd ed. (Houndmills: Palgrave Macmillan, 2006), 108.
90. Sanders, *Losing an Empire,* 232.
91. Kenny and Woolley, "Some Lessons from British Participation," 160.
92. Percy Cradock, *In Pursuit of British Interests: Reflections on Foreign Policy under Margaret Thatcher and John Major* (London: John Murray, 1997), 160.
93. "Lebanon Needs Help," *The Times* (London), October 22, 1982.
94. Thatcher, *Downing Street Years,* 334. See also 327, 328, and John Campbell, *Margaret Thatcher: The Iron Lady* (London: Vintage, 2008), 337.
95. See "Britain Asked to Send Troops to Lebanon," Stanhope, "Small British Team," and Henry Stanhope, "Lebanon Peace Force 'Will Double in Two Weeks,'" *The Times* (London), December 11, 1982.
96. "House of Commons PQs," June 22, 1982, http://www.margaretthatcher.org/.
97. Stanhope, "Small British team."

192 • Notes

98. Margaret Thatcher, "TV Interview for CBS *Morning News*," June 23, 1982, http://www.margaretthatcher.org/.
99. Sharp, *Thatcher's Diplomacy*, 25.
100. Ibid., 63, 67.
101. Ibid., 68. See also, p. 95.
102. *The Times* "Lebanon Needs Help."
103. "No Power, No Peacekeeping," *The Times* (London), December 8, 1982.
104. Kenny and Woolley, "Some Lessons from British Participation," 160.
105. Sharp, *Thatcher's Diplomacy*, 99.
106. Ibid., 74–84.
107. See Geoffrey Kemp, "The American Peacekeeping Role in Lebanon," in *Multinational Force*, ed. McDermott and Skjelsbaek, 232. See also Sanders, *Losing an Empire*, 232.
108. Nelson, "Multinational Peacekeeping," 12.
109. Pia Christina Wood, "The Diplomacy of Peacekeeping: France and the Multinational Forces to Lebanon, 1982–84," *International Peacekeeping* 5, no. 2 (Summer 1998): 19–37.
110. Shultz, *Turmoil and Triumph*, 46, 63.
111. Hubert Védrine, *Les mondes de François Mitterrand. À l'Élysée 1981–1995* (Paris: Fayard, 1996), 321.
112. Nelson, "Multinational Peacekeeping," 11. Steven Rattner, "300 Legionnaires Given Send-Off for Beirut," *The New York Times*, August 20, 1982.
113. François Mitterrand, *Réflexions sur la politique extérieure de la France* (Paris: Fayard, 1986), 9. See also Jean Lacouture, *Mitterrand: Une histoire de Français II, Les vertiges du sommet* (Paris: Seuil, 1998), 141.
114. Evan Galbraith, *Ambassador in Paris: The Reagan Years* (Washington, D.C.: Regnery Gateway, 1987), 114.
115. Roland Dumas, *Affaires étrangères I, 1981–1988* (Paris: Fayard, 2007), 78. See also Lacouture, *Mitterrand*, 149.
116. Lacouture, *Mitterrand*, 149.
117. Ibid., 147. See also, Dumas, *Affaires étrangères I*, 78; Galbraith, *Ambassador in Paris*, 14.
118. Wood, "The Diplomacy of Peacekeeping," 20.
119. Ibid., 23.
120. Anthony McDermott and Kjell Skjelsbaek, "The Ambiguous Role of France," in *Multinational Force*, ed. McDermott and Skjelsbaek, 143.
121. Védrine, *Les mondes de François Mitterrand*, 321.
122. Wood, "The Diplomacy of Peacekeeping," 20.
123. Claude Cheysson, "Mitterrand, La Guerre du Golfe et L'Islamisme: Témoignages et interventions," in *Mitterrand et la sortie de la guerre froide*, ed. Samy Cohen (Paris: Presses Universitaires de France, 1998), 349.
124. Védrine, *Les mondes de François Mitterrand*, 308.
125. Ibid., 321.
126. McDermott and Skjelsbaek, *Multinational Force*, 144.

127. Lacouture, *Mitterrand,* 202, 204.
128. Ghassan Salamé, "Globalisme et régionalisme dans la politique mitterrandienne de l'après-guerre froide," in *Mitterrand et la sortie de la guerre froide*, ed. Cohen, 226.
129. Wood, "The Diplomacy of Peacekeeping," 19–20.
130. Ibid., 20.
131. Védrine, *Les mondes de François Mitterrand,* 317.
132. Lacouture, *Mitterrand,* 196, 206. See also Védrine, *Les mondes de François Mitterrand,* 312, 313.
133. Shultz, *Turmoil and Triumph*, 68–69.
134. Rattner, "300 Legionnaires."
135. Védrine, *Les mondes de François Mitterrand,* 314.
136. Shultz, *Turmoil and Triumph*, 106.
137. John Vincour, "Doubts in Lebanon," *The New York Times*, September 24, 1983.
138. Ibid.
139. John Vincour, "Mitterrand's Global Role Troubles His Supporters," *The New York Times*, October 9, 1983.
140. Védrine, *Les mondes de François Mitterrand,* 306. See also McDermott and Skjelsbaek, *Multinational Force,* 144.
141. Bassma Kodmani-Darwish, "François Mitterrand face aux défis de l'islamisme," in *Mitterrand*, ed. Cohen, 306.
142. Kodmani-Darwish, "François Mitterrand face aux défis de l'islamisme," 306; McDermott and Skjelsbaek, *Multinational Force,* 144.
143. McDermott and Skjelsbaek, *Multinational Force,* 144.
144. Wood, "The Diplomacy of Peacekeeping," 25.
145. Shultz, *Turmoil and Triumph*, 63.
146. McDermott and Skjelsbaek, *Multinational Force,* 143. See also Mitterrand, *Réflexions*, 113.
147. McDermott and Skjelsbaek, *Multinational Force,* 145–46.
148. Ibid., 144.
149. Nelson, "Multinational Peacekeeping," 11.
150. Ferraris, *Manuale della politica estera italiana,* 384.
151. Mammarella and Cacace, *La politica estera dell'Italia,* 245.
152. Carlo M. Santoro, *La Politica Estera di una Media Potenza: L'Italia dall'Unità ad oggi* (Bologna: Il Mulino, 1991), 182.
153. Mammarella and Cacace, *La politica estera dell'Italia,* 241–43; Romano, *Guida alla politica estera*, 208.
154. Mammarella and Cacace, *La politica estera dell'Italia,* 242.
155. Ibid., 243–44. See also Ferraris, *Manuale della politica estera italiana,* 348.
156. Ferraris, *Manuale della politica estera italiana,* 318. Giovanni Spadolini, *L'Italia Nell'Occidente* Vol. II (Roma: Edizione La Voce, 1984), 14–15.
157. Mammarella and Cacace, *La politica estera dell'Italia,* 243.
158. Ferraris, *Manuale della politica estera italiana,* 384.

194 • Notes

159. Valter Coralluzzo, *La Politica Estera Dell'Italia Repubblicana (1946–1992)* (Milano: FrancoAngeli, 2000), 294.

160. Ibid., 297.

161. Ferraris, *Manuale della politica estera italiana,* 350.

162. Franco Angioni and Maurizio Cremasco, "Italy's Role in Peacekeeping Operations," in *The Multinational Force in Beirut,* ed. McDermott and Skjelsbaek, 150.

163. Ferraris, *Manuale della politica estera italiana,* 378.

164. It was also a less competitive arena for engagement than central Europe. Romano, *Guida alla politica estera,* 214.

165. Spadolini, *L'Italia Nell'Occidente,* Vol. II, 10.

166. Santoro, *La Politica,* 213.

167. Spadolini, *L'Italia Nell'Occidente,* Vol. II, 17. See also p. 24.

168. Ferraris, *Manuale della politica estera italiana,* 377.

169. Angioni and Cremasco, "Italy's Role in Peacekeeping Operations," 150.

170. Rattner, "300 Legionnaires."

171. Ferraris, *Manuale della politica estera italiana,* 378.

172. Spadolini, *L'Italia Nell'Occidente,* Vol. I, 41–43. See also p. 242.

173. Angioni and Cremasco, "Italy's Role in Peacekeeping Operations," 151.

174. Ferraris, *Manuale della politica estera italiana,* 384.

175. Ibid., 318, 320.

176. Stefano Folli, "Prefazione" in Spadolini, *L'Italia Nell'Occidente,* Vol. I, 12–13.

177. Mammarella and Cacace, *La politica estera dell'Italia,* 244. See also Spadolini, *L'Italia Nell'Occidente,* Vol. II, 24, 27.

178. Mammarella and Cacace, *La politica estera dell'Italia,* 244.

179. Rattner, "300 Legionnaires."

180. Shultz, *Turmoil and Triumph,* 106.

181. Rattner, "300 Legionnaires."

182. Coralluzzo, *La Politica Estera Dell'Italia Repubblicana,* 295.

183. Ibid. See also, Mammarella and Cacace, *La politica estera dell'Italia,* 244.

184. Santoro, *La Politica,* 207.

185. Angioni and Cremasco, "Italy's Role in Peacekeeping Operations," 150.

186. Coralluzzo, *La Politica Estera Dell'Italia Repubblicana,* 294.

187. Nelson, "Multinational Peacekeeping," 12–13.

188. Alessandro Massai, "Il Controllo Parlamentare e le Operazioni della Forza di Pace," a cura di Alessandro Migliazzi, *Le Forze Multinazionali nel Libano e nel Sinai* (Milano: Giuffrè, 1988), 152–53.

189. Ibid., 154, 159–60.

190. Nelson, "Multinational Peacekeeping," 13.

191. Lepgold, "Britain in Desert Storm," 70–71.

192. Campbell, *Margaret Thatcher,* 666.

193. Freedman and Karsh, Lawrence Freedman and Efraim Karsh, *The Gulf Conflict, 1990–1991: Diplomacy and War in the New World Order* (Princeton, NJ: Princeton University Press, 1995), 90.

194. Ibid., 111.
195. Ibid., 149. While the Thatcher government committed British troops, John Major oversaw the war itself. John Major, *The Autobiography* (New York: Harper Collins, 2007), 224.
196. Cradock, *In Pursuit of British Interests*, 26. For an American assessment, see James Addison Baker, *The Politics of Diplomacy: Revolution, War, and Peace, 1989–1992* (New York: Putnam, 1995), 279.
197. Ibid., 27. See also p. 51–53.
198. Cradock, *In Pursuit of British Interests,* 41.
199. For arms control concerns, see Cradock, *In Pursuit of British Interests,* 84–85.
200. Thatcher, *Downing Street Years*, 820.
201. Freedman and Karsh, *The Gulf Conflict,* 113.
202. Campbell, *Margaret Thatcher,* 665.
203. Cradock, *In Pursuit of British Interests,* 180.
204. Lepgold, "Britain in Desert Storm," 73.
205. Thatcher, *Downing Street Years*, 817.
206. Cradock, *In Pursuit of British Interests,* 171.
207. Campbell, *Margaret Thatcher,* 664.
208. Cradock, *In Pursuit of British Interests,* 28.
209. Thatcher, *Downing Street Years*, 173.
210. Lepgold, "Britain in Desert Storm," 75. See also Dobson, *Anglo-American Relations,* 151.
211. Lepgold, "Britain in Desert Storm," 84.
212. Ibid., 69–70.
213. Ibid., 82.
214. Steven Prokesch, "WAR IN THE GULF: BRITAIN; British Chief Assails Hussein, Saying He Is 'Without Pity,'" *The New York Times*, January 23, 1991. See also, Freedman and Karsh, *The Gulf Conflict,* 346.
215. Freedman and Karsh, *The Gulf Conflict,* 347.
216. Ibid.
217. Freedman and Karsh, *The Gulf Conflict,* 110.
218. Campbell, *Margaret Thatcher,* 663.
219. Douglas Hurd, *Memoirs* (London: Abacus, 2003), 431.
220. Cradock, *In Pursuit of British Interests,* 175. Emphasis added.
221. Thatcher, *Downing Street Years*, 817.
222. Ibid., 821.
223. http://www.un.org/en/documents/charter/chapter7.shtml.
224. Campbell, *Margaret Thatcher,* 663.
225. Cradock, *In Pursuit of British Interests,* 172.
226. Thatcher, *Downing Street Years*, 817.
227. Campbell, *Margaret Thatcher,* 664.
228. Baker, *The Politics of Diplomacy,* 278.
229. Freedman and Karsh, *The Gulf Conflict,* 167, 238, 261, 264–67, 270–74.

196 • Notes

230. Isabelle Grunberg, "Still a Reluctant Ally: France's Participation in the Gulf War Coalition," in *Friends in Need*, ed. Bennett, Lepgold, and Unger, 115.

231. Freedman and Karsh, *The Gulf Conflict,* 349.

232. Grunberg, "Still a Reluctant Ally," 123.

233. Pascal Boniface, "Révolution stratégique mondiale, continuité et inflexions de la politique française de sécurité," in *Mitterrand et la sortie de la guerre froide,* ed. Samy Cohen (Paris: Presses Universitaires de France, 1998), 157–85.

234. Ibid., 176.

235. George H. W. Bush and Brent Scowcroft, *A World Transformed* (New York: Knopf, 1998), 267.

236. Grunberg, "Still a Reluctant Ally," 126–27.

237. Baker, *The Politics of Diplomacy,* 371.

238. Salamé, "Globalisme et régionalisme dans la politique mitterrandienne de l'après-guerre froide," in *Mitterrand*, ed. Cohen, 236.

239. Denis Lacorne, "Le rang de la France: Mitterrand et la guerre du Golfe," in *Mitterrand*, ed. Cohen, 333.

240. Grunberg, "Still a Reluctant Ally," 119.

241. Ibid., 121.

242. Hubert Védrine, *Les mondes de François Mitterrand. À l'Élysée 1981–1995* (Paris: Fayard, 1996), 524.

243. For a contrasting perspective, see Lacorne, "Le rang de la France," 324–25.

244. Védrine, *Les mondes de François Mitterrand,* 526. See also pp. 524, 533.

245. Claude Cheysson, "Mitterrand, La Guerre du Golfe et L'Islamisme: Témonages et interventions," in *Mitterrand*, ed. Cohen, 348. See also Lionel Jospin, *Le temps de répondre. Entretiens avec Alain Duhamel* (Paris: Stock, 2002), 66.

246. Bush and Scowcroft, *A World Transformed,* 326. See also Baker, *The Politics of Diplomacy,* 314.

247. Bush and Scowcroft, *A World Transformed,* 127.

248. Grunberg, "Still a Reluctant Ally," 235. See also Lacorne, "Le rang de la France," 340.

249. Védrine, *Les mondes de François Mitterrand,* 527. See also Bozo, *La politique étrangère de la France depuis 1945,* 98.

250. Salamé, "Globalisme et régionalisme dans la politique mitterrandienne de l'après-guerre froide," 235.

251. Freedman and Karsh, *The Gulf Conflict,* 117; Lacorne, "Le rang de la France," 335; Grunberg, "Still a Reluctant Ally," 117.

252. Lacorne, "Le rang de la France," 337.

253. Ibid., 338–39.

254. Ibid., 335.

255. Cogan, *Oldest Allies, Guarded Friends,* 4.

256. Védrine, *Les mondes de François Mitterrand,* 523.

257. Grunberg, "Still a Reluctant Ally," 128.

258. Natalie La Balme, "L'influence de l'opinion publique dans la gestion des crises," in *Mitterrand*, ed. Cohen, 415. See also Freedman and Karsh, *The Gulf Conflict,* 352.

259. Védrine, *Les mondes de François Mitterrand,* 540.

260. Grunberg, "Still a Reluctant Ally," 128.

261. Ibid., 128.

262. Védrine, *Les mondes de François Mitterrand,* 524.

263. Lacorne, "Le rang de la France," 343.

264. Védrine, *Les mondes de François Mitterrand,* 527. See also p. 524.

265. Baker, *The Politics of Diplomacy,* 298.

266. Coralluzzo, *La Politica Estera Dell'Italia Repubblicana,* 311–12; Freedman and Karsh, *The Gulf Conflict,* 356.

267. Virgilio Ilari, "La politica militare italiana," *L'Italia nella politica internazionale* (Bologna: Il Mulino, 1991), 273.

268. A senior U.S. official at the Rome Embassy told me with regard to the Gulf War that " . . . we regarded the Italian decision as a major one." Anonymous interview, 3/5/08. For criticisms that Italy did not provide ground troops, see Mammarella and Cacace, *La politica estera dell'Italia,* 252. See also Coralluzzo, *La Politica Estera Dell'Italia Repubblicana,* 309, 335–36. There is some debate on the question of Italian ground troops. Valter Coralluzzo (p. 327) argues that the United States sought Italian ground troops and Italy was technically able to provide them. Giampiero Giacomello and Fabrizio Coticchia point out, however, that the United States had no more need for light troops, which was all Italy had. Giampiero Giacomello and Fabrizio Coticchia, "In Harm's Way: Why and When a Modern Democracy Risks the Lives of Its Uniformed Citizens," *European Security* 16, no. 2 (June 2007), 181.

269. Coralluzzo, *La Politica Estera Dell'Italia Repubblicana,* 331. For other instances, see ibid., 321; Freedman and Karsh, *The Gulf Conflict,* 261, 262, 271.

270. For reasons why Italy should not have valued its relationship with the United States, see Sergio Romano, *Lo scambio ineguale. Italia e Stati Uniti da Wilson a Clinton* (Rome, Laterza, 1995), 68–71.

271. Baker, *The Politics of Diplomacy,* 604.

272. Bush and Scowcroft, *A World Transformed,* 294.

273. Coralluzzo, *La Politica Estera Dell'Italia Repubblicana,* 311. See also p. 314.

274. Ibid., 322.

275. Ibid., 308.

276. Anonymous interview, 3/5/08.

277. Coralluzzo, *La Politica Estera Dell'Italia Repubblicana,* 310.

278. Jeffrey R. Lord and Kristin M. Lord, "Additional Cases from the Gulf Crisis and Burden Sharing in UNPROFOR," in *Friends in Need*, ed. Bennett, Lepgold, and Unger, 331.

279. Coralluzzo, *La Politica Estera Dell'Italia Repubblicana,* 311. See also p. 322.

280. Ibid., 333.

281. See Baker, *The Politics of Diplomacy,* 195.

282. For Germany, see Gunther Hellman, "Absorbing Shocks and Mounting Checks: Germany and Alliance Burden Sharing in the Gulf War," in *Friends in Need,* ed. Bennett, Lepgold, and Unger.

283. Baker, *The Politics of Diplomacy,* 372.

198 • Notes

284. Coralluzzo, *La Politica Estera Dell'Italia Repubblicana,* 326.
285. Ibid., 314.
286. Lord and Lord, 332.
287. Laura Guazzone, "Italy and the Gulf Crisis: European and Domestic Dimensions," *The International Spectator* 26, no. 4 (October–December 1991), 73.
288. Mammarella and Cacace, *La politica estera dell'Italia,* 252.
289. Guazzone, "Italy and the Gulf Crisis," 70–71.
290. Christopher Duggan, *The Force of Destiny: A History of Italy since 1796* (London: Penguin, 2007), 580–81.
291. Ginsborg, *History of Contemporary Italy,* 442.
292. Guazzone, "Italy and the Gulf Crisis," 71.
293. Ibid., 73. For full text, see http://www.senato.it/documenti/repository/istituzione/costituzione_inglese.pdf.
294. Guazzone, "Italy and the Gulf Crisis," 74.
295. Roberto Aliboni, "L'Italia, il Golfo e il Mediterraneo," *L'Italia nella politica internazionale* (Bologna: Il Mulino, 1991), 111. See also, Coralluzzo, *La Politica Estera Dell'Italia Repubblicana,* 321–22.
296. Guazzone, "Italy and the Gulf Crisis," 72.
297. Coralluzzo, *La Politica Estera Dell'Italia Repubblicana,* 327 (see also, note 187).
298. Guazzone, "Italy and the Gulf Crisis," 71.
299. For an overview, see John L. Hirsch and Robert B. Oakley, *Somalia and Operation Restore Hope: Reflections on Peacemaking and Peacekeeping* (Washington, D.C.: United States Institute of Peace Press, 1995).
300. Paul Lewis, "Key UN Members Agree to U.S. Force in Somalia Mission," *The New York Times,* December 3, 1992.
301. Hirsch and Oakley, *Somalia and Operation Restore Hope,* 37.
302. Ibid., 45, note 17.
303. Ibid., 45.
304. Lawrence Freedman, "Defence Policy," in *The Major Effect,* ed. Kavanagh and Anthony Seldon (London: Macmillan, 1994), 277.
305. William Wallace, "Foreign Policy," in *Major Effect,* 295–96.
306. Wallace (p. 285) notes that Bush and Major shared a relationship of "mutual respect" and (pp. 290, 293) Major enjoyed a number of visits to the Bush White House. Some also argued that the presidential campaign story would not have lingering effects. See Peter Riddell, "Will Clinton Be 'Special'?" *The Times* (London) December 7, 1992.
307. Raymond Seitz, *Over Here* (London: Weidenfeld and Nicolson, 1998), 321.
308. James Bone and Martin Fletcher, "UN Gains Firm Grip on American-Led Forces in Somalia," *The Times* (London), December 4, 1992.
309. *Parliamentary Debates,* 12/4/92, col. 561, http://www.publications.parliament.uk/pa/pahansard.htm (Hereafter I will cite this series as *PD*).

Notes • 199

310. Freedman, "Defence Policy," 278.
311. The British military faced budget cuts during this period but not of the magnitude to make the claim credible. See Freedman, "Defence Policy," 269–70.
312. Bone and Fletcher, "UN Gains Firm Grip on American-Led Forces".
313. "Rescue for Somalia," *The Times* (London), August 20, 1982.
314. William Wallace makes clear that Major did not put the same stress on prestige as Thatcher had. See Wallace, "Foreign Policy," 285–86.
315. "Force for Humanity," *The Times* (London), August 6, 1992; "Shoot to Feed," *The Times* (London), December 1, 1992; "Gentle Giant," *The Times* (London), December 9, 1992.
316. David Owen, "When It Is Right to Fight," *The Times* (London), August 4, 1992.
317. *PD*, 12/4/92.
318. Freedman, "Defence Policy," 280; Wallace, "Foreign Policy," 287.
319. "UK's Labour Calls for More Aid to Somalia," *Financial Times*, August 21, 1992. See also *PD*, 12/4/92, cols. 503, 509–10.
320. Baroness Chalker, "The Struggle to Alleviate Plight of the Somalis," *Financial Times*, August 5, 1992.
321. Frances Williams, "UN Gives Action Plan for Somalia," *Financial Times*, October 13, 1992.
322. *PD*, 12/9/92, col. 671.
323. Paul Lewis, "U.N. Council Essentially Agrees to U.S. Command in Somalia," *The New York Times*, December 2, 1992.
324. Hirsch and Oakley, *Somalia and Operation Restore Hope,* 45.
325. George Graham, "Bush Orders 28,000 Troops into Somalia to Aid Relief," *Financial Times*, December 5, 1992.
326. Védrine, *Les mondes*, 162–66.
327. Dominique D'hombres, "ETATS-UNIS L'ELECTION DE BILL CLINTON La relation Paris-Washington à l'épreuve de la transition," *Le Monde*, November 6, 1992.
328. Ibid.
329. Pierre Joxe, "Le Processus de Décision," in *Mitterrand*, ed. Cohen, 428.
330. On the former claim, see Jean-Marie Colombani, "Un entretien avec Alain Joxe 'Le monde de l'empire unique n'est pas acceptable,'" *Le Monde*, December 22, 1992.
331. Gérard Prunier, "The Experience of European Armies in Operation Restore Hope," in Clarke and Herbst, *Learning from Somalia*, 135.
332. Ibid., 139.
333. Ibid.
334. Daniel Vernet, "The Dilemma of French Foreign Policy," *International Affairs* 68, no. 4 (1992), 663.
335. Guy Martin, "Continuity and Change in Franco-African Relations," *Journal of Modern African Studies* 33, no. 1 (1995): 1–20.

200 • Notes

336. Ibid., 8.

337. Jean-Marie Colombani, "L'opération militaire internationale et le débat en France sur l'ingérence humanitaire Nourrir la Somalie, mourir pour la Bosnie?" *Le Monde*, December 12, 1992.

338. "L'OPERATION MILITAIRE EN SOMALIE M. Giscard d'Estaing: l'Europe aurait dû être 'leader,'" *Le Monde*, December 12, 1992.

339. "L'OPERATION MILITAIRE EN SOMALIE M. Juppé (RPR): la France a 'suivi' et non 'précédé' en Somalie," *Le Monde*, December 15, 1992.

340. Prunier, "The Experience of European Armies," 135.

341. Samy Cohen and Natalie La Balme, "Ni bellicistes, ni pacifists: Les Français et l'intervention militaire extérieure," in *L'Opinion, l'humanitaire et la guerre: Une perspective comparative,* ed. Samy Cohen (Paris: Fondation Pour Les Études de Défense, 1996), 21.

342. "SOMALIE M. Chirac se dit 'favorable' à l'intervention," *Le Monde*, December 10, 1992.

343. The center-right garnered 46.8 percent of the vote in the 1988 election. William Safran, *The French Polity,* 5th ed. (New York: Longman, 1998), 75.

344. Theirry Brehier, "A l'occasion du départ de la 'Jeanne' 'La France entend être présente dès lors qu'il y a à respecter le droit ou à préserver des vies humaines,' affirme M. Bérégovoy," *Le Monde*, December 10, 1992.

345. Prunier, "The Experience of European Armies," 135. See also La Balme, "La influence," 418 and Jean-François Bayart, "'Bis repitita': La politique africaine de François Mitterrand de 1989 à 1995," in *Mitterrand,* ed. Cohen, 276.

346. "L'OPERATION MILITAIRE EN SOMALIE M. Fillon (RPR): une intervention 'inutile,'" *Le Monde*, December 12, 1992.

347. The December 10 National Assembly debate on Somalia did not focus on the government's decision. Pascale Robert Diard, "L'intervention militaire en Somalie A l'Assemblée nationale Des députés choqués par les 'débordements médiatiques,'" *Le Monde*, December 11, 1992.

348. For a critical discussion, see Philippe Guillot, "France, Peacekeeping and Humanitarian Intervention," *International Peacekeeping* 1, no. 1 (Spring 1994): 30–43.

349. Brehier, "A l'occasion du départ de la 'Jeanne.'"

350. Ibid.

351. Alain Frachon, "Pour sauver de la famine des centaines de milliers de personnes Le Conseil de sécurité a approuvé à l'unanimité l'intervention militaire internationale en Somalie Une 'résolution historique,'" *Le Monde*, December 5, 1992.

352. "SOMALIE: la lutte contre la famine M. Boutros-Ghali juge 'indispensable' le recours à la force pour assurer la distribution de l'aide," *Le Monde*, November 26, 1992; "Le courage d'agir," *Le Monde*, December 3, 1992.

353. Alain Frachon and Afsane Bassir-Pour, "SOMALIE La situation sur le terrain a convaincu M. Bush qu'il fallait intervener," *Le Monde*, November 28, 1992.

354. Jacques Isnard, "Les interrogations des militaires Nourrir à coups de canon?" *Le Monde*, December 9, 1992; Diard, "L'intervention militaire en Somalie"; Brehier, "A l'occasion du départ de la 'Jeanne.'"
355. Prunier, "The Experience of European Armies," 135.
356. "L'OPERATION MILITAIRE EN SOMALIE M. Fillon (RPR): une intervention 'inutile.'"
357. "Anche l' Italia nell' operazione Somalia," *Corriere della Sera*, November 29, 1992.
358. Ferraris, *Manuale della politica estera italiana,* 486; Clarke and Herbst, 137.
359. Robert Graham and Steven Butler, "Italy Approves Despatch of Troops," *Financial Times*, December 10, 1992. See also, Hirsch and Oakley, *Somalia and Operation Restore Hope,* 37–38.
360. Anonymous interview, 3/5/08.
361. Claudio Lindner, "'Pronti a partire', conferma Ando," *Corriere della Sera*, November 30, 1992; Ferraris, *Manuale della politica estera italiana,* 485.
362. Filippo Andreatta, "Italy at a Crossroads: The Foreign Policy of a Medium Power after the End of Bipolarity," *Daedalus* 130, no. 2 (Spring 2001), 52.
363. Paola Di Caro, "'Italiani sgraditi': polemica con gli USA," *Corriere della Sera*, December 10, 1992.
364. Prunier, "The Experience of European Armies," 137, 142.
365. Andreatta, "Italy at a Crossroads," 46.
366. Bruno Loi, *Peace-keeping, pace o guerra? Una risposta italiana: l'operazione Ibis in Somalia* (Firenze: Vallecchi, 2004), 22. See also, Andreatta, "Italy at a Crossroads," 57.
367. Franco Venturini, "L' armata dei dubbi," *Corriere della Sera*, December 7, 1992.
368. Prunier, "The Experience of European Armies," 137.
369. Hirsch and Oakley, *Somalia and Operation Restore Hope,* 74.
370. Loi, *Peace-keeping,* 26.
371. Sergio Romano, "Prefazione," in Loi, *Peace-keeping*, 6.
372. Osvaldo Croci, "The Italian Intervention in Somalia: A New Italian Foreign Policy After the Cold War?" in *Italian Politics: Ending the First Republic,* ed. Carol Mershon and Gianfranco Pasquino (Boulder, CO: Westview, 1995), 201.
373. Romano, "Prefazione," 6.
374. Margherita De Bac, "Il Papa benedice la guerra alla fame," *Corriere della Sera*, December 6, 1992; Ferraris, *Manuale della politica estera italiana,* 485.
375. Ilari, "La politica militare italiana," 212.
376. Ferraris, *Manuale della politica estera italiana,* 485 (note 563).
377. Loi, *Peace-keeping,* 26.
378. Romano, "Prefazione," 6.
379. Ibid.
380. Ibid., 6.
381. Angelo Del Boca, *Una sconfitta dell'intelligenza: Italia e Somalia* (Roma: Laterza, 1993), 116. See also, p. 157.

202 • Notes

382. Ibid., 126–64.
383. For criticisms of inaction in the period leading up to the creation of UNITAF, see ibid., 129, 132–33, 140.

Chapter 4

1. For an overview, see Ivo H. Daalder and Michael E. O'Hanlon, *Winning Ugly: NATO's War to Save Kosovo* (Washington, D.C.: Brookings Institution, 2000).
2. For a recent judgment (with additional citations on this point), see Daniel R. Lake, "The Limits of Coercive Airpower: NATO's 'Victory' in Kosovo Revisited," *International Security* 34, no. 1 (Summer 2009), 84, 109.
3. Daalder and O'Hanlon, *Winning Ugly*, 147–49.
4. House of Commons Defence Committee, *Fourteenth Report: Lessons of Kosovo*, Vol. I, Session 1999–2000, London, 2000, lvii.
5. Louise Richardson, "A Force for Good in the World: Britain's Role in the Kosovo Crisis," in *Alliance Politics, Kosovo, and NATO's War: Allied Force or Forced Allies?* Ed. Pierre Martin and Mark R. Brawley (New York: Palgrave Macmillan, 2001), 145. See also Daalder and O'Hanlon, *Winning Ugly*, 36, 132, 158.
6. John Kampfner, *Blair's Wars* (London: Simon and Schuster, 2003), 12.
7. Tony Blair, "Speech by the Prime Minister on Foreign Affairs," Tuesday December 15, 1998, http://www.number10.gov.uk/.
8. Ibid. Another reason is cooperation on defense and intelligence. Peter Riddell, rev. ed. *Hug Them Close: Blair, Clinton, and the "Special Relationship"* (London: Politico's, 2004), 26.
9. Riddell, *Hug Them Close*, 15.
10. Anthony Seldon with Chris Ballinger, Daniel Collings, and Peter Snowdon, *Blair* (London: The Free Press, 2004), 389.
11. Interview with Dana Allin, 6/19/09.
12. Richardson, "A Force for Good in the World," 152–53.
13. Interview with Oliver Daddow, 6/30/09.
14. *The Strategic Defence Review* (London: Her Majesty's Stationery Office, 1998), 10.
15. Ibid. See also p. 7.
16. *Parliamentary Debates*, 2/24/99, col. 409, http://www.publications.parliament. uk/pa/pahansard.htm (hereafter I will cite this series as *PD*); *PD*, 3/23/99, cols. 163, 164; House of Commons Foreign Affairs Select Committee, *Fourth Report: Kosovo*, Vol. I, Session 1999–2000, London, 2000, 73.
17. Interview with Dana Allin, 6/19/09; Anonymous interview, 7/15/09a.
18. Richardson, "A Force for Good in the World," 150.
19. House of Commons Foreign Affairs Select Committee, *Fourth Report*, 73.
20. Anonymous interview, 7/15/09b. Another anonymous interviewee raised the possibility that those involved did not know that they were putting NATO's

credibility on the line when they were doing so. Anonymous interview, 7/15/09a.

21. Daalder and O'Hanlon, *Winning Ugly*, 9.
22. *Strategic Defence Review*, 5.
23. Kampfner, *Blair's Wars*, 61.
24. Interview with Oliver Daddow, 6/30/09.
25. *Strategic Defence Review*, 9.
26. *PD*, 1/18/99, col. 571.
27. *PD*, 3/23/99, 161. Italics added.
28. *PD*, 3/23/99, col. 165.
29. Interview with Tim Judah, 7/17/09.
30. Anonymous interview, 7/15/09b.
31. Interview with Oliver Daddow, 6/30/09.
32. Anonymous Interview, 7/15/09a.
33. Interview with Dana Allin, 6/19/09.
34. Interview with Oliver Daddow, 6/30/09.
35. *PD* 10/19/98, col. 955.
36. *PD*, 2/16/99, col. 722.
37. *PD*, 1/18/99, col. 576.
38. Interview with Oliver Daddow, 6/30/09. Anonymous interview, 7/15/09a.
39. "Update: Global Reaction to Kosovo Crisis," United States Information Agency, April 28, 1999, http://www.ess.uwe.ac.uk/Kosovo/Kosovo-Current_News122.htm.
40. Ibid.
41. *PD*, 10/19/98, col. 955.
42. *PD*, 1/18/99, col. 568; *PD*, 2/1/99, col. 600; *PD*, 3/23/99, col. 163.
43. *PD*, 1/18/98, col. 569.
44. Anonymous interview, 7/15/09a; Interview with Dana Allin, 6/19/09; Interview with Oliver Daddow, 6/30/09; Anonymous interview, 7/15/09b; Interview with Robert Worcester, 7/2/09.
45. Daalder and O'Hanlon, *Winning Ugly*, 132; Interview with Robert Worcester, 7/2/09.
46. Richardson, "A Force for Good in the World," 158–60.
47. *PD*, 1/18/99, 565.
48. *PD*, 3/23/99, 161.
49. Riddell, *Hug Them Close*, 99–101.
50. Tony Blair, "Doctrine of the International community," The Economic Club, Chicago, April 24, 1999, http://www.number10.gov.uk/.
51. Independent International Commission on Kosovo, *Kosovo Report: Conflict, International Response, Lessons Learned* (Oxford: Oxford University Press, 2000), 4; House of Commons Foreign Affairs Select Committee, *Fourth Report*, 138. See also, Richardson, "A Force for Good in the World," 160.
52. Anonymous interview, 7/15/09a; Interview with Dana Allin, 6/19/09.
53. Kampfner, *Blair's Wars*, 15.

204 • Notes

54. Ibid., 16. See also page 14.
55. *Strategic Defence Review*, 7.
56. Seldon, *Blair*, 395.
57. Ibid.
58. See Paddy Ashdown, *The Ashdown Diaries Volume II: 1997–1999* (London: Allen Lane, 2001), 412–13.
59. Interview with Oliver Daddow, 6/30/99. Clare Short (*An Honourable Deception?* p. 93) documents the extensive efforts that went into building "Blair's image as a humanitarian war leader."
60. Mahon, *PD*, 3/23/99, 172.
61. Interview with Dana Allin, 6/19/09.
62. Independent International Commission on Kosovo, *Kosovo Report*, 180–182; Kampfner, *Blair's Wars,* 55. While Tim Judah is right that these actions do not prove motives other than humanitarian ones, they do cast doubt on the force of these motives. Another, more controversial issue is casualty aversion and the 15,000-foot bombing ceiling. See John Norris, *Collision Course: NATO, Russia, and Kosovo* (Westport, CT: Praeger, 2005), 5; Benjamin S. Lambeth, *NATO's Air War for Kosovo: A Strategic and Operational Assessment* (Santa Monica: RAND, 2001), 140.
63. Independent International Commission on Kosovo, *Kosovo Report*, 159.
64. In the period from May 1, 1998, to October 1, 1998, Blair made no speeches to the House of Commons on Kosovo. Only once in that period did Blair say anything about Kosovo longer than four sentences and it was in a response to an urge to action by the Liberal Democrat Paddy Ashdown during question time. In his response Blair said his government was pressing for action because "we do not believe that we could afford to have disorder spreading in that part of the world." He did not mention the humanitarian logic. *PD*, 6/3/98, col. 360. See also *PD*, 6/17/98, cols. 368–69; *PD*, 5/20/98, col. 958.
65. Ashdown, *The Ashdown Diaries,* 236, 263–64, 267, 371–73. Blair initiated discussion of Kosovo with Ashdown only once during the period according to Ashdown's diary. The conversation took place on September 30, 1998. Ashdown does not record Blair raising the humanitarian logic. Ashdown, *The Ashdown Diaries,* 294–95.
66. Katharina P. Coleman, *International Organizations and Peace Enforcement: The Politics of International Legitimacy* (Cambridge: Cambridge University Press, 2007), 200.
67. Coleman, *International Organizations,* 200. See also House of Commons Foreign Affairs Select Committee, *Fourth Report*, 132.
68. Coleman, *International Organizations,* 200.
69. Independent International Commission on Kosovo, *Kosovo Report*, 145.
70. Ashdown, *The Ashdown Diaries,* 267.
71. Independent International Commission on Kosovo, *Kosovo Report*, 174.
72. *PD*, 10/19/98, col. 957; 2/1/99, col. 604; *PD*, 3/23/99, col. 168.

73. Madeleine Albright with Bill Woodward, *Madam Secretary* (New York: Miramax Books, 2003), 384.
74. Independent International Commission on Kosovo, *Kosovo Report*, 4.
75. House of Commons Foreign Affairs Select Committee, *Fourth Report*, 128. See also p. 126.
76. Anonymous interview, 7/15/09b.
77. Blair, "Doctrine of the International Community."
78. Tony Blair, "Oral Evidence Transcript," *The Iraq Inquiry*, London, January 29, 2010, 26, http://www.iraqinquiry.org.uk/transcripts.aspx.
79. Anonymous interview, 7/15/09b.
80. Daalder and O'Hanlon, *Winning Ugly*, 149.
81. Strobe Talbott, *The Russia Hand: A Memoir of Presidential Diplomacy* (New York: Random House, 2002), 317. See also Daalder and O'Hanlon, *Winning Ugly*, 118; John Norris, *Collision Course*, 5, 21, 95.
82. For Iraq, see Claire Trean, "Pourquoi la France n'ose pas afficher ses divergences avec les Etats-Unis," *Le Monde*, 21 décembre 1998. More broadly, see Maurice Vaïsse, *La puissance ou l'influence: La France dans le monde depuis 1998* (Paris: Fayard, 2009), 214, 217–18.
83. Hubert Védrine, *Face à l'hyperpuissance: Textes et discourse 1995–2003* (Paris: Fayard, 2003), 113. For earlier statements, see pp., 90, 104–05.
84. Védrine, *Face à l'hyperpuissance*, 10, 105.
85. Jacques Chirac, *Mon combat pour la paix: textes et interventions* (Paris: Odile Jacob, 2007), 84. See also Védrine*, Face*, 153.
86. Even Bill Clinton recognized this to be the case. See Gilles Delafon and Thomas Sancton, *Dear Jacques, Cher Bill: Au coeur de l'Elysée et de la Maison Blanche, 1995–1999* (Paris: Plon, 1999), 16. For a detailed survey, see pp. 58–119.
87. Ibid., 358.
88. Ibid., 356. See also pp. 13, 233, 297, 308.
89. Craig R. Whitney, "NATO Threatens Military Action to Stem the Violence in Kosovo," *The New York Times*, January 29, 1999.
90. Interview with Louis Gautier, 6/4/09.
91. Anonymous interview, 6/10/99b.
92. Eric Rouleau, trans. Barry Smerin, "French Diplomacy Adrift in Kosovo," *Le Monde Diplomatique*, December 1999, http://mondediplo.com/1999/12/04rouleau.
93. Vaïsse *La puissance ou l'influence*, 214–15. See also, Janet Bryant, "France and NATO from 1966 to Kosovo: Coming Full Circle," *European Security* 9, no. 3 (Autumn 2000): 21–37.
94. Interview with Louis Gautier, 6/4/09.
95. Alex Macleod, "France: Kosovo and the Emergence of a New European Security," in *Alliance Politics*, ed. Martin and Brawley, 118.
96. Gilles Andréani, "Force et diplomatie à propos de la guerre du Kosovo," *Annuaire français de relations internationals* (2000), 166.

206 • Notes

97. Paul Quilès et François Lamy, "RAPPORT D'INFORMATION N 2022, sur le conflit du Kosovo, PAR LA COMMISSION DE LA DÉFENSE NATIONALE ET DES FORCES ARMÉES, ASSEMBLÉE NATIONALE," 15 décembre 1999.
98. In one interview I was told that NATO credibility was not a factor. Interview with Jean-Pierre Maulny, 5/27/09.
99. Andréani, "Force et diplomatie," 176.
100. "Un tournant historique," *Le Monde*, March 25, 1999.
101. Quilès et Lamy. Emphasis added.
102. Ibid.
103. "Discours de M. Jacques CHIRAC, Président de la République prononcé à l'occasion de la réunion de Rambouillet sur le Kosovo," Rambouillet, Yvelines, 6 février 1999, http://www.elysee.fr/elysee/elysee.fr/francais_archives/interventions/discours_et_declarations.
104. "Déclaration de M. Jacques CHIRAC, Président de la République, sur le Kosovo lors du Conseil européen extraordinaire à Berlin," Berlin, Allemagne, le mercredi 24 mars 1999, http://www.elysee.fr/elysee/elysee.fr/francais_archives/interventions/discours_et_declarations.
105. "SITUATION AU KOSOVO Déclaration du Gouvernement et débat sur cette déclaration," ASSEMBLÉE NATIONALE - SÉANCE DU 26 MARS 1999, http://www.assemblee-nationale.fr/11/cri/html/19990203.asp.
106. Macleod, "France," 117.
107. "Audition de M. Alain Richard, Ministre de la Défense, sur la participation de la France aux opérations de l'OTAN en République fédérale de Yougoslavie," Commission de la Défense, Vendredi 26 mars 1999, http://www.assemblee-nationale.fr/11/cr-cdef/98-99/c9899025.asp.
108. In addition to those I discuss here and the dissenting views I discuss later, one anonymous interviewee said regional stability was very important in the government's decision.
109. Interview with Jean-Pierre Maulny, 5/27/09.
110. Interview with Louis Gautier, 6/4/09. When I asked, "What about the dangers that the conflict might expand?" Gautier replied, "The falling dominoes had already occurred and this time it might be Macedonia. We had to be in a role of preventing fires rather than putting them out after the fact."
111. Chirac, *Mon Combat*, 9; Lionel Jospin, *Le temps de répondre. Entretiens avec Alain Duhamel* (Paris: Stock, 2002), 194.
112. Védrine, *Face*, 90. See also 108, 118, 123.
113. Delafon and Sancton, *Dear Jacques,* 100.
114. Isabelle Lasserrre, *L'Impuissance Française: 1989–2007 Une diplomatie qui a fait son temps* (Paris: Flammarion, 2007), 118.
115. Macleod, "France," 114.
116. "SITUATION AU KOSOVO."
117. Andréani, "Force et diplomatie," 166.
118. Conférence de presse conjointe de M. Jacques CHIRAC Président de la République et de M. William J. CLINTON Président des Etats-Unis

d'Amérique, Skopje, Macédoine, le dimanche 28 février 1999, http://www.elysee.fr/elysee/elysee.fr/francais_archives/interventions/discours_et_declarations. See also Claire Trean, "Les Albanais du Kosovo ont annoncé leur accord avec le plan international de paix; Slobodan Milosevic est contraint de prendre position," *Le Monde*, March 17, 1999.

119. Interview with Louis Gautier, 6/4/09. Of others I interviewed one expressly said prestige was not a big factor in this case and another said it was important. Interview with Jean-Pierre Maulny, 5/27/09; Anonymous interview, 6/3/09.

120. Chirac, *Mon combat*, 21; Vaïsse, *La puissance ou l'influence*, 155.

121. Jacques Isnard, "La force d'extraction au Kosovo sera un test pour la France, désignée nation-pilote," *Le Monde*, December 12, 1998; Chirac, *Mon combat*, 22.

122. Rouleau, "French Diplomacy," 7.

123. Interview with Jean-Pierre Maulny, 5/27/09.

124. "Discours de M. Jacques CHIRAC, Président de la République prononcé à l'occasion de la réunion de Rambouillet sur le Kosovo," February 6, 1999.

125. "Audition de M. Alain Richard."

126. Védrine, *"Face,"* 94.

127. Macleod, "France," 124. For the wording of the NATO question, see "Update: Global Reaction to Kosovo Crisis."

128. Wesley K. Clark, *Waging Modern War: Bosnia, Kosovo, and the Future of Combat* (New York: Public Affairs, 2001), 428; Macleod, "France," 124.

129. Macleod, "France," 123.

130. Interview with Louis Gautier, 6/4/09.

131. Interview with François Bujon de l'Estang, 6/10/09a; Interview with Jean-Pierre Maulny, 5/27/09.

132. "Le destin de la France n'a jamais été de se replier sur son hexagone," *Le Monde*, March 4, 1999.

133. Védrine, *Face*, 152.

134. Ibid., 144.

135. "SITUATION AU KOSOVO."

136. Interview with François Bujon de l'Estang, 6/10/09a.

137. Interview with Louis Gautier, 6/4/09.

138. Claire Trean, "De nouveau, l'indignation impuissante des Occidentaux; L'OTAN continue de privilégier l'idée d'une autonomie négociée," *Le Monde*, January 19, 1999.

139. Natalie Nougayrede, "Il n'y a pas de politique spécifiquement française au Kosovo," *Le Monde*, January 21, 1999.

140. Emmanuel Wallon, "Kosovo: guérir du syndrome de répétition," *Le Monde*, February 27, 1999.

141. Védrine, *Face*, 95.

142. "Discours de M. Jacques CHIRAC, Président de la République, lors de la présentation des voeux du Corps diplomatique," Palais de l'Elysée, le jeudi 7 janvier 1999, http://www.elysee.fr/elysee/elysee.fr/francais_archives/interventions/discours_et_declarations.

208 • Notes

143. "Conférence de presse conjointe de M. Jacques CHIRAC, Président de la République, de M. Lionel JOSPIN, Premier ministre et de M. Romano PRODI, Président du Conseil italien," Florence, Italie, le mardi 6 octobre 1998, http://www.elysee.fr/elysee/elysee.fr/francais_archives/interventions/discours_et_declarations.

144. Coleman, *International Organizations,* 198–99.

145. Patrick Jarreau, Olivier Mazerolle, Pierre Luc Seguillon, "Il est de l'ordre de la critique légitime de mettre en cause l'unilatéralisme américain," *Le Monde,* March 16, 1999.

146. Interview with Jean-Pierre Maulny, 5/27/09.

147. Anonymous interview, 6/3/09.

148. Interview with Louis Gautier, 6/4/09; Interview with François Bujon de l'Estang, 6/10/09a; Anonymous interview, 6/10/09b.

149. Anonymous interview, 6/10/09b.

150. Independent International Commission on Kosovo, *Kosovo Report,* 159.

151. Interview with Louis Gautier, 6/4/09.

152. Interview with Jean-Pierre Maulny, 5/27/09.

153. Michael J. Brenner and Guillaume Parmentier, *Reconcilable Differences: U.S.-France Relations in the New Era* (Washington, D.C.: Brookings Institution Press, 2002), 35.

154. For an overview, see Osvaldo Croci, "Forced Ally? Italy and 'Operation Allied Force,'" in *Italian Politics, 2000: The Faltering Transition,* ed. Mark Gilbert and Gianfranco Pasquino (New York: Berghahn Books, 2000), 33–50.

155. Daalder and O'Hanlon, *Winning Ugly,* 147–49. For a slightly lower figure, see John E. Peters et al., *European Contributions to Operation Allied Force* (Santa Monica: RAND, 2001), 19, 21.

156. Peters, *European Contributions,* 21–22.

157. Dino Martirano, " L'Italia Fornira' Le Basi Ma Non Bombardera,'" *Corriere della Sera*, March 24, 1999.

158. Marco Nese, "Aerei Italiani Colpiscono in Kosovo," *Corriere della Sera*, April 15, 1999.

159. Massimo D'Alema (intervista di F. Rampini), *Kosovo. Gli italiani e la guerra* (Milano: Mondadori, 1999), 39.

160. Peters, *European Contributions,* 30.

161. The two most thorough studies—by Peters and Daalder and O'Hanlon—do not mention the restriction.

162. Maurizio Cremasco, "Italy and the Management of International Crises," in *Alliance Politics, Kosovo, and NATO's War: Allied Force or Forced Allies?* Ed. Pierre Martin and Mark R. Brawley (New York: Palgrave Macmillan, 2001), 172.

163. Peters, *European Contributions,* 30.

164. For a brief summary, see Croci, "Forced Ally?" 33.

165. Franco Venturini, "Il Paradosso Americano," *Corriere della Sera*, December 17, 1998.

166. See Roberto Aliboni e Daniela Pioppi, "Il caso Öcalan, l'Italia e i rapporti euro-turchi," in *L'Italia e la politica internazionale, 2000,* ed., Roberto Aliboni et al. (Bologna: Il Mulino, 2000). See also Maria Latella, " D'Alema-Clinton, L'Ombra Del Cermis," *Corriere della Sera*, March 5, 1999, and Ennio Carretto, "D'Alema A Clinton: Dovete Punire I Colpevoli," *Corriere della Sera*, March 6, 1999.

167. Dino Vaiano, "La Fedelta' Alla Nato Non Si Discute," *Corriere della Sera*, March 8, 1999. See also Franco Venturini, " Il Legame USA-Italia Non Si Discute," *Corriere della Sera*, March 10, 1999, and Franco Venturini, " Sfida Alla Superpotenza Sfida," *Corriere della Sera*, March 10, 1999.

168. Roberto Menotti, "Italy," in *Enlarging NATO: The National Debates*, ed. Gale A. Mattox and Arthur R. Rachwald (Boulder, CO: Lynne Rienner, 2001), 94–95.

169. Ibid., 94.

170. Ibid.

171. Anonymous interview, 12/12/08. See also Interview with Marta Dassù, 4/1/09; Interview with Carlo Scognimiglio, 4/23/09.

172. Massimo D'Alema, "Italy, Europe and the New Nato," *International Herald Tribune*, January 22, 1999.

173. "Intervento del Presidente del Consiglio Massimo D'Alema—Camera dei Deputati," 25/01/99, http://www.sitiarcheologici.palazzochigi.it/. See also Maria Latella, "D'Alema-Clinton: L'Ombra Del Cermis," *Corriere della Sera*, March 5, 1999.

174. Lamberto Dini suggests Italy's value for NATO was critical in its prior decision to vote in favor of the 1998 Actord authorizing the use of force. Lamberto Dini (intervista di Maurizio Molinari), *Fra Casa Bianca e Botteghe Oscure: Fatti e retroscena di una stagione alla Farnesina* (Milano: Guerini, 2001), 68.

175. Saulino Felice, "D'Alema Evita La Crisi," *Corriere della Sera*, March 27, 1999.

176. "Intervento del Presidente del Consiglio Massimo D'Alema—Camera dei Deputati," 26/03/1999, http://www.sitiarcheologici.palazzochigi.it/. See also "Discussione di mozioni sulla crisi del Kosovo."

177. See "Intervento del Presidente del Consiglio Massimo D'Alema—Camera dei Deputati," 04/13/1999, and "Intervento del Presidente del Consiglio Massimo D'Alema—Cerimonia commemorativa NATO, Washington" 4/23/1999, http://www.sitiarcheologici.palazzochigi.it/.

178. Roberto Menotti, "I rapporti politici transatlantici e la trasformazione della NATO," in *L'Italia e la politica internazionale, 2000,* ed. Roberto Aliboni et al. (Bologna: Il Mulino, 2000), 357.

179. Stefano Folli, " Svolta Di Politica Estera Anche Per Ragioni Interne," *Corriere della Sera*, January 19, 1999, and Stefano Folli, "Solidarieta' Chiesta Al Paese E Sopratutto Alla Coalizione," *Corriere della Sera*, March 31, 1999.

180. Croci, "Forced Ally?" 42.

181. Anonymous interview, 12/12/08.

210 • Notes

182. Interview with Massimo D'Alema, 4/16/09; Interview with Giuliano Amato, 4/22/09; Interview with Carlo Scognamiglio, 4/23/09.
183. Interview with Carlo Scognamiglio, 4/23/09. See also, Carlo Scognamiglio Pasini, *La Guerra del Kosovo* (Milano: Rizzoli, 2002), 57.
184. Interview with Roberto Menotti, 12/1/08; Anonymous interview, 3/18/09; Interview with Marta Dassù, 4/1/09; Anonymous interview, 4/29/09.
185. Dini, *Fra Casa Bianca,* 46.
186. Giuliano Amato told me that he had no direct evidence that D'Alema's past impacted his decision on Kosovo but he also noted that it is hard to believe it was unimportant. Then he said, "Of course, any other Prime Minister would have adopted the same policy for the same reason we have discussed: Italy had to be there." Interview with Giuliano Amato, 4/22/09.
187. Interview with Massimo D'Alema, 4/16/09.
188. "Il club dei suicidi," *Quaderni speciali di Limes: Kosovo*, 5–10.
189. Cremasco, "Italy and the Management of International Crises," 172. See also "Incontro con una delegazione dei rappresentanti dei pescatori di Chioggia," 05/24/1999, http://www.sitiarcheologici.palazzochigi.it/.
190. Alfonso Desiderio, "Che cosa rischia l'Italia," *Quaderni speciali di Limes: Kosovo, L'Italia in Guerra*, Supplemento al no. 1/1999, 87–92.
191. Maurizio Caprara e Marco Nese, "Roma Da' Le Basi, Sinistra Divisa," *Corriere della Sera*, October 13, 1998. Andrea Nicastro, "Rischi Per l'Italia?," *Corriere della Sera*, March 23, 1999.
192. See, for example, "Intervento del Presidente del Consiglio Massimo D'Alema—Camera dei Deputati," 04/13/1999, http://www.sitiarcheologici.palazzochigi.it/.
193. Angelo Panzeri, "Bloccati Alla Frontiere 70 Profughi Dal Kosovo. E' Di Nuovo Emergenza," *Corriere della Sera*, October 13, 1998; Roberto Buonavoglia, "Puglia, E' Di Nuovo Emergenza Sbarchi," *Corriere della Sera*, October 18, 1998; "Gorizia, Nuovi Arrivi Di Profughi Del Kosovo," *Corriere della Sera*, October 26, 1998; Roberto Zuccolini, "Questa Volta Gli Albanesi Devono Impegnarsi Sul Serio," *Corriere della Sera*, October 27, 1998; Roberto Buonavoglia, "Immigrati, Ancora Sbarchi In Puglia," *Corriere della Sera*, December 28, 1998; and Carlo Vulpi and Roberto Buonavoglia, "Ondata Di Profughi Sulle Coste Pugliesi," *Corriere Della Sera*, January 18, 1999.
194. "CONFERENZA STAMPA del Presidente del Consiglio Massimo D'Alema," 10/25/98, http://www.sitiarcheologici.palazzochigi.it/.
195. Renato Mannheimer, "Quasi L' 80 Per Cento Degli Italiani In Allarme Per La Nuova Ondata Di Arrivi," *Corriere della Sera*, March 29, 1999. See also D'Alema, *Kosovo*, 15, 19, 20; Marco Nese, "Task Force-Profughi," *Corriere della Sera*, April 12, 1999.
196. Angelo Panebianco, "Un Paese Alla Prova," *Corriere della Sera*, March 30, 1999. See also "Intervento del Presidente del Consiglio Massimo D'Alema—Camera dei Deputati," 1/25/99.
197. D'Alema, *Kosovo*, 11.

Notes • 211

198. Marco Nese, "D'Alema: L'Italia Al Fianco Della Nato," *Corriere della Sera*, January 19, 1999.
199. "Dichiarazione del Presidente del Consiglio Massimo D'Alema," 03/30/1999, http://www.sitiarcheologici.palazzochigi.it/.
200. Ernesto Galli Della Loggia,"Italia Paese Balcanico," *Corriere della Sera*, March 25, 1999.
201. Ettore Greco, "La politica italiana durante il conflitto del Kosovo," in Aliboni, *L'Italia e la politica internazionale*, 138.
202. Ibid., 139.
203. Stefano Folli, "Svolta Di Politica Estera Anche Per Ragioni Interne," *Corriere della Sera*, January 19, 1999. Franco Venturini, "Una Scelta Sofferta," *Corriere della Sera*, March 24, 1999.
204. In addition to those cited below, see Interview with Roberto Menotti, 12/1/08; Anonymous interview, 3/30/09.
205. Anonymous interview, 12/11/08.
206. Interview with Carlo Scognamiglio, 4/23/09. See also Scognamiglio Pasini, *La Guerra*, 54.
207. Interview with Massimo D'Alema, 4/16/09.
208. Anonymous interview, 12/12/08; Anonymous interview, 3/18/09.
209. Ennio Carretto, "Riforma ONU, L'Italia Vince La Sfida," *Corriere della Sera*, November 24, 1999.
210. "Intervento del Presidente del Consiglio Massimo D'Alema—Camera dei Deputati," 1/25/99, http://www.sitiarcheologici.palazzochigi.it/.
211. Massimo Gaggi e Franco Venturini, "Soldati Nei Balcani E Non Bombe," *Corriere della Sera*, February 7, 1999.
212. Andrea Nicastro, "Ma Non Possiamo Rimanere Indifferenti Alle Stragi," *Corriere della Sera*, March 22, 1999.
213. Gaggi e Venturini, "Soldati Nei Balcani."
214. "Intervento del Presidente del Consiglio Massimo D'Alema—Camera dei Deputati," 26/03/1999, http://www.sitiarcheologici.palazzochigi.it/.
215. "Discussione di mozioni sulla crisi del Kosovo."
216. D'Alema, *Kosovo*, 21–22.
217. "Fu un errore bombardare Belgrado," *Il Riformista*, 24 Marzo 2009. For a similar interpretation, see Marta Dassù, *Mondo privato e altre storie* (Torino: Bollati Boringhieri, 2009), 88.
218. Ibid.
219. Cremasco, "Italy and the Management of International Crises," 177.
220. Croci, "Forced Ally?" 42.
221. Only one interviewee expressed skepticism that this was an important factor. Anonymous interview, 3/18/09.
222. Anonymous interview, 12/12/08. I heard a similar view during an anonymous interview, 12/11/08.
223. Interview with Marta Dassù, 4/1/09.
224. Ibid.

212 • Notes

225. Anonymous interview, 3/30/09.
226. Interview with Massimo D'Alema, 4/16/99.
227. Ibid.
228. Renato Mannheimer, "Sondaggio: Vincono I No Alle Bombe," *Corriere della Sera*, April 27, 1999.
229. Ibid. See also Cremasco, "Italy and the Management of International Crises," 170.
230. D'Alema, *Kosovo*, 109.
231. Many believe that the government was targeting the far-left with its peace initiatives and its claim that Italian aircraft would only be used for defensive purposes. Dini, *Fra Casa Bianca*, 70; Cremasco, "Italy and the Management of International Crises," 172; Roberto Zuccolini, "Fermiamo Subito I Bombardamenti," *Corrriere della Sera*, May 19, 1999.
232. Interview with Ettore Greco, 3/27/09.
233. Fabrizio Coticchia and Giampiero Giacomello, "Esiste una Via Italiana alla Cultura di Difesa?" *Biblioteca della Libertà*, XLIII, no. 193 (October–December 2008): 109–22.
234. "Dichiarazione del Presidente del Consiglio Massimo D'Alema," 03/30/1999.
235. "Discussione di mozioni sulla crisi del Kosovo."
236. http://www.quirinale.it/costituzione/costituzione.htm.
237. See Natalino Ronzitti, "L'intervento in Iraq e il diritto internazionale," in *L'Italia e la politica internazionale, 2004*, ed. Alessandro Colombo and Natalino Ronzitti (Bologna: Il Mulino, 2004), 67–78.
238. Dini, *Fra Casa Bianca*, 65.
239. Gianna Fragonara, "Cossutta: Il Parlamento Discuta L'Intervento, Noi Diremo No," *Corriere della Sera*, March 23, 1999; "Ingrao: Costituzione Stracciata, c'e' Troppa Soggezzione Degli USA," *Corriere della Sera*, March 25, 1999; Maria Latella, "Sanguineti: D'Alema, Non Sei Di Sinistra," *Corriere della Sera*, March 25, 1999.
240. Francesco Alberti, "Tortorella: No Massimo, Cosi' Non Ti Fermerai," *Corriere della Sera*, April 15, 1999.
241. "Discussione di mozioni sulla crisi del Kosovo," Senato, Legislatura 13—Aula—Resoconto stenografico della seduta n. 584 del 26 MARZO 1999.
242. See "Lettera aperta di Massimo D'Alema—l'Unità," 5/16/1999, http://www.sitiarcheologici.palazzochigi.it/. See also "Dichiarazione del Presidente del Consiglio Massimo D'Alema," 03/30/1999.
243. "Intervento del Presidente del Consiglio Massimo D'Alema—Senato della Repubblica," 05/26/1999. See also "Fu un errore bombardare Belgrado."
244. "Ranieri In Missione Yugoslava, " *Corriere della Sera*, January 17, 1999.
245. "Dichiarazione del Presidente del Consiglio Massimo D'Alema," 03/30/1999. See also "INCONTRO CON LA STAMPA del Presidente del Consiglio Massimo D'Alema," 03/23/1999; Intervento del Presidente del Consiglio Massimo D'Alema—Camera dei Deputati," 26/03/1999.

246. Luigi Offeddu, "D'Alema, Appello Al Leader Serbo," *Corriere della Sera*, March 30, 1999; Ennio Carretto, "Se Inizia Il Ritiro, L'Attacco Finira," *Corriere della Sera*, April 24, 1999; "D'Alema Orgoglioso Per La Dura Prova," *Corriere della Sera*, June 6, 1999. See also D'Alema, *Kosovo*, 98.

247. Dini, *Fra Casa Bianca,* 66.

248. Roberto Zuccolini, "L'Ira Di Cossiga," *Corriere della Sera* , March 27, 1999.

249. "Intervista a Massimo D'Alema—La Stampa, Barbara Spinelli," 12/17/98, http://www.sitiarcheologici.palazzochigi.it/.

250. Anonymous interview, 12/12/08. See also Interview with Ettore Greco, 3/27/09.

251. Interview with Massimo D'Alema, 4/16/09; Interview with Giuliano Amato, 4/22/09; Interview with Carlo Scognamiglio, 4/23/09.

252. Interview with Carlo Scognamiglio, 4/23/09.

Chapter 5

1. Sarah Kreps, "When Does the Mission Determine the Coalition? The Logic of Multilateral Intervention and the Case of Afghanistan," *Security Studies* 17, no. 3 (July 2008): 531–67.

2. Bob Woodward, *Bush at War* (New York: Simon and Schuster, 2002), 63. See also p. 203.

3. Damian Whitworth and Richard Webster, "The Battle Is Joined," *The Times (London)*, October 8, 2001. See also, "Operation *Enduring Freedom* and the Conflict in Afghanistan: An Update," House of Commons Library Research Paper, 01/81, 31 October 2001, pp. 26–29, 102. (Hereafter I will refer to this document as HCLRP 01/81).

4. James F. Dobbins, *After the Taliban: Nation-Building in Afghanistan* (Dulles: Potomac Books, 2008), 44–45, 88, 102–3, 129–31; Michael Evans and Philip Webster, "Britain and U.S. Row over Troops," *The Times* (London), November 20, 2001.

5. Michael Evans and Martin Fletcher, "Britain Picks Euro-Army for Peacekeeping Mission," *The Times* (London), January 9, 2002. See also Paul D. Williams, *British Foreign Policy under New Labour, 1997–2005* (Houndmills: Palgrave Macmillan, 2005), 53.

6. John Kampfner, *Blair's Wars* (London: The Free Press, 2004), 87–88.

7. Alastair Campbell with Richard Stott, *The Blair Years: Extracts from the Alastair Campbell Diaries* (London: Hutchinson, 2007), 507. See also Peter Riddell, *Hug Them Close: Blair, Clinton, Bush and the "Special Relationship"* (London: Politico's, 2004), 134.

8. Christopher Meyer, *DC Confidential* (London: Phoenix, 2006), 175.

9. Philip Stephens, *Tony Blair: The Making of a World Leader* (New York: Viking, 2004), xiii.

10. Campbell, *Blair Years*, 566–67, 568.

11. John Dumbrell, *A Special Relationship: Anglo-American Relations from the Cold War to Iraq,* 2nd ed. (Houndmills: Palgrave Macmillan, 2006) 149.

214 • Notes

12. Stephens, *Tony Blair*, 198.
13. Riddell, *Hug Them Close,* 150–51.
14. Tom Lansford, *All for One: Terrorism, NATO and the United States* (Aldershot: Ashgate, 2002), 97; Paul D. Williams, *British Foreign Policy under New Labour, 1997–2005* (Houndmills: Palgrave Macmillan, 2005), 207.
15. Stephens, *Tony Blair,* 199. See also Kampfner, *Blair's Wars*, 121.
16. Meyer, *DC Confidential*, 205.
17. Campbell, *Blair Years*, 581.
18. Interview with Lawrence Freedman, 7/23/09.
19. HCLRP, 01/81, p. 83.
20. Anonymous interview, 6/23/09.
21. Interview with Theo Farrell, 7/1/09.
22. Ibid.
23. "September 11 Attacks: Prime Minister's Statement Including Question and Answer Session," September 12, 2001, http://www.number-10.gov.uk/output/Page12009.asp. See also Anthony Seldon with Peter Snowdon and Daniel Collings, *Blair Unbound* (London: Simon and Schuster, 2007), 15.
24. "Prime Minister's Statement to the House of Commons Following the September 11 Attacks," September 14, 2001, http://www.number-10.gov.uk/output/Page12009.asp.
25. Ibid. See also "Prime Minister Tony Blair Statement in Response to Terrorist Attacks in the United States," September 11, 2001, http://www.number-10.gov.uk/output/Page12009.asp; Campbell, *Blair Years*, 565.
26. "11 September 2001: The Response," House of Commons Library Research Paper, 01/72, October 3, 2001, p. 34. Emphasis added.
27. "Prime Minister's Statement to the House of Commons Following the September 11 Attacks." See also "Prime Minister's Briefing to the Press En Route to New York," September 21, 2001, http://www.number-10.gov.uk/output/Page12009.asp; Campbell, *Blair Years*, 560.
28. See "Prime Minister's Statement to the House of Commons Following the September 11 Attacks." See also Campbell, *Blair Years*, 561–62; Seldon, *Blair Unbound*, 59–60.
29. Riddell, *Hug Them Close,* 143.
30. Seldon, *Blair Unbound*, 14.
31. Williams, *British Foreign Policy*, 45. See also, HCLRP, 01/81, pp. 12–13.
32. Christopher Hill, "Putting the World to Rights: Tony Blair's Foreign Policy Mission," in *The Blair Effect, 2001–5,* ed. Anthony Seldon and Dennis Kavanagh (Cambridge: Cambridge University Press, 2005), 389.
33. Lansford, *All for One*, 78.
34. "Prime Minister's Statement on Military Action in Afghanistan," October 7, 2001, http://www.number-10.gov.uk/output/Page12009.asp. See HCLRP, 01/81, p. 10.
35. "Prime Minister's Statement to the House of Commons," October 8, 2001, http://www.number-10.gov.uk/output/Page12009.asp. See also Philip Webster,

Roland Watson, and Richard Beeston, "Blair's Finger on the Trigger," *Times* (London), September 21, 2001; Seldon, *Blair Unbound*, 57.

36. House of Commons Hansard Debates, October 16, 2001, column 1054, http://www.publications.parliament.uk/pa/pahansard.htm. (Hereafter I will refer to this series as HCHD.) See also column 1063.

37. For the Conservative position, see the speech by Michael Ancram (Shadow Foreign Secretary) in HCHD, October 16, 2001, columns 1064–65.

38. Michael Evans, "SAS Ready to Respond to U.S. for British Specialists," *The Times* (London), October 22, 2001.

39. Michael Evans and Philip Webster, "Tories Break Political Truce on Afghanistan," *The Times* (London), December 18, 2001.

40. HCLRP, 01/81, p. 47.

41. Anonymous interview, 6/23/09.

42. Interview with Lawrence Freedman, 7/23/09.

43. Interview with Theo Farrell, 71/09.

44. Anonymous interview, 6/23/09.

45. Interview with Theo Farrell, 7/1/99.

46. Zahid Hussein, Roland Watson, and Philip Webster, "Wanted: Dead or Alive," *The Times* (London), September 18, 2001.

47. Ibid.

48. Poll cited in HoCRP, 01/81, pp. 87. The same table shows that 73 percent favored British military support on September 21.

49. Robin Cook, *The Point of Departure: Diaries from the Front Bench* (London: Pocket Books, 2003), 43.

50. Damian Whitworth and Paul Webster, "The Battle Is Joined," *The Times* (London), October 8, 2001.

51. David Charter and Melissa Kite, "Blair's War Effort Raked by Friendly Fire," *The Times* (London), November 2, 2001.

52. Michael Evans and Philip Webster, "Tories Break Political Truce on Afghanistan," *The Times* (London), December 18, 2001; Charles Kennedy, "Without the UN We Can Never Have a Just End to the Afghan Nightmare," *The Times* (London), October 18, 2001; and Charter and Kite, "Blair's War Effort Raked by Friendly Fire."

53. Interview with Robert Worcester, 7/2/09.

54. Anonymous interview, 6/23/09.

55. Williams, *British Foreign Policy*, 17. See also p. 31.

56. Ibid., 17–18.

57. "Prime Minister's Statement on Military Action in Afghanistan," October 7, 2001. See also Seldon, *Blair Unbound*, 58.

58. Philip Webster, "Don't Wobble, Warns Blair," *The Times* (London), October 29, 2001.

59. Riddell, *Hug Them Close,* 141.

60. HCHD, 12/12/01, column 847.

61. Williams, *British Foreign Policy*, 20.

216 • Notes

62. Ibid., 21, 169.
63. Clare Short, *An Honourable Deception? New Labour, Iraq, and the Misuse of Power* (London: Simon and Schuster, 2004), 119–22.
64. Andrew Cottey, "Afghanistan and the New Dynamics of Intervention: Counter-Terrorism and Nation-Building," in *SIPRI Yearbook, 2003* (Oxford: Oxford University Press, 2003), 180–81. See also Ahmed Rashid, *Descent into Chaos* (London: Allen Lane, 2008), 93–94.
65. See HCLRP, 01/72, pp. 43–50.
66. Short, *Honourable Deception*, 111.
67. Interview with Theo Farrell, 7/1/09.
68. Anonymous interview, 6/23/09.
69. "Prime Minister's statement to the House of Commons following the September 11 attacks."
70. HCLRP, 01/72, p. 23.
71. "Prime Minister's statement on military action in Afghanistan," October 7, 2001. See also "Prime Minister's statement to the House of Commons," October 8, 2001.
72. Anonymous interview, 6/23/09.
73. Interview with Theo Farrell, 7/1/99.
74. Raphaelle Baque, Sean McCormack, and Patrick Jarreau, "Jacques Chirac réaffirme à Washington l'offre de coopération de la France," *Le Monde*, September 20, 2001.
75. "Les chefs réligieux afghans et pakistanais menacent les Etats-Unis d'un djihad," *Le Monde*, September 21, 2001.
76. Claire Trean, "Paris avait eté informé de l'imminence d'une intervention," *Le Monde*, October 9, 2001.
77. Nora Bensahel, *The Counterterror Coalitions: Cooperation with Europe, NATO, and the European Union* (Santa Monica: RAND, 2003), 57.
78. Ibid., 11.
79. Ibid., 58.
80. Daniel Vernet, "La France propose á l'Union européenne un plan d'action pour l'après–talibans," *Le Monde*, October 10, 2001.
81. Henri de Bresson, "Jacques Chirac appelle à maintenir la mobilisation antiterroriste," *Le Monde*, November 19, 2001. See also Bensahel, *Counterterror Coalitions,* 57.
82. "Une première expédition de 300 soldats français," *Le Monde*, December 19, 2001. Lansford, *All for One*, 126.
83. Henri Vernet et Thomas Cantaloube, *Chirac contre Bush: L'autre guerre* (Paris: JC Lattès, 2004), 53.
84. Ibid., 54.
85. Védrine, *Face*, 223.
86. Ibid., 163. See also Lionel Jospin, *Le temps de répondre. Entretiens avec Alain Duhamel* (Paris: Stock, 2002), 238.
87. Vernet et Cantaloube, *Chirac*, 61.

Notes • 217

88. Ibid., 62.
89. Entretien avec Pierre Hassner conduit par Jean-Christophe THIABAUD et Thomas HOFNUNG, "La guerre est un cameleon," *Politique Internationale* 94 (Hiver 2001–2002); François Heisborg, "Quelle menaces pour l'Europe?" *Annuaire Français de Relations Internationales* 3 (2002), 54. Patrice de Beer, "Le orientations necèssaires de George Bush," *Le Monde*, September 22, 2001. Steve Erlanger, "Bush's Move on ABM Pact Gives Pause to Europeans," *The New York Times*, December 13, 2001. See also Tom Lansford, "Whither Lafayette? French Military Policy and the American Campaign in Afghanistan," *European Security* 11, no. 3 (Autumn 2002), 133.
90. Védrine, *Face*, 163.
91. Heisborg, "Quelle menaces pour l'Europe?" 54–55.
92. For this claim, see Lansford, *All for One*, 122.
93. "Allies Firm Up Military Roles NATO U.S. Makes Intelligence, Naval and Airspace Requests," *Financial Times*, October 4, 2001.
94. A relevant French Government Minister was the only person I interviewed to cite such concerns—he referred specifically to the U.S. lack of use of NATO despite the activation of Article V on September 12, 2001. Anonymous interview, 6/10/09b.
95. Interview with Pierre Hassner, 6/2/09. See also anonymous interview, 5/19/09; Interview with François Bujon de l'Estang, 6/10/09b.
96. Anonymous interview, 5/19/09.
97. Interview with François Bujon de l'Estang, 6/10/09a.
98. Anonymous interview, 6/10/09b.
99. "Intervention lors des Questions d'actualité à l'Assemblée nationale au sujet de la riposte militaire en Afghanistan," 10/9/01, http://www.archives.premier-ministre.gouv.fr. See also "Intervention de Lionel Jospin, Premier ministre sur TF1," 9/12/01, http://www.archives.premier-ministre.gouv.fr.
100. "Allocution lors de l'ouverture de la session annuelle de l'Institut des Hautes Études de Défense Nationale," 9/24/01, http://www.archives.premier-ministre.gouv.fr. See also Lionel Jospin, *Le temps de répondre. Entretiens avec Alain Duhamel* (Paris: Stock, 2002), 161.
101. Heisborg, "Quelle menaces pour l'Europe?"," 48.
102. "Intervention télévisée de M. Jacques CHIRAC, Président de la République, à la suite des opérations militaires en Afghanistan," 10/7/01, http://www. elysee.fr/elysee/elysee.fr/francais_archives.
103. "Discours de M. Jacques CHIRAC, Président de la République, lors de la visite à la base aérienne 125 à Istres," 10/25/01, http://www.elysee.fr/elysee/elysee.fr/francais_archives.
104. "Réponse de Lionel Jospin lors du débat à l'Assemblée nationale sur la situation en Afghanistan," 11/21/01, http://www.archives.premier-ministre.gouv.fr.
105. Jospin, *Le Temps*, 239.
106. "Entretien du Ministre des Affaires Étrangères, M. Hubert Vedrine, avec le quotidien 'L'Humanite,'" 10/10/01, http://www.doc.diplomatie.gouv.fr. See

218 • Notes

also "Conseil Affaires Generales point de presse du Ministre des Affaires Etrangeres M. Hubert Vedrine," 10/8/01, http://www.doc.diplomatie.gouv.fr.

107. See the interventions by Jean-Pierre Chevènement and Edouard Balladur in "Déclaration du gouvernement sur la situation consecutive aux attentats du 11 Septembre et débat sur cette déclaration," 10/03/01, http://www.assemblee-nationale.fr/11/.

108. "Intervention sur la situation en Afghanistan, Assemblée nationale," 11/21/01, http://www.archives.premier-ministre.gouv.fr.

109. Ibid. See also "56eme session de l'Assemblée Generale des Nations Unies, entretien du Ministre des Affaires Étrangères, M. Hubert Védrine, avec la presse francaise," 11/10/01, http://www.doc.diplomatie.gouv.fr.

110. Interview with François Bujon de l'Estang, 6/10/09a.

111. Anonymous interview, 5/19/09.

112. Ibid.

113. Anonymous interview, 6/10/09b.

114. Jacques Chirac, *Mon Combat Pour La Paix: Textes et interventions* (Paris: Odile Jacob, 2007), 9. See also p. 34.

115. Jospin, *Le temps*, 194.

116. "Audition du Ministre des Affaires Étrangères, M. Hubert Védrine, devant la commission des affaires éntrangeres, de la defense et des forces armées du Senat," 11/17/01, http://www.doc.diplomatie.gouv.fr.

117. Jacques Isnard of *Le Monde* reported that a high-ranking official in the French military said the United States was purposely trying to marginalize France relative to Britain because Paris was less likely to instinctively support Washington than London. Jacques Isnard, "Afghanistan: les déconvenues des armées françaises," *Le Monde*, December 12, 2001.

118. Vernet et Cantaloube, *Chirac,* 69.

119. "Point de presse conjoint de M. Jacques CHIRAC, Président de la République, et de M. Hamid KARZAI, Président de l'administration intérimaire d'Afghanistan," 02/28/02.

120. "Réponse de Lionel Jospin lors du débat à l'Assemblée nationale sur la situation en Afghanistan," 11/21/01. For a similar view, see Claire Trean, "Durcissement de la guerre et mobilisation diplomatique," *Le Monde*, November 3, 2001.

121. Lansford, *All for One,* 98. See also Lansford, "Whither," 126, 127, 134.

122. Anonymous interview, 6/3/09.

123. Anonymous interview, 5/19/09.

124. Interview with François Bujon de l'Estang, 6/10/09a.

125. Elizabeth Pond, *Friendly Fire: The Near-Death of the Transatlantic Alliance* (Washington, D.C.: Brookings Institution Press, 2003), 10.

126. Jean-François Bureau, "L'opinion publique et la defense en France," *Annuaire stratégique et militaire, 2002* (Paris: Odile Jacob, 2002), 227.

127. "Americans and Europeans Differ Widely on Foreign Policy Issues," April 17, 2002, http://people-press.org.

128. See "Réponse aux Sénateurs lors de la séance exceptionnelle sur la situation consécutive aux attentats perpétrés aux Etats-Unis," 10/10/01, http://www.archives.premier-ministre.gouv.fr. See also, Jospin, *Le temps*, 184.

129. Caroline Monnot, "Les militants communistes critiquent les positions de la direction sur l'Afghanistan," *Le Monde*, October 29, 2001.

130. Interview with François Bujon de l'Estang, 6/10/09a.

131. Anonymous interview, 6/10/09b.

132. "Entretien du Ministre des Affaires Étrangères, M. Hubert Védrine, avec 'France 3—France Europe Express,'" 11/4/01, http://www.doc.diplomatie.gouv.fr.

133. "Point de presse conjoint de M. Jacques Chirac Président de la République et de M. George Walker Bush Président des Etats-Unis d'Amérique," 9/18/01, http://www.elysee.fr/elysee/elysee.fr/francais_archives.

134. "Intervention de Lionel Jospin, Premier ministre sur TF1 Mercredi 12 septembre 2001," 9/12/01, http://www.archives.premier-ministre.gouv.fr; "Entretien du Ministre des Affaires Etrangères, M. Hubert Védrine, Avec 'Le Grand Jury RTL-LCI-Le Monde,'" 9/16/01, http://www.doc.diplomatie.gouv.fr.

135. See "Allocution de M. Jacques CHIRAC Président de la République devant la communauté française à Washington," 9/19/01, http://www.elysee.fr/elysee/elysee.fr/francais_archives.

136. "Audition du Ministre des Affaires Étrangères, M. Hubert Védrine, et du Ministre de la Defense, M. Alain Richard, devant les Commissions de la Defense Nationale et Des Étrangères de l'Assemblée Nationale," 10/9/01, http://www.doc.diplomatie.gouv.fr.

137. Chirac, *Mon Combat Pour La Paix,* 191–92.

138. "Réponse aux Sénateurs lors de la séance exceptionnelle sur la situation consécutive aux attentats perpétrés aux Etats-Unis," 10/10/01.

139. "Afghanistan, entretien du Ministre des Affaires Étrangères, M. Hubert Védrine, avec 'RFI' et 'France Inter,'" 11/14/01, http://www.doc.diplomatie.gouv.fr.

140. "Réponse de Lionel Jospin lors du débat à l'Assemblée nationale sur la situation en Afghanistan," 11/21/01.

141. Anonymous interview, 6/10/09b.

142. Interview with François Bujon de l'Estang, 6/10/09a.

143. Anonymous interview, 5/19/09.

144. Paola di Caro, "Conseguenze attacco terroristico agli USA," *Corriere della Sera*, September 13, 2001. Marco Nese, "L'Italia da tre basi, pronti uomini e mezzi," *Corriere della Sera*, September 27, 2001; "Resoconto stenografico dell'intervento del Presidente del Consiglio Silvio Berlusconi, tenuto al Senato nella seduta del 28 Settembre 2001," September 28, 2001, http://www.sitiarcheologici.palazzochigi.it.

145. Marco Nese, "L'Italia dia basi aeree, porti e soldati," *Corriere della Sera*, October 4, 2001. See also Senato della Repubblica, "Resoconto stenografico della seduta n.050 del 09/10/2001," October 9, 2001, http://www.senato.it.

220 • Notes

See also Francesco Verderami, "Washington chiede all'Italia sessanta tank per il fronte," *Corriere della Sera,* October 18, 2001.

146. Maurizio Caprara, "A Bush offrirò tutte le nostre forze militari," *Corriere della Sera,* October 12, 2001. See also Paola di Caro, "Berlusconi da a Bush solidarietà e mezzi," *Corriere della Sera,* October 15, 2001, for a very similar statement.

147. "Afghanistan, militari italiani pronti per la fase due potrebbero participare a un contingente di pace," *Corriere della Sera,* October 16, 2001.

148. Marco Nese, "Libertá duratura, anche l'Italia presto in azione," *Corriere della Sera,* November 5, 2001. See also Antonio Martino in Senato della Repubblica, "Resoconto stenografico della seduta n. 060 del 7/11/2001," November 7, 2001, http;//www.senato.it.

149. Marco Nese, "Misione Afghanistan: navi, aerei e 2700 uomini," *Corriere della Sera,* November 8, 2001; on the arrival, see "Golfo: arrivate le navi italiane," *Corriere della Sera,* December 5, 2001.

150. Senato, November 7, 2001.

151. Dobbins, *After the Taliban,* 51. Marco Nese, "Missione Afghanistan," *Corriere della Sera,* November 15, 2001.

152. Marco Nese, "Opereremo solo come forza di pace," *Corriere della Sera,* November 19, 2001. See also Alessio Altichieri, "Non vogliamo altre truppe straniere, non ce n'é bisogno," *Corriere della Sera,* November 20, 2001.

153. Andrea Nicastro, "Kabul italiani già in azione," *Corriere della Sera,* January 21, 2002.

154. Leopoldo Nuti, "The Richest and Farthest Master is Always Best: U.S.-Italian Relations in Historical Perspective," in *The Atlantic Alliance under Stress: U.S.-European Relations after Iraq,* ed. David M. Andrews (Cambridge: Cambridge University Press, 2005), 193. Many European leaders reacted negatively to the far-right parties in Berlusconi's government (the National Alliance and Northern League).

155. Melinda Henneberger, "A Bush Admirer Longs to Join America's A-List," *The New York Times,* October 20, 2001.

156. "Resoconto stenografico dell'intervento del Presidente del Consiglio, Silvio Berlusconi tenuto alla Camera nella seduta del 12 Settembre, 2001," September 12, 2001, http://www.sitiarcheologici.palazzochigi.it.

157. For criticism, see Franco Venturini, "Se l'Italia vuole avere voce," *Corriere della Sera,* October 15, 2001.

158. Henneberger, "Bush Admirer."

159. Francesco Verderami, "Il cavaliere manderà dei generali al commando di Tampa," *Corriere della Sera,* October 16, 2001.

160. Michele Nones, "L'industria della difesa italiana fra collaborazioni europee e transatlantiche," in *L'Italia e la politica internazionale 2002,* ed. Alessandro Colombo and Natalino Ronzitti (Bologna: Il Mulino, 2002), 116–27.

161. Senato, October 9, 2001.

162. Senato, November 7, 2001.

163. Senato, October 9, 2001; Senato, November 7, 2001.

164. Anonymous interview, 12/18/08.

165. Anonymous interview, 12/9/08.

166. Anonymous interview, 3/18/09.

167. Interview with Lucio Caracciolo, 4/28/09b.

168. "Resoconto stenografico dell'intervento del Presidente del Cosiglio Silvio Berlusconi, tenuto alla Camera nella seduta del 12 Settembre 2001," September 12, 2001, http://www.sitiarcheologici.palazzochigi.it.

169. Paola di Caro, "G8 contro i terroristi, Berlusconi candida l'Italia," *Corriere della Sera,* September 13, 2001; Roberto Zuccolini e Dario di Vico, "Dibattito dopo attentato terroristico agli USA," *Corriere della Sera,* September 16, 2001.

170. Giovanni Bianconi, "Scatta anche in Italia il piano di massima allerta," *Corriere della Sera*, October 8, 2001; Fiorenza Sarzanini, "Il governo aumenta i controlli sugli Arabi," *Corriere della Sera*, October 10, 2001.

171. Enzo Biagi, "La paura globale," *Corriere della Sera*, September 20, 2001. See also, Luigi Accattoli, "Martini: tregua, ma é legittimo il diritto di difesa," *Corriere della Sera,* October 23, 2001; Giovanni Bianconi, "Colpiranno di nuovo ma questa volta in Europa," *Corriere della Sera,* October 28, 2001; and Guido Olimpio, "Dalla Cecenia all'Italia piano segreto di Osama," *Corriere della Sera,* November 24, 2001; Guido Olimpio, "Le petroliere e i porti nel mirino dei terroristi," *Corriere della Sera*, November 26, 2001.

172. Paolo Biondani e Luigi Ferrarella, "Smantellata cellula italiana di Bin Laden," *Corriere della Sera*, October 10, 2001. See also Paolo Biondani, "Spuntano le donne kamikaze," *Corriere della Sera*, October 12, 2001.

173. Fiorenza Sarzanini, "Segnalati ai servizi la possibilità di attacchi ai confini con Francia e Austria," *Corriere della Sera*, October 30, 2001.

174. Fiorenza Sarzanini, "La minaccia Halloween, gli 007 temono anche per l'Italia," *Corriere della Sera*, October 31, 2001.

175. Franco and Venturini. "La stagione delle scelte," *Corriere della Sera*, November 5, 2001.

176. Biagi, " La paura globale."

177. Maurizio Caprara, "Dini: in America c'è scetticismo verso di noi ma non mi pare giustificato," *Corriere della Sera,* October 8, 2001.

178. "Discorso del Presidente Sivlio Berlusconi, Senato della Repubblica," October 9, 2001, http://www.sitiarcheologici.palazzochigi.it.

179. Senato, October 9, 2001.

180. Senato, November 7, 2001; See also Antonio Macaluso, "Martino: se la guerra sará lunga il paese ci criticherá," *Corriere della Sera*, November 10, 2001.

181. "Messaggio del Presidente del Consiglio Sivlio Berlusconi ai soldati italiani impegnati nell'operazione 'Enduring Freedom,'" November 18, 2001, http://www.sitiarcheologici.palazzochigi.it.

222 • Notes

182. Anonymous interview, 12/9/08.
183. Interview with Silvio Fagiolo, 4/21/09.
184. Anonymous interview, 3/18/09.
185. Anonymous interview, 12/18/08.
186. Anonymous interview, 4/28/09a.
187. Interview with Lucio Caracciolo, 4/28/09b.
188. "Resoconto stenografico dell'intervento del Presidente del Consiglio Silvio Berlusconi, tenuto alla Camera nella seduta del 12 Settembre 2001," September 12, 2001, http://www.sitiarcheologici.palazzochigi.it.
189. Venturini, "Se l'Italia."
190. Verderami, "Il Cavaliere manderá."
191. "Super-vertice sulla guerra a Gand, l'Italia rimane esclusa," *Corriere della Sera*, November 18, 2001; Felice Saulino,"D'Alema: con me l'Italia era piu' stimata," *Corriere della Sera,* October 20, 2001. See also Stefano Folli, "Ma il rapporto con gli USA é la priorità del governo," *Corriere della Sera*, October 20, 2001; Stefano Folli, "NATO finita, via le basi o andremo in serie B," *Corriere della Sera*, October 25, 2001.
192. Maurizio Caprara, "Vertice a tre a Londra, l'Italia di nuovo esclusa," *Corriere della Sera*, November 3, 2001. See also Massimo Nava, "Rivalità e dispetti, la difficile convivenza tra Chirac e il Cavaliere," *Corriere della Sera*, November 4, 2001, and Paola di Caro, "Nessuna esclusione sinistra smentita dai fatti," *Corriere della Sera,* November 5, 2001.
193. Franco Venturini, "La stagione della scelta," *Corriere della Sera*, November 5, 2001.
194. Saulino Felice, "Cacciari: evitiamo ipocrisie e diamo il sostegno, come nei paesi seri," *Corriere della Sera,* November 5, 2001.
195. Senato, November 7, 2001.
196. Marco Nese, "Missione pericolosa, ci vogliono regole," *Corriere della Sera,* December 23, 2001.
197. Anonymous interview, 12/18/08. Another Foreign Ministry official told me that Italy had to be involved to "preserve our international weight" but had to be careful because others might ask too much of it. Anonymous interview, 12/9/08.
198. Anonymous interview, 3/18/09.
199. Anonymous interview, 3/18/09; Interview with Lucio Caracciolo, 4/28/09b.
200. Interview with Silvio Fagiolo, 4/21/09.
201. Anonymous interview, 4/28/09a.
202. Renato Mannheimer, "Missione Afghanistan, cresce il partito del dubbio," *Corriere della Sera*, November 9, 2001.
203. Roberto Zuccolini e Dario Di Vico, "Reagire o pacifcare; il dilemma dei cattolici," *Corriere della Sera,* September 16, 2001; Giuliano Gallo, "A Roma l'estrema destra sfila con i Verdi e i comunisti," *Corriere della Sera*, October 9, 2001.

204. Luigi Accattoli, "Martini: tregua ma è legittimo diritto alla difesa," *Corriere della Sera,* October 23, 2001. Carlo Vulpio, "Rutelli e Fassino tra i militari: siamo con voi," *Corriere della Sera*, November 10, 2010.
205. Gianna Fragonara, "Marcia della pace, tra assenze e timori," *Corriere della Sera,* October 14, 2001.
206. Francesco Alberti and Roberto Zuccolini, "Berlusconi: Manifestiamo contro il terrorismo," *Corriere della Sera*, October, 17, 2001.
207. Angelo Panebianco, "Siamo tutti italiani o no?" *Corriere della Sera*, November 6, 2001.
208. Paola di Caro, "G8 contro i terroristi," *Corriere della Sera*, September 13, 2001.
209. Marzio Breda, "Contro i terroristi non bastano le armi," *Corriere della Sera*, October 10, 2201. See also Gianna Fregonara, "Voto sulla guerra," *Corriere della Sera*, November 5, 2001.
210. Daria Gorodinsky, "D'Alema e Rutelli," *Corriere della Sera*, October 13, 2001.
211. Saulino Felice, "Salvi: siamo come l'Italia di Crispi," *Corriere della Sera*, November 6, 2001. See also Piero Ostellino, "Una pagina ben scritta dalle Camere," *Corriere della Sera*, November 8, 2001.
212. Stefano Folli, "Giorno solenne alla Camere, forse un passaggio storico," *Corriere della Sera*, November 8, 2001.
213. Campbell, *Blair Years*, 569.
214. Anonymous interview, 12/18/08. Another Foreign Ministry official made a similar point. Anonymous interview, 12/9/08.
215. Anonymous interview, 3/18/09.
216. Anonymous interview, 4/28/09a.
217. Interview with Lucio Caracciolo, 4/28/09b.
218. Ferruccio De Bortoli and Oriana Fallaci, "Lettera da New York," *Corriere della Sera*, September 29, 2001; Melinda Henneberger, "Provocateur Is Back to 'Spit' on Detractors of U.S.," *New York Times*, October 30, 2001.
219. Paola di Caro, "L'Occidente è una civiltà superiore," *Corriere della Sera*, September 27, 2001.
220. "Discorso del Presidente Silvio Berlusconi, Senato della Repubblica," October 9, 2001, http://www.sitiarcheologici.palazzochigi.it/www.governo.it/dicembre %202002/www.governo.it/index.html. See also, Lamberto Dini during Senato, October 9, 2001.
221. Senato, November 7, 2001.
222. "Messaggio inviato dal Presidente del Consiglio Berlusconi, al Presidente della Commissione Parlamentare per l'Infanzia della Camera dei Deputati Maria Burani Procaccini," November 19, 2001, http://www.sitiarcheologici. palazzochigi.it.
223. Senato, October 9, 2001.
224. Paolo Conti, "Massacro a Mazar: sono questi I nostri alleati?," *Corriere della Sera*, November 30, 2001.

224 • Notes

225. I did hear that it was important that a UNSC resolution explicitly authorized the use of force. Anonymous interview, 12/9/08.
226. Anonymous interview, 12/18/08.
227. Anonymous interview, 3/18/09.

Chapter 6

1. For an overview, see Philip H. Gordon and Jeremy Shapiro, *Allies at War: America, Europe, and the Crisis over Iraq* (New York: McGraw Hill, 2004). For the U.S. perspective, see Bob Woodward, *Plan of Attack* (New York: Simon and Schuster, 2004).
2. Peter Riddell, rev. ed., *Hug Them Close: Blair, Clinton, Bush and the "Special Relationship"* (London: Politico's, 2004), 191.
3. Alastair Campbell with Richard Stott, *The Blair Years: Extracts from the Alastair Campbell Diaries* (London: Hutchinson, 2007), 630.
4. "The Downing Street Memo," in Mark Danner, *The Secret Way to War: The Downing Street Memo and the Iraq War's Buried History* (New York: New York Review Books, 2006), 90.
5. Ibid., 92.
6. Woodward, *Plan of Attack,* 178–79.
7. Campbell, *Blair Years,* 645.
8. Anthony Seldon with Peter Snowdon and Daniel Collings, *Blair Unbound* (London: Simon and Schuster, 2007), 161.
9. http://www.mod.uk/DefenceInternet/FactSheets/OperationsFactsheets/OperationsInIraqFactsandFigures.htm.
10. Campbell, *Blair Years,* 630. See also Campbell, 632, 636, 640, 656. See also Christopher Meyer, *DC Confidential: The Controversial Memoirs of Britain's Ambassador at the Time of 9/11 and the Iraq War* (London: Phoenix, 2006), 241; William Wallace and Tim Oliver, "A Bridge Too Far: The United Kingdom and the Transatlantic Relationship," in *The Atlantic Alliance Under Stress,* ed. David M. Andrews (Cambridge: Cambridge University Press, 2005), 152; John Kampfner, *Blair's Wars* (London: The Free Press, 2004), 235.
11. Philip Stephens, *Tony Blair: The Making of a World Leader* (New York: Viking, 2004), xiii. See also Seldon, *Blair Unbound,* 86; Robin Cook, *The Point of Departure: Diaries from the Front Bench* (London: Pocket Books, 2003), 102.
12. Cook, *Point of Departure,* 104, 205.
13. Riddell, *Hug Them Close,* 300.
14. Cook, *Point of Departure,* 199.
15. Christopher Meyer recalled that American policies on steel, air, and defense sales were not ideal for Britain but he blames the disagreement on " . . . a failure in London at the highest level to have a clear vision of the national interest and to negotiate accordingly." That is, Meyer blames poor statecraft rather than Washington's resistance to London's pressures. Meyer, *DC Confidential,* 61.

Notes • 225

16. Peter Riddell says Blair had "privileged status" in Washington as a result of his government's reaction to 9/11 and contribution to the U.S.-led war in Afghanistan. Riddell, *Hug Them Close,* 163.

17. Seldon, *Blair Unbound,* 92–93, 178, 180. See also Campbell, *Blair Years,* 613; Stephens, *Tony Blair,* 212; Seldon, *Blair Unbound,* 95.

18. On the Bush promise, see Campbell, *Blair Years,* 635. On the follow-through, see Campbell, *Blair Years,* 680. See also Woodward, *Plan of Attack,* 347.

19. Kampfner, *Blair's Wars,* 297.

20. Seldon, *Blair Unbound,* 92–93. See also Campbell, *Blair Years,* 631, 635, 636; Woodward, *Plan of Attack,* 183. For a more skeptical British view, see Meyer, *DC Confidential,* 250. Seldon, *Blair Unbound,* 106, cites a private interviewee who said that Number 10 believed that "Bush would never even have tried to use the UN without Blair."

21. Riddell, *Hug Them Close,* 206.

22. See Campbell, *Blair Years,* 659; Seldon, *Blair Unbound,* 147; Woodward, *Plan of Attack,* 297.

23. Cook, *Point of Departure,* 309.

24. Meyer, *DC Confidential,* 248. See also Seldon, *Blair Unbound,* 99; Christopher Hill, "Putting the World to Rights: Tony Blair's Foreign Policy Mission," in *The Blair Effect, 2001–5,* ed. Anthony Seldon and Dennis Kavanagh (Cambridge: Cambridge University Press, 2005), 388.

25. Riddell, *Hug Them Close,* xiv.

26. See, for example, Charles Kennedy's statements in HCHD, 18 March 2003, column 785. Robin Cook recorded varied views at the time. See Cook, *Point of Departure,* 99, 102, 106.

27. Clare Short, *An Honourable Deception? New Labour, Iraq, and the Misuse of Power* (London: Free Press, 2004), 184. See also pp. 129, 142, 152, 170, and 177.

28. Williams, *British Foreign Policy,* 193.

29. "I Had Dinner with Condi," in Danner, *Secret Way to War,* 131.

30. Ibid.

31. Campbell, *Blair Years,* 636.

32. Cook, *Point of Departure,* 2, 213. Cook seems to have opposed the war primarily because he valued Britain's relationship with the European Union more highly than its relationship with the United States. See Cook, *Point of Departure,* 115, 130, 139.

33. Ibid., 116. On January 7, 2003, Blair told British Ambassadors and diplomats that "[t]he price of influence is that we do not leave the U.S. to face the tricky issues alone." Quoted in Riddell, *Hug Them Close,* 1.

34. Seldon, *Blair Unbound,* 86–87.

35. Meyer, *DC Confidential,* 239.

36. HCHD, March 18, 2003, column 770–71.

37. Blair, "Oral Evidence," 46, 52.

226 • Notes

38. Kevin Tebbit and Michael Boyce, "Oral Evidence Transcript," *The Iraq Inquiry*, London, December 3, 2009, 26, 38, 45–46; Geoffrey Hoon, "Oral Evidence Transcript," *The Iraq Inquiry*, London, January 19, 2010, 20; Jonathan Powell, "Oral Evidence Transcript," *The Iraq Inquiry*, London, January 18, 2010, 22–23; Jack Straw, "Oral Evidence Transcript," *The Iraq Inquiry*, London, January 21, 50–51, http://www.iraqinquiry.org.uk/transcripts.aspx.

39. Anonymous interview, 6/17/09; Interview with Clare Short, 7/6/09; Interview with Philip Stephens, 7/14/09; Anonymous interview, 7/21/09. Rosemary Hollis disagreed, suggesting that Blair probably deceived himself as to his level of influence. Interview with Rosemary Hollis, 7/1/09.

40. Interview with Alan Dobson, 7/17/09. Rosemary Hollis noted the importance of U.S. power in Blair's calculus, which is compatible with Dobson's point.

41. In addition to those I cite below, see Anonymous interview, 6/17/09; Interview with Rosemary Hollis, 7/1/09; Anonymous interview, 7/8/09; Interview with Philip Stephens, 7/14/09; Interview with Robin Niblett, 7/22/09. An anonymous Blair minister did not emphasize the UK-U.S. alliance. Anonymous interview, 7/21/09. Robin Niblett pointed out that those seeking to defend the Blair government's actions might not admit to the importance of the U.S.-UK alliance for fear of feeding domestic criticism that Blair had been Bush's "poodle." Interview with Robin Niblett, 7/22/09.

42. Interview with Clare Short, 7/6/09.

43. Interview with Peter Riddell, 7/24/09.

44. Interview with Bernard Jenkin, 7/20/09.

45. Williams, *British Foreign Policy*, 194, 196.

46. Seldon, *Blair Unbound*, 138.

47. Cook, *Point of Departure,* 213.

48. One might question whether Blair's distorted, individual view of Iraq's WMD dominated. Wallace and Oliver, "A Bridge Too Far," 152, 169. Anthony Seldon (p. 166) provides a response: "Those who think Blair bounced the Cabinet are wrong: it had discussed Iraq every time it met from September 2002 onwards." The Iraq Inquiry testimony further suggests a large degree of consensus within the Cabinet on the fundamentals of the issue (excluding Clare Short and Robin Cook, of course).

49. HCHD, March 18, 2003, column 762. See also Campbell, *Blair Years,* 640.

50. Hans Blix, *Disarming Iraq: The Search for Weapons of Mass Destruction* (London: Bloomsbury, 2004), 201, 257.

51. Seldon, *Blair Unbound*, 138. See also Blix, *Disarming Iraq,* 194.

52. Kampfner, *Blair's Wars,* 206. See also Seldon, *Blair Unbound*, 195. Campbell, *Blair Years,* 702.

53. Kampfner, *Blair's Wars,* 264–67. See also Seldon, *Blair Unbound*, 151.

54. Kampfner, *Blair's Wars,* 363–68, 371–76.

55. Meyer, *DC Confidential,* 283.

56. Kampfner, *Blair's Wars,* 268.
57. "Review of Intelligence on Weapons of Mass Destruction, Report of a Committee of Privy Counsellors," London, Her Majesty's Stationery Office, 14 July 2004, 73.
58. Blix, *Disarming Iraq,* 240.
59. Cook, *Point of Departure,* 221. See also Short, *An Honourable Deception?* 147–48.
60. Short, *An Honourable Deception?* 147–48, 228–29.
61. Hill, "Putting the World to Rights," 398.
62. Riddell, *Hug Them Close,* xiii.
63. Kampfner, *Blair's Wars,* 210.
64. Seldon, *Blair Unbound,* 143. Blix told the UNSC that Iraq's December declaration " . . . had not provided material or evidence that solved any of the unresolved disarmament issues." See Blix, *Disarming Iraq,* 108, 139. UNMOVIC's March 2003 quarterly report had a similar effect. See Blix, *Disarming Iraq,* 199.
65. Riddell, *Hug Them Close,* 213.
66. Cook, *Point of Departure,* 221. See also Riddell, *Hug Them Close,* 216–17.
67. "Iraq: Options Paper," in Danner, *Secret Way to War,* 95.
68. "Review of Intelligence," 73.
69. "Foreign Secretary Straw on 'Crawford/Iraq'," in Danner, *Secret Way to War,* 146.
70. HCHD, 18 March 2003, column 770.
71. Kampfner, *Blair's Wars,* 282.
72. "Review of Intelligence," 120.
73. On the importance of the fear that WMD might be handed off to terrorist groups, see Campbell, *Blair Years,* 669; Meyer, *DC Confidential,* 234–35; Seldon, *Blair Unbound,* 85.
74. HCHD, March 18, 2003, column 768. See also column 767.
75. HCHD, March 18, 2003, column 775.
76. Campbell, *Blair Years,* 671.
77. Kampfner, *Blair's Wars,* 159.
78. Blair, "Oral Evidence," 78–79. See also Powell, "Oral Evidence Transcript," 47; Hoon, "Oral Evidence Transcript," 25. Blair was by far the most concerned with the Iraq/terrorism threat but admitted it was a future, potential threat not an actual one. Blair, "Oral Evidence," 69–70.
79. Straw, "Oral Evidence Transcript," 55.
80. Interview with Clare Short, 7/6/09; Anonymous interview, 7/8/09; Anonymous interview, 7/21/09.
81. Anonymous interview, 7/21/09. Anonymous interview, 7/8/09. In fact, Bernard Jenkin expressed the concern at the time that Hussein might use WMD against British interests, specifically bases on Cyprus. Interview with Bernard Jenkin, 7/20/09.
82. Anonymous interview, 7/21/09.

228 • Notes

83. Interview with Bernard Jenkin, 7/20/09; Anonymous interview, 6/17/09.
84. In addition to those I cite below, I heard similar views in my interview with Rosemary Hollis, 7/1/09; Interview with Robin Niblett, 7/22/09.
85. Interview with Philip Stephens, 7/14/09.
86. Interview with Peter Riddell, 7/24/09.
87. Anonymous interview, 7/8/09.
88. Riddell, *Hug Them Close,* 241. See also Tim Dunne, "Britain and the Gathering Storm over Iraq," in *Foreign Policy: Theories, Actors, Cases,* ed. Steve Smith, Amelia Hadfield, and Timothy Dunne (Oxford: Oxford University Press, 2008), 341.
89. Campbell, *Blair Years,* 671.
90. Riddell, *Hug Them Close,* 203. See also Cook, *Point of Departure,* 188, 251.
91. Campbell, *Blair Years,* 669. See *Britain at the Polls, 2001,* ed. Anthony Stephen King (London: Chatham House, 2002).
92. Kampfner, *Blair's Wars,* 309. See also Campbell, *Blair Years,* 681.
93. Interview with Robert Worcester, 7/2/09.
94. Anonymous interview, 6/17/09; Interview with Rosemary Hollis, 7/1/09; Interview with Robin Niblett, 7/22/09.
95. Interview with Clare Short, 7/6/09.
96. Anonymous interview, 7/8/09; Interview with Peter Riddell, 7/24/09.
97. Interview with Bernard Jenkin, 7/20/09.
98. Williams, *British Foreign Policy,* 17.
99. Riddell, *Hug Them Close,* 8.
100. HCHD, March 18, 2003, column 773.
101. Cook, *Point of Departure,* 294.
102. Ibid., 291.
103. Williams, *British Foreign Policy,* 187. See also Seldon, *Blair Unbound,* 152; Cook, *Point of Departure,* 293; Kampfner, *Blair's Wars,* 273.
104. HCHD, March 18, 2003, column 773.
105. Blair, "Oral Evidence," 65. See also Straw, "Oral Evidence Transcript," 17, 25.
106. Ibid.
107. Ibid., column 761.
108. HCHD, March 18, 2003, column 902.
109. "Review of Intelligence," 105.
110. Greenstock, "Oral Evidence Transcript," 100; Straw, "Oral Evidence Transcript," 56–57; Alastair Campbell, "Oral Evidence Transcript," *The Iraq Inquiry,* London, January 12, 2010, I-62; David Manning, "Oral Evidence Transcript," *The Iraq Inquiry,* London, November 20, 2009, 30, http://www.iraqinquiry.org.uk/transcripts.aspx.
111. See Article 51, http://www.un.org/aboutun/charter/chapter7.shtml.
112. Williams, *British Foreign Policy,* 197–99.
113. Goldsmith argued that the root authorization to use force was found in UNSC Resolutions 678 and 687 and he required that Blair certify Iraq's failure to

comply with Resolution 1441. For a summary, see "Review of Intelligence," 93–97. For Goldsmith's prior warning, see Blair, "Oral Evidence," 96.

114. Riddell, *Hug Them Close,* 259.

115. For the view at the time in Britain, see Short, *An Honourable Deception?* 186. See also "International Law Expert Says U.S. Should Delay an Iraq Attack Until It Gains Security Council Backing," March 4, 2003, http://www.cfr.org/publication.html?id=5646.

116. "Note from Michael Wood (FCO Legal Adviser) to the Foreign Secretary's Private Secretary re Iraq: Legal basis for use of force," January 24, 2003, Declassified Document, Iraq Inquiry; "Letter from Elizabeth Wilmshurst (FCO Deputy Legal Adviser) to Michael Wood (FCO Legal Adviser) on early retirement/resignation," March 18, 2003, http://www.iraqinquiry.org.uk/transcripts/declassified-documents.aspx.

117. "Iraq: Options Paper," 97. See also, "Foreign Secretary Straw on 'Crawford/Iraq,'" 146.

118. Blair, "Oral Evidence," 145.

119. "Full Text: Iraq Legal Advice (part two)," *The Guardian*, April 28, 2005, http://www.guardian.co.uk/politics/2005/apr/28/election2005.uk1. See also Blair, "Oral Evidence," 138.

120. "Full Text: Iraq Legal Advice (part two)."

121. Interview with Bernard Jenkin, 7/20/09.

122. Interview with Philip Stephens, 7/14/09. Interview with Clare Short, 7/6/09.

123. Anonymous interview, 7/8/09.

124. Interview with Peter Riddell, 7/24/09.

125. Anonymous interview, 7/21/09.

126. Peter Riddell agreed that the military imperative doomed the Chilean proposal to allow inspectors more time. Interview with Peter Riddell, 7/24/09.

127. Interview with Philip Stephens, 7/14/09.

128. Interview with Rosemary Hollis, 7/1/09; Interview with Clare Short, 7/6/09.

129. Riddell, *Hug Them Close,* 18. See also p. 293.

130. Campbell, *Blair Years,* 612. From the Iraq Inquiry, see Boyce, 14, 37; Hoon, 49; Manning, 19; Powell, 18, 78.

131. Manning, "Oral Evidence Transcript," 39.

132. Seldon, *Blair Unbound*, 148.

133. Riddell, *Hug Them Close,* 249.

134. Greenstock, "Oral Evidence Transcript," 76–77; Manning, "Oral Evidence Transcript," 81, 84, 104; Meyer, "Oral Evidence," 51–52, 94; Powell, "Oral Evidence Transcript," 82; Edward Chaplin and Peter Ricketts, "Oral Evidence Transcript," *The Iraq Inquiry*, London, December 1, 2009, 44, 47; Michael Jay, "Oral Evidence Transcript," *The Iraq Inquiry*, London, 22–23, 24, http://www.iraqinquiry.org.uk/transcripts.aspx. Blair denied U.S. impatience was a factor, arguing that the British military were equally concerned with initiating

230 • Notes

military action as soon as possible. Blair, "Oral Evidence," 102. Straw offered a more ambiguous statement, "Oral Evidence," 85. Defense Secretary Geoffrey Hoon directly contradicted Blair, noting that British forces became operational just prior to the start of the war in March and would have benefited from more time prior to the initiation of hostilities. Hoon, "Oral Evidence Transcript," 143. See also Boyce, "Oral Evidence Transcript," 68.

135. Greenstock, "Oral Evidence Transcript," 76–77.

136. Ibid., 76, 79; Manning, "Oral Evidence Transcript," 81; Christopher Meyer, November 26, 2009, "Oral Evidence Transcript," *The Iraq Inquiry*, London, 51–52, 92, http://www.iraqinquiry.org.uk/transcripts.aspx.

137. Blair and Straw—among others—blame the lack of explicit UNSC authorization on the French. Blair, "Oral Evidence," 102; Straw, "Oral Evidence Transcript," 84, 101. Substantial evidence, however, including Blair's statement to the Inquiry, shows that the French government clarified that it would veto a resolution that would allow the United States and UK to judge when Iraq had failed to comply. Blair, "Oral Evidence," 124–25. See also Blix, *Disarming Iraq,* 246. The French almost certainly would have supported a resolution providing authorization for the use of force in the event that Blix judged Iraq to have not met the benchmarks. Even if the French insisted on a UNSC vote after Blix's judgment, it is inconceivable that they would have vetoed authorization had Blix judged Iraq to have failed to meet the benchmarks.

138. Some, such as Jack Straw, imply that allowing inspectors more time would have meant that Iraq would keep its WMD, having faced down the United States and UK. Straw, "Oral Evidence Transcript," 114–15. It is unclear how more time for inspections would have translated into the evaporation of the American and British resolve to deal with Iraq's WMD that existed in March 2003.

139. Boyce, "Oral Evidence Transcript," 63.

140. Campbell, *Margaret Thatcher,* 630.

141. "French Leader Offers America Both Friendship and Criticism," *The New York Times*, September 9, 2002.

142. Gordon and Shapiro, *Allies at War,* 142.

143. Dominique De Villepin, *Un autre monde* (Paris: L'Herne, 2003), 60–61. See also Gordon and Shapiro, *Allies at War,* 123. For Bruno Le Maire De Villepin's statement emerged from the realization that the United States had firmly decided on war. Bruno Le Maire, *Le Ministre* (Paris: Grasset, 2004), 137.

144. Gordon and Shapiro, *Allies at War,* 125. See, for example, Chirac's statement on the January 22 anniversary of the Elysée Treaty. Gordon and Shapiro, 126.

145. Gordon and Shapiro, *Allies at War,* 138, 140.

146. Ibid., 150.

147. Gordon and Shapiro (p. 153) interpret "whatever the circumstances" as referring to the array of votes in the UNSC.

Notes • 231

148. Ibid. See also Blix, *Disarming Iraq,* 246.
149. Gordon and Shapiro, *Allies at War,* 154.
150. Ibid., 64.
151. Ibid., 52.
152. Georges-Henri Soutou, "Three rifts, two reconciliations: Franco-American relations during the Fifth Republic," in *The Atlantic Alliance Under Stress,* ed. David M. Andrews (Cambridge: Cambridge University Press, 2005), 117.
153. Henri Vernet et Thomas Cantaloube, *Chirac contre Bush: L'autre guerre* (Paris: JC Lattès, 2004), 21.
154. Gilles Delafon et Thomas Sancton, "L'Irak ne pourra nous diviser," *Le Monde*, February 19, 2003.
155. Vernet and Cantaloube, *Chirac contre Bush,* 170.
156. De Villepin, *Un autre monde*, 46; Chirac, *Mon Combat*, 253–54.
157. Interview with Etienne de Durand, 5/15/09.
158. Interview with Bruno Tertrais, 5/13/09b.
159. Anonymous interview, 5/20/09.
160. Anonymous interview, 6/9/09.
161. Interview with Nicole Gnesotto, 6/3/09.
162. Anonymous interview, 5/20/09.
163. Blix, *Disarming Iraq,* 127, 128, 194.
164. Vernet and Cantaloube, *Chirac contre Bush,* 194.
165. Chirac, *Mon Combat*, 247; De Villepin *Un autre monde,* 40.
166. "Discours de M. Jacques Chirac, Président de la République, lors de la présentation des voeux du Corps diplomatique," January 7, 2003, http://www.elysee.fr/elysee/elysee.fr/francais_archives.
167. Chirac, *Mon Combat*, 235.
168. *New York Times*, "French Leader Offers America Both Friendship and Criticism."
169. Ibid.
170. The French view was apparent during the negotiations for 1441 and the French expressed it to their American counterparts. See Vernet and Cantaloube, *Chirac contre Bush,* 114.
171. Vernet and Cantaloube, *Chirac contre Bush,* 144. See also Gordon and Shapiro, *Allies at War,* 120. Within days Gourdault-Montagne's assessment became the consensus view. Vernet and Cantaloube, *Chirac contre Bush,* 154.
172. Blix, *Disarming Iraq,* 246.
173. Ibid., 89, 246, 252. See also Le Maire, *Le Ministre,* 203.
174. *New York Times*, "French Leader Offers America Both Friendship and Criticism."
175. Gordon and Shapiro, *Allies at War,* 83. See also p. 85.
176. Blix, *Disarming Iraq,* 252.
177. *New York Times*, "French Leader Offers America Both Friendship and Criticism." See also Gordon and Shapiro, *Allies at War,* 80; De Villepin, *Un autre monde,* 62, 86–87, 95.

232 • Notes

178. Gordon and Shapiro, *Allies at War,* 89–90, 146, 177.
179. Le Maire, *Le Ministre,* 23.
180. Vernet and Cantaloube, *Chirac contre Bush,* 124–25.
181. Gordon and Shapiro, *Allies at War,* 146.
182. De Villepin, *Un autre monde,* 58. See also p. 95–96. See also Le Maire, *Le Ministre,* 94.
183. Campbell, *Blair Years,* 662. See also Blix, *Disarming Iraq,* 128.
184. Blix, *Disarming Iraq,* 127.
185. "Déclaration sur l'Iraq de M. Jacques CHIRAC, Président de la République," March 18, 2003, http://www.elysee.fr/elysee/elysee.fr/francais_archives.
186. De Villepin, *Un autre monde,* 27. See also p. 31.
187. Robert J. Pauly, "French Security Agenda in the Post-9/11 World," in *Old Europe, New Europe and the U.S.* ed. Tom Lansford and Blagovest Tashev (Aldershot: Ashgate, 2005), 6.
188. Gordon and Shapiro, *Allies at War,* 179. See also Chirac, *Mon Combat,* 247; Pauly, "French Security Agenda," 13.
189. "Discours prononcé par M. Jacques CHIRAC, Président de la République, à l'occasion de la reception des Ambassadeurs," August 29, 2002, http://www.elysee.fr/elysee/elysee.fr/francais_archives.
190. *New York Times,* "French Leader Offers America Both Friendship and Criticism,"
191. Claire Trean, "Irak: France, Russie et Chine disent non à George W. Bush," *Le Monde,* September 30, 2002. Gordon and Shapiro, *Allies at War,* 10, 122.
192. Gordon and Shapiro, *Allies at War,* 145. See also Chirac, *Mon Combat,* 252.
193. Stephens, *Tony Blair,* 226; Gordon and Shapiro, *Allies at War,* 127.
194. Vernet and Cantaloube, *Chirac contre Bush,* 248.
195. "Conférence de presse de M. Jacques CHIRAC, Président de la République, à l'issue de la réunion informelle extraordinaire du Conseil européen," February 17, 2003, http://www.elysee.fr/elysee/elysee.fr/francais_archives.
196. "Déclaration de M. Chirac, March 18, 2003. See also "Conférence de presse de M. Jacques CHIRAC, Président de la République, à l'issue du Conseil européen," March 21, 2003, http://www.elysee.fr/elysee/elysee.fr/francais_archives.
197. The Policy Planning official noted that Chirac doubted that Iraq possessed WMD. Anonymous interview, 6/9/09.
198. Some stressed Hussein's lack of means to deliver WMD even if he had the will to do so: Interview with Frédéric Bozo, 5/11/09; Interview with Camille Grand, 5/13/09b.
199. Anonymous interview, 5/20/09. Also, interview with Nicole Gnesotto, 6/3/09.
200. Anonymous interview, 6/9/09.
201. Interview with Frédéric Bozo, 5/11/09.
202. Interview with Bruno Tertrais, 5/13/09b.

Notes • 233

203. Anonymous interview, 5/20/09.
204. Anonymous interview, 6/9/09; Interview with Nicole Gnesotto, 6/3/09.
205. Interview with Nicole Gnesotto, 6/3/09. Camille Grand made a similar point. Interview with Camille Grand, 5/13/09a.
206. Interview with Etienne de Durand, 5/15/09.
207. Interview with Frédéric Bozo, 5/11/09.
208. Gordon and Shapiro, *Allies at War,* 144. See also Claire Trean, "Les Européens repoussent la perspective d'une guerre en Irak," *Le Monde*, January 15, 2003.
209. "Le débat sur la guerre contre l'Irak mobilise les partis," *Le Monde*, September 13, 2002. See also "La France et l'Irak," *Le Monde*, October 10, 2002; "M. Hollande pour un veto de la France," *Le Monde*, January 7, 2003.
210. See, for example, Claire Trean, "Pour la France, rien ne justifie un débat à l'ONU sur le recours à la force," *Le Monde*, January 28, 2003. See also Claire Trean, "A ce stade, la France opposerait son veto à une résolution autorisant le recours à la force," *Le Monde*, February 8, 2003.
211. Vernet and Cantaloube, *Chirac contre Bush,* 133. See also p. 140.
212. Le Maire, *Le Ministre,* 94.
213. Claire Trean, "La France refuse tout glissement vers une logique de guerre," *Le Monde,* January 31, 2003.
214. Jacques Isnard, "Les armées françaises n'ont pas encore lancé de plan spécifique de preparation," *Le Monde,* January 9, 2003.
215. Gordon and Shapiro, *Allies at War,* 120.
216. On the relationship between public opinion and the communication of policy, see Vernet and Cantaloube, *Chirac contre Bush,* 150.
217. Interview with Frédéric Bozo, 5/11/09.
218. Interview with Bruno Tertrais, 5/13/09b. The claim found similar support from interview with Nicole Gnesotto, 6/3/09.
219. Anonymous interview, 6/9/09. I heard similar views expressed in the interview with Camille Grand, 5/13/09a; Interview with Nicole Gnesotto, 6/3/09.
220. "Conférence de presse conjointe de M. Jacques CHIRAC, Président de la République, de M. Paul BIYA, Président du Cameroun, de M. Thabo MBEKI, Président d'Afrique du Sud, et de M. Kofi ANNAN, Secrétaire général de l'Organisation des Nations Unies, à l'issue de la 22e Conférence des Chefs d'Etat d'Afrique et de France," February 21, 2003, http://www.elysee.fr/elysee/elysee.fr/francais_archives.
221. "Déclaration de M. Chirac," March 18, 2003.
222. De Villepin, *Un autre monde,* 40.
223. Gordon and Shapiro, *Allies at War,* 126.
224. Ibid., 121.
225. On French persuasion, see Béatrice Gurrey, "La Bataille Onusienne de Jacques Chirac," *Le Monde*, March 18, 2003.
226. Claire Tréan, "Analyse Le précédent du Kosovo peut difficilement être invoqué," *Le Monde*, March 15, 2003.

234 • Notes

227. "Irak: Chirac fait reculer Bush," *Le Monde*, October 19, 2002; Patrice de Beer, "Le jour de gloire de Jacques Chirac," *Le Monde*, November 5, 2002; Claire Tréan, "Diplomatie: la France reprend des couleurs," *Le Monde*, November 13, 2002.

228. Interview with Camille Grand, 5/13/09a.

229. Interview with Bruno Tertrais, 5/13/09b; Interview with Nicole Gnesotto, 6/3/09; Anonymous interview, 5/20/09.

230. Anonymous interview, 6/9/09.

231. Anonymous interview, 6/9/09; Anonymous interview, 5/20/09; Interview with Camille Grand, 5/13/09a.

232. Anonymous interview, 6/9/09.

233. Paola di Caro, "Se bisognerá intervenire, sono certo che agiremo insieme," *Corriere della Sera*, November 22, 2002.

234. Paola di Caro, "Berlusconi: niente italiani in prima linea," *Corriere della Sera*, November 23, 2002. See also "Berlusconi e Bush, intesa contro Saddam," *Corriere della Sera,* January 31, 2003; Paola di Caro, "Berlusconi: si alla pace ma senza nasconderci," *Corriere della Sera*, February 7, 2003; and "Berlusconi: potrei incontrare Tarek Aziz," *Corriere della Sera*, February 8, 2003.

235. Maurizio Caprara, "Frattini: se lo decideranno le Nazioni Unite l'Italia contribuira' al disarmo forzato dell Iraq," *Corriere della Sera*, January 21, 2003.

236. Maurizio Caprara, "Il Dipartimento di Stato," *Corriere della Sera,* October 18, 2002.

237. Roberto Zuccolini, "L'Italia non mandera' soldati in Iraq," *Corriere della Sera*, March 15, 2003.

238. Francesco Verderami, " L'amarezza di Ciampi," *Corriere della Sera*, October 3, 2002.

239. Daria Gorodisky, "No alla guerra e accuse al governo, l'opposizione ritrova unitá," *Corriere della Sera*, March 19, 2003.

240. Giles Tremlett and Sophie Arie, "War in the Gulf: Spain/Italy," *The Guardian*, March 29, 2003.

241. Carlo Bonini, "I nostril 007 e i generali di Saddam," *La Repubblica*, April 23, 2003.

242. Ettore Greco, "La politica estera dell'Italia," in *L'Italia e la politica internazionale*, ed., Alessandro Colombo and Natalino Ronzitti (Bologna: Il Mulino, 2004), 49.

243. Franco Frattini with Carlo Panella, *Cambiamo Rotta: La Nuova Politica Estera Dell'Italia* (Casale Monferrato: Piemme, 2004), 158.

244. Paola di Caro, "Il premier: grave per tutti se l'America dovrá agire da sola," *Corriere della Sera*, September 24, 2002.

245. Paola di Caro, "Berlusconi: ha vinto la volontá di stare uniti," *Corriere della Sera*, February 18, 2003.

246. Paola di Caro, "Berlusconi: un dovere difenderci," *Corriere della Sera*, September 14, 2002.

247. Paola di Caro, "Ma Saddam si piegherá gli conviene," *Corriere della Sera*, September 15, 2002.

248. Osvaldo Croci, "Much Ado about Little: The Foreign Policy of the Second Berlusconi Government," *Modern Italy* 10, no. 1 (May 2005), 68.

249. Paola di Caro, "Berlusconi-Bush: stretto contatto sulla crisi," *Corriere della Sera*, February 12, 2003. See also "Bush e Berlusconi: ogni sforzo per evitare la guerra," *Corriere della Sera*, February 9, 2003.

250. Di Caro, "Berlusconi-Bush." See also "Berlusconi: spazio per una soluzione pacifica," *Corriere della Sera*, February 19, 2003.

251. Maurizio Caprara, "Un compito per l'Italia nell'Iraq liberato," *Corriere della Sera*, January 29, 2003.

252. Stefano Folli, "Un messaggio obliquo inviato anche al Quirinale," *Corriere della Sera*, January 31, 2003.

253. Leslie Wayne, "Lockheed Team to Build Presidential Copters," *The New York Times*, January 29, 2005.

254. Caprara, "Frattini."

255. Stefano Folli, "L'appoggio all' America unico punto fermo," *Corriere della Sera*, March 19, 2003. See also "Berlusconi ricomincia dalla politica estera," *Corriere della Sera*, August 22, 2002.

256. Renato Zuccolini, "Guerra all' Iraq, Bush chaima Berlusconi," *Corriere della Sera*, March 12, 2003.

257. Daria Gorodisky, "Ulivo freddo sulla proposta," *Corriere della Sera*, January 20, 2003.

258. Francesco Verderami, "La paura del Premier: rovina il semestre italiano al'UE," *Corriere della Sera*, January 25, 2003.

259. Interview with Silvio Fagiolo, 4/21/09a. I heard a similar perspective during an anonymous interview, 3/10/09.

260. Interview with Raffaello Matarazzo, 4/24/09a; Interview with Roberto Menotti, 4/24/09b.

261. Interview with Silvio Fagiolo, 4/21/09a.

262. Interview with Lucio Caracciolo, 4/28/09b.

263. Interview with Silvio Fagiolo, 4/21/09a; Anonymous interview, 4/21/09b; Interview with Fiorello Provera, 4/27/09.

264. Interview with Silvio Fagiolo, 4/21/09a.

265. Interview with Fiorello Provera, 4/27/09.

266. Anonymous interview, 3/30/09.

267. Franco Frattini with Carlo Panella, *Cambiamo Rotta: La Nuova Politica Estera Dell'Italia* (Casale Monferrato: Piemme, 2004), 155.

268. Feruccio De Bortoli, "L'apporto italiano? Quasi simbolico," *Corriere della Sera*, February 2, 2003.

269. Fiorenza Sarzanini, "Allerta del Sismi," *Corriere della* Sera, November 14, 2002.

270. Paola di Caro, "Berlusconi cerca di convicere Putin," *Corriere della Sera*, February 3, 2003.

271. Maria Latella, "Temo terribili stragi con le armi di Saddam," *Corriere della Sera*, January 31, 2003.

272. Fabio Cavalera, "Cortei sinceri, anche noi per la pace," *Corriere della Sera*, February 17, 2003.

236 • Notes

273. Senato della Repubblica, "Comunicazione del Ministro degli affair esteri sulle linee della politca estera italiana," 29/01/2003, http://www.senato.it.
274. Gianna Fregonara, "Ciampi-Berlusconi: consulto sull'Iraq," *Corriere della Sera*, February 2, 2003.
275. Marco Galluzzo, "Berlusconi: non ci sono piu' dubbi Saddam mente," *Corriere della Sera*, February 6, 2003.
276. Franco Venturini, "Casini: autolesionista una guerra senza l'ONU," *Corriere della Sera*, February 9, 2003.
277. Paola di Caro, "Premere su Saddam per la pace," *Corriere della Sera*, February 15, 2003.
278. Paola di Caro, "Useró tutte le forze per evitare il conflitto," *Corriere della Sera,* September 26, 2003.
279. Paola di Caro, "Berlusconi teme che non si possa evitare la guerra," *Corriere della Sera*, February 10, 2003.
280. Franco Venturini, "Casini: autolesionista una guerra senza l'ONU," *Corriere della Sera*, February 9, 2003.
281. Lorenzo Fuccaro, "Iraq, Bush invita Berlusconi a Camp David," *Corriere della Sera,* September 11, 2002.
282. Senato della Repubblica, "Comunicazioni del Presidente del Consiglio dei ministri sulla questione irachena e sul Vertice di Pratica di Mare e conseguente discussione," 09/25/2002.
283. Senato della Repubblica, "Seguito della discussione sulle linee di politica estera e discussione di mozioni connesse," 2/19/2003.
284. Ibid.
285. Paola di Caro, "Berlusconi: le ispezioni? Risultati scarsi," *Corriere della Sera*, March 7, 2003. See also, Gianna Fregonara, "Scali degli aerei americani, tutto regolare," *Corriere della Sera,* March 2, 2003.
286. Senato, 9/25/2002.
287. Anonymous interview, 3/30/09.
288. Anonymous interview, 4/21/09b.
289. Interview with Roberto Menotti, 4/24/09b; Anonymous interview, 3/10/09.
290. Interview with Silvio Fagiolo, 4/21/09a.
291. Renato Mannheimer, "Un italiano su due contro la guerra 'in ogni caso,'" *Corriere della Sera*, September 16, 2002.
292. Maria Latella, "Temo terribili stragi con le armi di Saddam," *Corriere della Sera*, January 31, 2003.
293. Renato Mannheimer, "Attacco all'Iraq, crescono i no," *Corriere della Sera*, February 14, 2003.
294. Luigi Accattoli, "Vaticano: non si puo' imporre sempre la legge del piu' forte," *Corriere della Sera*, September 10, 2002; "Il Pontefice: la guerra non risolve i conflitti," *Corriere della Sera*, January 14, 2003.
295. Gianna Fregonara, "Berlusconi vola da Bush," *Corriere della Sera*, January 28, 2003.
296. Gianna Fregonara, "L'Ulivo si compatta sull'Iraq," *Corriere della Sera*, September 10, 2002.

297. On UN authorization, see Marco Galluzzo, "Guerra, l'ONU dica no," *Corriere della Sera*, October 18, 2002; Gianna Fregonara, "Iraq e articolo 18, tensioni nell' Ulivo," *Corriere della Sera*, February 4, 2003; Stefano Folli, "Le tre carte del Polo," *Corriere della Sera*, February 18, 2003. On bases, see Maria Latella, "Il dubbio del Centrosinistra: e giusto dire no al sorvolo USA?," *Corriere della Sera*, February 6, 2003.

298. Paola di Caro, "La promessa del premier: si alla mediazione," *Corriere della Sera*, March 5, 2003.

299. Stefano Folli, "Tra Bush e i cattolici la via stretta del premier," *Corriere della Sera*, March 15, 2003.

300. Massimo Teodori, *Benedetti americani: dall'Alleanza atlantica alla guerra al terrorismo* (Milano: Mondadori, 2003), 165–66.

301. Anonymous interview, 4/21/09b. Others agreed that electoral politics played little role: Interview with Roberto Menotti, 4/24/09b; Anonymous interview, 3/10/09.

302. Interview with Silvio Fagiolo, 4/21/09a.

303. Anonymous interview, 3/30/09.

304. Interview with Fiorello Provera, 4/27/09.

305. Franco Venturini, "Frattini: un dovere restare fedele alle scelte delle Nazioni Unite," *Corriere della Sera*, January 19, 2003.

306. Paola di Caro, "Premere su Saddam per la pace," *Corriere della Sera*, February 15, 2003.

307. Maurizio Caprara, "Ingrao: il mondo ha il fiato sospeso e qui si fanno calcoli personali," *Corriere della Sera*, October 15, 2002.

308. Maria Latella, "D'Alema sulle barricate, insulti alla Camera a Giovanardi," *Corriere della Sera*, March 19, 2003.

309. Maria Latella, "Andreotti: il no nella Costituzione e piu forte delle scelte ONU," *Corriere della Sera*, March 13, 2003.

310. Cavalera, "Cortei sinceri."

311. Senato della Repubblica, "Seguito della discussione sulle comunicazioni del Governo sulle linee della politca estera," 06/02/2003.

312. Senato della Repubblica, "Conferenza dei Presidenti dei gruppi parlamentari, convocazione," 18/03/2003.

313. Marco Galluzzo, "Berlusconi: non ci sono più dubbi, Saddam mente," *Corriere della Sera*, February 6, 2003.

314. Di Caro, "Berlusconi: le ispezioni?" For contrary views in the Italian Foreign Ministry, see Paola di Caro, "Il rapporto tra gli alleati si può salvare," *Corriere della Sera*, March 17, 2003.

315. Marco Galluzzo, "Gasparri: mai ipotizzato di andare al di la' delle Nazioni Unite," *Corriere della Sera*, March 17, 2003.

316. Senato della Repubblica, "Discussione sulle comunicazionu del Presidente del Consiglio dei ministri sui recenti sviluppi della crisi irachena," 19/03/2003.

317. Ibid.

318. Anonymous interview, 3/10/09.

238 • Notes

319. Interview with Silvio Fagiolo, 4/21/09a.
320. Anonymous interview, 3/30/09.
321. Interview with Lucio Caracciolo, 4/28/09.
322. Interview with Fiorello Provera, 4/27/09.
323. Anonymous interview, 4/21/09b.
324. Marzio Breda, "Ciampi: spetta all' Onu gestire il dopoguerra," *Corriere della Sera*, April 5, 2003.

Chapter 7

1. David Sylvan and Stephen Majeski, *U.S. Foreign Policy in Perspective: Clients, Enemies, and Empire* (Abingdon: Routledge, 2009), 184.
2. Of course, as proposition four only fit one case, it did not receive the same degree of support as proposition one or proposition two.
3. Chapter 2 outlines the basis for classifying the different factors.
4. Andrew Bennett, Joseph Lepgold, and Danny Unger, *Friends in Need: Burden Sharing in the Persian Gulf War* (New York: St. Martin's Press, 1997), 347.
5. "Henry John Temple, Lord Palmerston," in *Oxford Dictionary of Quotations,* ed. Elizabeth Knowles (Oxford: Oxford University Press, 2009), http://www.oxfordreference.com.
6. The nine cases are France/Lebanon, Italy/Lebanon, France/Persian Gulf, Italy/Persian Gulf, France/Kosovo, Italy/Kosovo, France/Afghanistan, Italy/Afghanistan, and France/Iraq.
7. For the pundit's perspective, see Jean-Marie Colombani and Walter Wells, *Dangerous De-Liaisons: What's Really Behind the War Between France and the U.S.* (Hoboken: Melville House, 2004), 36.
8. Other examples from the case studies include the Clinton administration's willingness to delay strikes on Iraq after consulting Tony Blair's government and the Clinton administration's decision to postpone an ultimatum to Serbia, taking into account French concerns.
9. Very small coalitions (like Afghanistan in 2001) can also implicate allies' prestige; unfortunately, they have negative consequences for alliance value as outlined previously.
10. For a framework for making such decisions, see Meghan L. O'Sullivan, *Shrewd Sanctions: Statecraft and State Sponsors of Terrorism* (Washington, D.C.: Brookings Institution Press, 2003), 29.

Index

9/11 terrorist attacks, 5, 105–6, 108–25, 127–31, 137, 139, 143, 146, 148, 161–62, 225
See also Afghanistan *and* Iraq

Afghanistan, 4–5, 7, 10, 12, 105–31, 135, 148, 158, 165, 177–78
9/11 terrorist attacks, 5, 105, 108–22, 124–25, 127–31
Al-Qaeda, 105–11, 113, 116–18, 121–22, 124–25, 129–31
anti-Western sentiment, 108
humanitarian concerns, 111–12, 114, 116, 120–22, 129–30
International Security Assistance Force (ISAF), 105–6, 109, 114, 117, 120, 122–23
just punishment, 112–14
North Atlantic Treaty Organization (NATO), 4, 105, 123–24, 148
Northern Alliance, 105, 112, 130
Operation Enduring Freedom (OEF), 105–11, 113–23, 125–31, 135, 148
Operation Veritas (Britain), 108
regional stability, 111, 115, 117
Taliban, 5, 10, 105–12, 114, 117–22, 124, 128–31, 135, 148
terrorism, 5, 105–6, 108–11, 113–14, 116–22, 124–5, 129
United Nations (UN), 105, 120, 126
War on Terror, 106
Agnelli, Susanna, 94

Albania, 78–79, 87, 98
Operation Alba, 98–99
Albright, Madeleine, 83, 86
Algeria, 36–37, 117
Front de libération nationale (FLN), 37
terrorist attacks, 117
alliance dependence, 13–15, 32, 38, 44, 48, 149, 152, 175
alliance value, 9, 11, 15–16, 18–25, 27–30, 32–35, 37–38, 40–41, 43–44, 47–48, 51–52, 55–56, 59–60, 63–64, 67, 70–71, 73, 76–78, 81, 84–87, 93–95, 103, 107, 113, 115–16, 121–23, 128, 130–31, 134, 136–37, 145–49, 157–60, 167–68, 171–73, 175–78
dependence, 13–15, 32, 38, 44, 48, 149, 152, 175
influence, 15–16, 32, 41, 52, 56, 64, 66–67, 76, 86, 94–95, 106–7, 115, 134–37, 149, 159, 177
See also by country
alliances, 9, 11–16, 19–20, 22–25, 27–30
Allin, Dana, 77, 79, 81
Alliot-Marie, Michèle, 149
Al-Qaeda, 105–11, 113, 116–18, 121–22, 124–25, 129–31, 137, 140–41, 150–51, 161
See also Afghanistan *and* Iraq
Amato, Giuliano, 70–73, 176
anarchy, 14–15
Andò, Salvo, 71
Andréani, Gilles, 87, 89

240 • Index

Andreotti, Giulio, 59–63
Angioni, Franco, 49, 51
Arafat, Yasser, 45
Ashdown, Paddy, 83
Auerswald, David, 13
Australia, 1, 29

Baker, James, 7, 56, 59–61
balance of threat (Walt), 14
Baltrusaitis, Daniel, 14
Barre, Siad, 72
Bennett, Andrew, 13, 175
Bérégovoy, Pierre, 69
Berlusconi, Silvio, 1, 121–31, 133,
    157–68, 172
Bertinotti, Fausto, 102
Biden, Joe, 4
Blair, Tony, 1, 27–8, 76–85, 106–14,
    126, 133–47, 152, 159, 162,
    168, 171
Blix, Hans, 151–52, 154
Bosnia-Herzegovina, 64–65, 77–79,
    86–89, 94–95
    Contact Group on Bosnia, 89, 94–95
    Dayton Accords (1995), 95
Bossi, Umberto, 161, 165
Boutros-Ghali, Boutros, 69
Boyce, Admiral Sir Michael, 134
Bozo, Fréderic, 35, 153–55
Britain, 1–2, 5, 7–9, 11–13, 17, 25,
    28–29, 31–34, 40–43, 51–55, 58,
    61, 63–66, 75–84, 89, 98–99,
    103, 105–13, 118, 123, 126, 131,
    133–47, 152, 168–70, 172
    alliance value, 12, 25, 27–28, 32–4,
        40–41, 43, 52–53, 55, 64, 76–78,
        84, 106–7, 109, 113, 131,
        133–37, 145–47, 168, 177
    electoral politics, 34, 43, 55, 65–66,
        80–81, 84, 110–11, 113–14,
        141–42, 172
    national interest, 17, 32–34, 41–43,
        53–55, 64–66, 78–79, 82, 84,
        103, 106, 108–9, 112–13, 134,

137–41, 145–46, 168
    prestige, 42, 53, 65, 80,103, 107,
        109–10, 118, 131, 137, 172
    "special relationship," 12, 32, 53,
        106, 126, 135
    threat, 27–28, 32–34, 41–43, 53, 55,
        64–65, 78–79, 84, 103, 107–9,
        111–13, 131, 137–41, 143–47, 168
burden-sharing, 1–4, 12–15, 23, 75,
    169, 175–77
Bush Doctrine, 149
Bush, George H. W., 5, 17, 31, 52–57,
    60, 63–64, 66–67, 69, 71, 85, 177
Bush, George W., 1, 4, 6, 12, 105–7,
    114–15, 118–19, 123, 133–37,
    148–52, 158–64, 168
Butler Review (Britain), 138–39, 143
    See also Iraq War

Cacace, Paolo, 48, 50
Campbell, Alastair, 106–7, 128, 134,
    136, 141, 147, 151
Campbell, John, 53, 55
Cantaloube, Thomas, 115, 118, 148
Caracciolo, Lucio, 124–26, 128, 160, 167
Casini, Pier Ferdinando, 162
Castellaneta, Giovanni, 126
CENTCOM. See United States Central
    Command
Central Intelligence Agency (CIA), 124
Chalker, Lynda, 66
Chamber of Deputies (Italy), 95, 98
chemical and biological weapons
    (CBW), 133, 137–40, 150, 153,
    160–63, 168
    See also Iraq War
Cheysson, Claude, 44–45, 47, 57
China, 83, 89, 152, 156
Chirac, Jacques, 1, 68, 85–93, 114–21,
    126, 131, 133, 147–57, 168,
    171–72, 178
Christian Democrats (Italy), 38–39,
    61, 72
CIA. See Central Intelligence Agency

Index • 241

Ciampi, Carlo, 158, 164, 166–67
Cimbala, Stephen, 4
Clark, Alan, 42
Clinton, Bill, 64, 66–67, 75–77,
   85–86, 99, 106, 115, 149
"coalition of the willing," 1, 6
   See also Iraq War
Cold War, 2, 12, 53, 60, 67, 71, 86,
   95, 127, 163
collective action theory, 13–14
Colombani, Jean-Marie, 68
Colombo, Emilio, 48, 51, 71
communism, 33, 35–38
Conservative Party (Britain), 27, 33–34,
   42–43, 54, 64–65, 80, 109–10,
   113, 140, 142, 147–48, 168
Consiglio Supremo di Difesa (Italy), 124,
   158, 166–67
constructivism, 10–11, 24–27, 29–30,
   34, 50, 74, 81, 155, 169, 171–73
Contact Group on Bosnia, 89, 94–95
   See also Bosnia-Herzegovina *and*
   Kosovo War
Cook, Robin, 78, 80–83, 111, 134–36,
   138–39, 142–43
Coralluzzo, Valter, 48, 50–51, 61–62
Corriere della Sera, 70–71, 95–98, 100,
   122, 124, 127–28, 130, 157, 159,
   161, 164–65
Cossiga, Francesco, 48
cost (in blood and treasure), 6, 8, 14,
   16–17, 96, 99, 109, 135–36, 179
Coticchia, Fabrizio, 100
Council of Ministers (France), 45
Cradock, (Sir) Percy, 41, 52–54
Craxi, Bettino, 71
Cremasco, Maurizio, 49, 51, 99
Croci, Osvaldo, 72, 95, 99
Cuban Missile Crisis, 35

D'Alema, Massimo, 93–103, 126,
   171–72
Daddow, Oliver, 82
Dassù, Marta, 99

Dayton Accords (1995), 95
   See also Bosnia-Herzegovina
de Durand, Etienne, 149, 153
de Gaulle, Charles, 35–37, 171
De Michelis, Gianni, 60–62, 159
D'Estaing, Valéry Giscard, 68
de Villepin, Dominique, 1, 147–49,
   151–52, 154–55
Dearlove, Richard, 111
Defence Intelligence Service (Britain), 140
Delafon, Gilles, 86, 88, 149
Delhaye, Bruno, 67–70
Della Loggia, Ernesto Galli, 97
Democratic Party of the Left (Italy), 72
détente, 38, 48
Di Caro, Paola, 159, 164
Dini, Lamberto, 94–95, 101, 123–24
Djibouti, 68
Dobson, Alan, 137
"dodgy dossier," 138–39
   See also Iraq War
domestic political structure, 7, 11,
   13–15, 32, 68–69, 72, 80–81, 90,
   93, 100, 112, 119, 127–28, 146,
   154–55, 160, 163–64, 167, 172,
   176–78
   See also electoral politics
Dumbrell, John, 41

El Baradei, Mohamed, 154
Economist, The, 45
electoral politics, 9, 11, 14, 18–20,
   22–24, 34, 36–37, 39–40, 43,
   50, 55, 58, 61, 63, 65–66, 68–70,
   72–74, 80–81, 90, 99–100, 103,
   110–11, 119, 121, 127–28,
   141–42, 147, 154–55, 157,
   163–65, 167, 171–73, 176,
   178–79
   domestic political structure, 7, 11,
   13–15, 32, 68–69, 72, 80–81, 90,
   93, 100, 112, 119, 127–28, 146,
   154–55, 160, 163–64, 167, 172,
   176–78

242 • Index

electoral politics—*continued*
  opposition support, 9, 19–20, 24,
    37, 40, 43, 46–47, 50, 54–55,
    58–59, 61, 63, 65, 68–70, 72–73,
    79–81, 93, 100, 109–11, 113,
    121, 127, 130, 140, 142, 154–55,
    157, 163–64, 167–68, 171–73,
    176–78
  See also by country
Ellis, Sylvia, 34
European Community, 41, 56, 64
European Union, 78–79, 114, 122,
    152, 163
  common foreign and security policy,
    57, 60, 77, 89–90, 92, 106, 152
  Vilnius declaration, 152

Fabbri, Fabio, 72–73
Fagiolo, Silvio, 125, 127, 160, 163–64,
    166
Falangist, Christian, 40
Falklands War, 41–43, 53, 65, 137
  Ascension Island, 41
Fallaci, Oriana, 128–29
Fanfani, Amintore, 38–39
Ferraris, Luigi Vittorio, 48–50
Farrell, Theo, 107, 109–10, 112
Fillon, François, 69–70
Fini, Gianfranco, 159
Fischer, Joschka, 86
Folli, Stefano, 95, 97, 127, 164
Forster, Peter, 4
France, 1–2, 5, 7–9, 11–13, 17, 25, 29,
    31, 35–37, 40, 44–48, 50–59, 61,
    65–70, 75–76, 85–94, 98–100,
    103, 105, 114–21, 123, 126, 131,
    133, 147–57, 163, 168–69, 172,
    177–78
  alliance value, 25, 35, 37, 44, 47,
    56–57, 59, 67, 70, 85–87, 93,
    114–17, 119–21, 148–50, 157,
    171, 177–78
  cohabitation government, 90, 93,
    119, 121

electoral politics, 36–37, 46, 58,
    68–70, 90, 119, 121, 154–55, 157
national interest, 17, 35, 37, 44–45,
    47, 57, 59, 67–68, 87–89, 92–93,
    116–17, 121, 131, 150–54,
    156–57, 168
"politique Arabe," 45, 47
prestige, 25, 36–37, 44–47, 57–59,
    67–68, 70, 88–89, 91–93, 114,
    116, 118–21, 131, 150, 152–54,
    156–57, 163
threat, 17, 35–37, 45, 56–57, 59,
    67, 87–8, 93, 116–18, 120–21,
    150–57, 168
Frattini, Franco, 157–59, 161, 165–66
Freedman, Sir Lawrence, 56, 107, 109
free-riding, 2, 79
French Communist Party. See *Parti
  Communiste Français*
French Socialist Party. See *Parti
  Socialiste*
Front National ("National Front" Party
  of France), 58, 90

Gasparri, Maurizio, 166
Gasperini, Luciano, 101
Gates, Robert, 4
Gautier, Louis, 86, 88–92
Gaviard, General Jean-Patrick, 147,
    154–55
Gemayel, Bashir, 40
Geneva Conference (1954), 33–34
geographic proximity, 16, 18, 78,
    87–88, 97
Germany, 9, 13–14, 17, 50, 52, 57,
    61, 89, 94, 98–99, 101, 126, 152,
    160, 163
Giacomello, Giampiero, 100
Gnesotto, Nicole, 150, 153
Goldsmith, Peter, 144
Gorbachev, Mikhail, 56
Gordon, Philip, 12, 147, 151, 155
Gourdault-Montagne, Maurice, 150
Grand, Camille, 156

Index • 243

Greco, Ettore, 97, 100
Greece, 78–79, 94, 101
Greenstock, (Sir) Jeremy, 6, 146
groupthink, 139
Guadalupe Summit France (1979), 50

Hague, William, 79
Hamas, 140
Hassner, Pierre, 116
Heisborg, François, 116
Hill, Christopher, 139
Hirsch, John, 63, 72
Hogg, Douglas, 64–65
Hollis, Rosemary, 145
Hoon, Geoffrey, 136–37
House of Commons (Britain), 40,
    64–65, 77–81, 83, 107–8, 110,
    136–37, 139–40
Howard, Michael, 80
Hurd, Douglas, 53–54
Hussein, Saddam, 5, 51, 53, 56–57, 60,
    77, 133, 137–43, 147, 149–51,
    153–55, 161–62, 175
Hutton inquiry (Britain), 138–39
    See also Iraq War

identity, 24–27, 29, 34, 37, 39, 43,
    46–48, 51, 62–63, 74, 81, 91,
    100–2, 111–12, 119, 128–31,
    142, 147, 155, 165–7, 171–73,
    176–77
Independent International Commission
    on Kosovo (IICK), 81–3
    See also Kosovo War
India, 89, 152
Indyk, Martin, 152
influence, 15–16, 32, 41, 52, 56, 64,
    66–67, 76, 86, 94–95, 106–7,
    115, 134–37, 149, 159, 177
International Criminal Court (ICC),
    115
International Security Assistance Force
    (ISAF), 105–6, 109, 114, 117,
    120, 122–23

See also Afghanistan and North
    Atlantic Treaty Organization
Iraq, 5, 13, 31, 52–60, 62, 64, 77,
    84–85, 94, 102
    invasion of Kuwait (1990), 5, 51–53,
        55, 57, 60, 140
    Kurds, 64, 102
    sanctions, 54–56, 143, 153
    Shi'a uprising (1991), 145
    UN inspections, 12, 77, 133, 138,
        144–47, 150–51, 154–55,
        161–62, 165, 168
    United Nations Special Commission
        (UNSCOM), 138
Iraq Inquiry (Chilcot Commission),
    136, 141, 143–46
    See also Iraq War
Iraq War (2003), 1, 4–8, 10–14, 27–30,
    133–69, 171–72, 176–78
    9/11 terrorist attacks, 137, 139, 143,
        146, 148, 161–62
    Al-Qaeda, 137, 140–41, 150–51, 161
    Butler review (Britain), 138–39, 143
    chemical and biological weapons
        (CBW), 133, 137–40, 150, 153,
        160–63, 168
    "coalition of the willing," 1, 6
    "dodgy dossier," 138
    humanitarian concerns, 142–45
    Hutton inquiry (Britain), 138–39
    international law, 143–45, 156–66
    Iraq Inquiry (Chilcot Commission),
        136, 141, 143–46
    Operation Iraqi Freedom (OIF),
        133–34, 136, 145, 153, 160
    regional stability, 151, 153
    UNSC resolution 1441, 133, 143–44,
        150–51, 155, 166
    weapons of mass destruction
        (WMD), 12, 28, 133, 137–41,
        143–44, 146–47, 149–51, 153–55,
        157–58, 161–63, 165–66
Islam, 49, 108, 124–25, 128–29,
    140, 151

244 • Index

Islam—*continued*
  radical Islam, 108, 124–25, 129,
    140, 151
  Israel, 40–41, 43–45, 47, 49, 51, 88,
    135, 152
  invasion of Lebanon (1982), 45–46,
    51
  Israeli-Palestinian conflict, 88, 135
  isolationism, 89, 116, 158
Italy, 1–2, 5, 7–9, 11–14, 17, 25, 29,
    31, 37–40, 48–51, 59–63, 70–73,
    75–76, 93–103, 105, 121–31,
    133, 152, 157–69, 171–72,
    176–77
  alliance value, 38, 40, 48–49, 60, 63,
    71, 94–96, 102–3, 122–24, 128,
    130–31, 158–60, 167–68, 176
  electoral politics, 39–40, 50, 61, 63,
    72–3, 99–100, 103, 127–28, 131,
    163–65, 167
  constitution, 62, 100–101, 165–67
  national interest, 38–40, 48–49, 51,
    60, 62–63, 71–72, 74, 94–99,
    102–3, 123–25, 129, 131,
    160–63, 167
  politica della sedia, 99
  prestige, 25, 48–51, 60–61, 63,
    71–73, 96, 98–99, 102–3,
    124–28, 130, 159–63
  presenzialismo, 72
  threat, 38–39, 60, 63, 71, 96–98,
    101–3, 124–25, 129–31, 158–63,
    165–68, 176
Italian Communist Party. See *Partito
  Comunista Italiano*
Italian Socialist Party. See *Partito
  Socialista Italiano*

Japan, 4, 57, 126
Jay, Michael, 136
Jenkin, Bernard, 137, 141–42, 144
Jenkins, Roy, 142
Jervolino, Rosa Russo, 96
Johnson, Lyndon B., 5, 31–33, 35–37, 40

Joint Intelligence Committee (JIC), 33,
    52, 55, 138–40
Jones, Brian, 139
Jospin, Lionel, 85–93, 114–21, 131
Joxe, Alain, 69
Joxe, Pierre, 67
Judah, Tim, 79
  Kosovo: War and Revenge, 79
Juppé, Alain, 68

Kagan, Robert, 4, 6, 12
Kampfner, John, 78, 138–39, 141
Karsh, Efraim, 56
Kelly, David, 139
Kennedy, John F., 32, 35–36
Kenny, J. A., 43
Khanh, Nguyen, 33
Kodmani-Darwish, Bassma, 46–47
Kosovo Liberation Army (KLA), 91
  See also Kosovo War
Kosovo Report, 83
  See also Kosovo War
Kosovo War (1999), 4, 7–8, 10, 13,
    75–103, 116, 171, 173, 176–77
  Contact Group on Bosnia, 89, 94–95
  humanitarian concerns, 5, 81–84,
    87, 91–93, 97, 101–3, 177
  Independent International
    Commission on Kosovo (IICK),
    81–83
  international law, 81, 83, 90–92,
    100–1
  Kosovar Albanians, 5, 75, 78–79,
    82–85, 90–91, 93, 97, 100–102
  Kosovo Liberation Army (KLA), 91
  Kosovo Report, 83
  Operation Allied Force (OAF), 75–81,
    83, 85–90, 93, 95–99, 101–2
  Raçak massacre, 81, 91, 101
  Rambouillet Agreement, 75, 80, 89,
    91–92, 98
  refugees, 79, 82, 96–98
  regional stability, 77–79, 84, 87–88,
    91–93, 95, 97–99, 103

UNSC resolution 1199, 83, 92
UNSC resolution 1203, 83
Kosovo: War and Revenge (Judah), 79
Kouchner, Bernard, 69
Kuwait, 5, 13, 31, 51–53, 55–60, 62, 140

La Pira, Giorgio, 38
Labour Party (Britain), 34, 43, 54–55, 65, 84, 110–11, 142–43
Lacorne, Denis, 58–59
Lamy, François, 87
Lansford, Tom, 118
Lanxade, Jacques, 67
Lasserre, Isabelle, 88
Le Maire, Bruno, 151, 154
Le Monde, 68–69, 87, 91, 114, 149, 154
Lebanon, 5, 8, 10, 12, 17, 31, 40–51, 171, 173
  humanitarian concerns, 43, 46, 50–51
  (the) Levant, 47
  Maronite Christians, 46–48, 51
  Multinational Force, 5, 31, 40–51, 171
  Multinational Force II, 5, 31, 40, 42–43, 46, 48, 50–51
  Palestine Liberation Organization (PLO), 31, 49
  "politique Arabe," 45, 47
  Sabra and Shatila massacres, 40, 43, 46, 50–51
legitimacy, 6–7, 44, 46, 56, 81, 83, 109–10, 117, 146, 162, 166, 179
Lennox-Boyd, Mark, 66
Lepgold, Joseph, 13, 53, 175
(the) Levant, 47
  See also Lebanon
Liberal Democrats (Britain), 81, 109–10, 142
Logevall, Frederik, 35
Loi, Bruno, 71

Macedonia, 78–79, 88
MacLeod, Alex, 88
Macmillan, Harold, 32
Maier, Herbert, 13–14
Major, John, 52, 63–66, 171
Malabarba, Luigi, 130
Mammarella, Giuseppe, 48, 50
Mannheimer, Renato, 96, 100, 127, 164
Manning, Sir David, 134, 136, 145
Manningham-Buller, Eliza, 111
Mantica, Alfredo, 159
Marini, Cesare, 98
Maronite Christians, 46–48, 51
  See also Lebanon
Martin, Guy, 68
Martino, Antonio, 122–23, 125, 129, 159, 161
Maulny, Jean-Pierre, 88–90, 92, 93
McDermott, Anthony, 45, 47
McMahon Act (1954), 35
McNamara, Robert, 135
Menon, Rajan, 4
Mérimée, Jean-Bernard, 69
Meyer, Christopher, 106–7, 135, 136
Migone, Gian Giacomo, 72
military contributions, 1–20, 25, 27–9, 31, 34–37, 39–40, 43, 46, 48, 53–57, 59–62, 75–76, 80–81, 83, 85, 87, 89–90, 92–93, 97, 99–102, 105–12, 114–17, 119, 127–31, 133–34, 136, 145, 147–49, 151–60, 163–65, 167–69, 171–73, 175–79
Milosevic, Slobodan, 75, 77–80, 82, 87–88, 101, 116
Minh, Ho Chi, 36, 38
Mitterrand, François, 44–47, 56–59, 66–70, 155, 171, 176, 177
MNF. *See* Multinational Force
Montenegro, 87
"More Flags" program, 31, 35
  See also Vietnam War
Moro, Aldo, 38–40, 172
Mullen, Admiral Mike, 4

246 • Index

multilateralism, 49, 85, 115, 148, 158
Multinational Force (MNF), 5, 31,
 40–51, 171
 See also Lebanon
Multinational Force II (MNF II), 5, 31,
 40, 42–43, 46, 48, 50–51
 See also Lebanon

National Assembly (France), 69, 85,
 87–90, 91, 117, 118, 120
national interest, 9, 11, 16–18, 19–20,
 22–23, 26, 30, 32–34, 35, 37,
 38–40, 41–45, 47–49, 51, 53–55,
 57, 59–60, 62–68, 71–72, 74,
 78–79, 82, 84, 87–89, 92–99,
 102–3, 106, 108–9, 112–13,
 116–17, 121, 123–25, 129, 131,
 134, 137–41, 145–46, 150–54,
 156–57, 160–63, 167–68
 See also by country
NATO. *See* North Atlantic Treaty
 Organization
Nenni, Pietro, 39
neoclassical realism, 9–11, 14, 23–29,
 169, 171, 179
Neo-Fascists (Italy), 38
New York Times, The, 46, 49, 50, 66,
 86, 151, 152
norms, 25–27, 29, 34, 43, 47–48, 51, 62,
 66, 69, 70, 74, 83, 85, 93, 102–3,
 111–12, 114, 119–20, 128–30,
 131, 142–44, 147, 155–56,
 165–67, 171, 172–73, 176–77
North Atlantic Treaty Organization
 (NATO), 2, 4, 29, 35, 38, 42,
 56, 60, 75–80, 82–98, 100–3,
 105, 116, 123, 126, 148–49,
 158–59, 165
 Afghanistan, 4, 105, 123–24, 148
 credibility, 75, 77–78, 84, 89, 103
 International Security Assistance
  Force (ISAF), 105–6, 109, 114,
  117, 120, 122–23
 Iraq, 148–49, 159

Kosovo War, 75–80, 82–98, 100–103
 Operation Allied Force (OAF),
  75–81, 83, 85–90, 93, 95–99,
  101–2
 Persian Gulf, 56, 60
 value, 77–78, 84–87, 94–96, 103,
  124, 159
 Vietnam, 35, 38
Northern Alliance, 105, 112, 130
 See also Afghanistan

Oakley, Robert, 63, 71, 72
Ocalan, Abdullah, 94
Olson, Mancur, 2
O'Neill, Tip, 167
Operation Alba, 98–99
 See also Albania
Operation Allied Force (OAF), 75–81,
 83, 85, 85–90, 93, 95–99, 101–2
 See also Kosovo *and* North Atlantic
  Treaty Organization
Operation Enduring Freedom (OEF),
 105–11, 113–23, 125–31, 135, 148
 See also Afghanistan
Operation Iraqi Freedom (OIF), 133–34,
 136, 145, 153, 160
 See also Iraq
Operation Provide Relief, 63
 See also Somalia
Operation Uphold Democracy, 8
Operation Veritas (Britain), 108
 See also Afghanistan
Organization for Economic
 Cooperation and Development
 (OECD), 49
Owen, David, 65

Palestine Liberation Organization
 (PLO), 31, 49
 See also Lebanon
Panebianco, Angelo, 97, 127
Parti Communiste Français (French
 Communist Party), 46, 58, 85,
 90, 119

Parti Socialiste (French Socialist Party), 46, 69, 154, 157
Partito Comunista Italiano (Italian Communist Party), 38, 39, 50, 61, 96, 100, 163
Partito Socialista Italiano (Italian Socialist Party), 72
Pershing missiles, 44
Persian Gulf War (1991), 2, 6–8, 10, 12–13, 17, 31, 51–65, 67–68, 71, 89, 91, 122, 138, 155, 158, 163, 175
    concerns about oil, 53, 55, 57, 59–60
    international law, 54–55, 58–59, 62
    invasion of Kuwait (1990), 5, 51–53, 55, 57, 60, 140
    legitimacy, 6, 7, 55–56
    North Atlantic Treaty Organization (NATO), 56, 60
    regional stability, 53, 60
    United Nations (UN), 54–55, 57, 61–63
    UNSC resolution 678, 62, 166
    UNSC resolution 687, 166
Peters, John E., 93
PLO. *See* Palestine Liberation Organization
Poland, 1
Polaris submarines, 32
Powell, Colin, 135, 159, 161, 165, 166
Powell, Jonathan, 85, 139
power, 2, 9, 11–18, 24–25, 32, 36–38, 42, 50, 52–53, 56–58, 60–61, 63, 67–68, 71, 76, 85, 88–89, 98–99, 109–111, 115, 118, 122, 134, 148, 152, 154, 158, 160, 163, 172, 175–76
    American power, 12, 32, 52, 67, 71, 76, 85, 134, 148, 158, 160, 172, 175
    relative power, 14–17, 109–10, 115, 172
public goods, 2

public opinion, 9, 11, 13–14, 18–20, 22–24, 29–30, 36, 39, 43, 46, 50, 58–59, 62, 70, 81, 90, 99–100, 110–11, 119, 127–28, 141–42, 154–55, 160, 163–65, 172, 177
    Britain, 43, 80–81, 110–11, 141–42
    France, 36, 46, 58–59, 70, 90, 119, 154–55
    Italy, 39, 50, 62, 99–100, 127–28, 163–65
Prashar, Baroness Usha, 146
Preble, Christopher, 4
presenzialismo, 72
prestige, 9, 11, 14, 16–18, 20, 22–25, 29, 36–37, 42, 44–51, 53, 57–61, 63, 65, 67–68, 70–73, 80, 88–89, 91–93, 96, 98–99, 102–3, 107, 109–10, 116, 118–21, 124–28, 130–31, 137, 150, 152–54, 156–57, 159–63, 171–73, 175–76, 178
    See also by country
Proletarian Unity Party (Italy), 50
Provera, Fiorello, 160, 165, 167
Prunier, Gérard, 69
Pym, Francis, 40, 42

Quilès, Paul, 87

Radicals (Italy), 50
Rambouillet Agreement, 75, 80, 89, 91–92, 98
    See also Kosovo War
Ranieri, Umberto, 98, 101
Rassemblement pour la République Party (France), 68–69
Reagan, Ronald, 5, 41, 44, 48–49, 52
Refounded Communists (Italy), 72
request, 7–8, 15, 29, 31–32, 37, 40, 44, 48, 50, 59, 66, 70–71, 105, 114, 118, 122, 155, 157, 160, 168, 175
Rice, Condoleezza, 115, 136
Richard, Alain, 88, 90
Richardson, Louise, 77

248 • Index

Riddell, Peter, 76, 108, 135, 137, 139, 141, 144, 145
"Roadmap for Peace," 135
Romano, Sergio, 72, 73, 124
Rose, Gideon, 24
Rumsfeld, Donald, 105, 106, 149
Rusk, Dean, 31, 33, 35
Russia, 83, 89, 94, 148, 152, 156
See also Soviet Union

Sabra and Shatila massacres, 40, 43, 46, 50–51
See also Lebanon
Salleo, Ferdinando, 123
sanctions, 41, 44, 48, 54–56, 143, 153
Iraq, 54, 55, 56, 143, 153
Soviet Union (USSR), 41, 44, 48
Sancton, Thomas, 86, 88, 149
Santoro, Carlo, 49, 50
Saragat, Giuseppe, 38
Saudi Arabia, 5, 52–57, 59
Scarlett, John, 138
Schifani, Renato, 123, 126, 162
Schroeder, Gerhard, 126, 162
Schuster, Jurgen, 13–14
Schwartz, Thomas, 35
Schwarzkopf, Norman, 52
Schweller, Randall, 24
Unanswered Threats, 24
Scognamiglio, Carlo, 93, 96, 98, 102
Seitz, Raymond, 64
Seldon, Anthony, 82, 134, 136, 137, 146
Sembler, Mel, 157, 160
Serbia, 5, 75–76, 78–80, 83, 85–86, 88, 91, 97, 103
See also Yugoslavia
Servizio per le Informazioni e la Sicurezza Democratica (Italy), 124
Shapiro, Jeremy, 12, 147, 151, 155
Short, Clare, 112, 135, 137–38, 142
Shultz, George, 41, 46, 47
Sica, Mario, 39
Skjelsbaek, Kjell, 45, 47

Skelton, Ike, 4
Smith, Ian Duncan, 140
Somalia, 5, 8, 10, 12, 17, 31–32, 63–73, 171, 178
Bakool Province, 67
humanitarian concerns, 63–66, 69–70, 72–73
Operation Provide Relief, 63
Unified Task Force (UNITAF), 5, 63–70, 73, 171, 176
United Nations (UN), 63, 65–66, 69, 73
United Nations Operation in Somalia (UNOSOM), 63
South Korea, 4, 14
Soutou, George-Henri, 148
Soviet Union (USSR), 2, 16, 32, 35–36, 38, 41–42, 44, 48–49, 56, 61, 130, 163
See also Russia
Spadolini, Giovanni, 48, 49–51
"special relationship," 12, 32, 53, 106, 126, 135
See also Britain *and* United States
Stanhope, Henry, 41
Stephens, Philip, 106, 134, 141, 145
Strategic Defence Review (Britain), 77, 78, 82
Straw, Jack, 107–9, 111, 136, 139, 141, 143, 147
Suez Crisis (1956), 32, 35

Talbott, Strobe, 85
Teodori, Massimo, 164
terrorism, 5, 105–6, 108–9, 111, 113–14, 116–18, 120–22, 124–25, 129, 133, 137, 140–41, 145, 147, 149–51, 153, 157, 161–62
Afghanistan, 5, 105–6, 108–11, 113–14, 116–22, 124–25, 129
Iraq, 133, 140–41, 145, 147, 149, 150–51, 153, 157, 160–62
recruitment, 151
Tertrais, Bruno, 149, 153, 155

Index • 249

Thant, General U, 39
Thatcher, Margaret, 40–43, 51–55,
  64–65, 171–73
threat, 2, 9, 11–20, 22–24, 27–29,
  32–34, 36–43, 45, 50, 53–61,
  63–65, 67, 69, 71, 74, 76–80,
  84, 87–88, 91, 93, 96–97, 101–3,
  107–9, 111–13, 116–18, 120–21,
  124–25, 129–31, 133, 137–41,
  143–47, 149, 150–63, 165–8,
  171–73, 175–76, 178
  external threat, 2, 15–16
  target threat, 16, 22, 175, 178
  See also by country
Times, The, 41–43, 64–65, 76, 108–9,
  135, 137, 141
Togliatti, Palmiro, 39
Tories. *See* Conservative Party (Britain)
Torikata, Yuko, 36
Tortorella, Aldo, 101
Trean, Claire, 91, 154
Turkey, 14, 79, 102, 148

Unanswered Threats (Schweller), 24
Unger, Danny, 13
Unified Task Force (UNITAF), 5,
  63–70, 73, 171, 176
  See also Somalia
unilateralism, 1, 85, 106–7, 115–16,
  121, 136, 162, 164
United Nations (UN), 6, 12, 39, 43,
  47, 55, 62–63, 65–66, 69, 77,
  83, 88, 92, 100–101, 120, 133,
  135, 141, 143, 144–45, 146–51,
  154–55, 158–59, 162–68
  Afghanistan, 105, 120, 126
  charter, 39, 55, 83, 92, 101, 144
  inspections, 133, 145–46, 154, 162
  Iraq, 133, 135, 141, 143–51,
    154–59, 161–68
  Kosovo, 77, 83, 85, 88, 92, 100–101
  Lebanon, 43, 47–48
  Persian Gulf, 54–55, 57, 61–63
  Somalia, 63, 65–66, 69, 73

Vietnam, 39
  "Uniting for Peace" mechanism, 83
United Nations Monitoring,
  Verification and Inspection
  Commission (UNMOVIC), 133,
  139, 144, 151
United Nations Operation in Somalia
  (UNOSOM), 63
United Nations Protection Force
  (UNPROFOR), 89
United Nations Security Council
  (UNSC), 39, 47, 54–55, 57,
  61–62, 65–66, 83, 85, 92, 98,
  100–102, 105, 126, 133–35, 143,
  144–48, 150–52, 154, 156–57,
  159, 160–61, 164, 166–68
  resolution 678, 62, 166
  resolution 687, 166
  resolution 1199, 83, 92
  resolution 1203, 83
  resolution 1441, 133, 143–44,
    150–51, 155, 166
  See also Kosovo War; Iraq War; *and*
    Persian Gulf War
United Nations Special Commission
  (UNSCOM), 138
  See also Iraq
United States
  National Missile Defense program, 106
  power, 12, 32, 52, 67, 71, 76, 85,
    134, 148, 158, 160, 172, 175
  "special relationship," 12, 32, 53,
    106, 126, 135
United States Central Command
  (CENTCOM), 122–23, 126

Vatican, the, 125, 127
Védrine, Hubert, 44–46, 57–59,
  85–86, 88, 90–91, 93, 115, 117,
  119–20
Venturini, Franco, 71, 97, 124, 126,
  161
Verdi ("The Greens"), 72, 100
Vernet, Henri, 115, 118, 148

250 • Index

Vietcong, 31
See also Vietnam War
Vietnam War, 1–2, 5, 7, 10, 12, 29–40,
 64, 169, 171–72
 communism, 33, 35–38
 humanitarian concerns, 37
 "More Flags" program, 31, 35
 military overextension, 33
 North Atlantic Treaty Organization
 (NATO), 35, 38
 regional instability, 36
 United Nations (UN), 39
 Vietcong, 31
Vincour, John, 46

Walker, Patrick Gordon, 33
Wall Street Journal, 160
Waltz, Kenneth, 14
"War on Terror," 106
Warsaw Pact, 42, 44
Washington Treaty, 44
weapons of mass destruction, 12, 28,
 133, 137–41, 143–44, 146–47,
 149–51, 153–55, 157–58,
 161–63, 165–66
 See also Iraq War
Weitsman, Patricia, 6
Wells, Walter, 6
Whitney, Craig, 86
Williams, Paul, 111, 136
Wilmshurst, Elizabeth, 144
Wilson, Harold, 32–34, 172
Wolfowitz, Paul, 123
Wood, Michael, 144
Wood, Pia Christina, 45
Woodward, Bob, 134
Woolley, Peter, 43
Worcester, Sir Robert, 111, 142
World War I, 76
World War II, 2, 7–9, 29, 36, 39,
 59–60, 76, 101, 144, 169

Yugoslavia, 75, 78–80, 90
 See also Serbia

Zeckhauser, Robert, 2